The Complete Book of Astrology

Caitlin Johnstone

HINKLER
BOOKS

To my little honey-ant Tjala, for not minding so much when the hopeful suggestion of 'park?' was once again denied; and to my darling Simon, for his midnight coffee kisses and Aries inspiration and for putting in the sleepless nights when I needed him the most.

The Complete Book of Astrology
First published in 2003 by Hinkler Books Pty Ltd
17–23 Redwood Drive
Dingley VIC 3172 Australia
www.hinklerbooks.com

© Hinkler Books Pty Ltd 2003
Illustration references drawn by Simon Hobbs

Reprinted 2003 (three times), 2004

ISBN 1 8651 5512 8

Typeset by Midland Typesetters, Maryborough, Victoria
Printed and bound in Australia

Contents

CONTENTS

Introduction

Welcome to the wonderful, astonishing and intriguing world of astrology. It's a world that some people dismiss as nonsense, yet millions of others cannot start their day, plan their lives or make a decision without consulting 'the stars'.

Astrology is having an increasingly profound impact on society, if the proliferation of star-reading magazine columnists is any guide. And the wealth of information available, the enthusiasm with which so many people use it and the anecdotal evidence of its effect surely lead to the conclusion that 'something' is there.

This book aims to give an analysis of the history, meaning and development of astrology, and show how you can use it in a meaningful way. It aims to provide an understanding of the science and logic behind astrology, presented in easy-to-understand, everyday language.

The book has been structured so that it is possible to read it through from beginning to end for an entire overview, or alternatively to dip into as a reference resource. It is intended for anyone who has little background in astrology, who perhaps knows little more than their own star sign, but is intrigued by its appeal. And it is detailed enough to be useful for the layperson with a greater interest in the subject.

When you reach the end of this book, you should have a thorough knowledge of astrology, and even be able to achieve milestones such as giving a rudimentary reading of an astrological natal chart. And along the way, hopefully you will enjoy your journey into this amazing world.

Before you Start . . .

Astrology is a science of observation. That is, it is a process developed over thousands of years of observing the stars and the influence their placement has over the personality at the time of birth. Its status as a science has been questioned time and time again. But there can be no doubting its worth in giving people another way to look at a troubling situation, or inspiring them to great achievements. It gives people a framework to search for meaning in their lives. In this way it can be seen as a form of psychotherapy, and very often, a successful one.

Chart interpretation is built around the influence of the planets as modified by three primary factors—signs, houses and aspects.

The signs, as is generally known, are the twelve familiar labels: Aries, Taurus, Gemini, Cancer, Leo, Virgo, Libra, Scorpio, Sagittarius, Capricorn, Aquarius and Pisces. The houses are sections of the sky, with the 360° of the sky divided into twelve equal pieces of 30° each. An interpretation is drawn from where the planets fall into the houses. Aspects are the angles that can be drawn from where the planets sit in the sky in relation to Earth. Unlike the constellations, which are fixed, the planets move around the sky. This means an interpretation can be drawn from where they sit in relation to each other from the fixed point of view of the chart. For example, if Jupiter sat at a 90° angle to

Mars, that would be a square aspect.

In astrology, the eight planets (not including Earth), the Sun and the Moon are referred to as the ten planets. Each sign is ruled by a particular planet. For instance, the planet Neptune rules Pisces, Jupiter rules Sagittarius, Mars rules Aries and so on.

There is also a link between each successive sign with each successive house. As an example, the first Sun sign is Aries, and the First House has many characteristics associated with Aries. In the same way, Taurus is associated with the Second House, Gemini with the Third House and so on. This means there is a similarity of meaning between particular planets, signs and houses. Sagittarius, Jupiter and the Ninth House all have similar characteristics, as do Pisces, Neptune and the Twelfth House, and Leo, the Sun and the Fifth House.

Another useful way of understanding astrology is to see the planet as the energy that needs to be expressed. The sign position indicates how that energy shows itself in the personality. The house positions show where the energy will manifest itself. And the aspects between planets reflect how various parts of the personality interact, indicating whether some parts are strengthened or weakened by other tendencies.

Astrological charts can appear very complicated and are usually interpreted by people with many years of study and experience. Yet with a good understanding of the twelve Sun signs, you will be able to make a basic reading of a natal chart, outlining a person's attributes and characteristics and giving some insight into their life path.

But this will come in time. We will take you on this journey in five stages:

✧ The Science of Astrology: This section shows you what a chart looks like and how the different parts represent sections of the sky. It explains in layperson's terms all the jargon that astrologers use, and shows you the symbols of astrology and their meaning. By the end of this chapter, you should be very comfortable finding your way around a chart.

✧ The Zodiac: This section takes you through the zodiac from Aries through to Pisces, from the First to the Twelfth House and from the Sun through to Pluto. It draws direct correlations between certain signs, houses and planets. In this way, we hope to make the process of absorbing all this complex information quicker and help you develop a good feel for the basic principles of astrology after only one read.

✧ Interpretation: This is where the fun really starts. In this section, we take your chart and dissect it piece by piece, interpret the parts and put it back together, giving you an in-depth overview of all its components.

✧ Dilemmas in Modern Astrology: dissects science from belief and answers a few frequently asked questions.

✧ Reference Material: includes handy look-up tables and an extensive glossary. As you become more confident in reading charts, you will find this a useful reference.

A History of Astrology

Most historians and astrologers agree that the beginnings of astrology can be traced back to Babylonia (present-day Iraq) about 3500 years ago, in the first half of the Hammurabi Dynasty. The Babylonians, noted for their advanced culture, had a well-developed science of observational astronomy. This provided them with a calendar for when to plant, harvest, hold religious festivals and so on through the year.

By about 1000 BC, the Babylonians had developed a sense of 'planetary omens' and put their minds to setting their knowledge down in literature. Each planet was given importance, and named in honour of their many gods and goddesses, such as Ishtar, now known as the Venus, and Nergal, now known as Mars. Since Nergal was the god of war, when this planet shone brightly the Babylonians took it as a sign that it was a good time to wage war. As Ishtar was the goddess of love, a spring night in which that planet shone high in the west after sunset was considered a good time for romance.

By 600 BC the Babylonians had devised the twelve-sign zodiac. They developed markers in the sky which roughly corresponded to the months of the year. The concept of making predictions based on the signs began to develop. Eventually this process became so complex that the Babylonians were able to make a map of the heavens to use in divination. The oldest known horoscope dates to 29 April 410 BC.

During the Greek and Roman classical eras, Babylonian astrologers sold their predictions throughout the civilised world. Greek astronomers scoffed at astrology, and in 44 BC, the Roman statesman Marcus Tullius Cicero wrote a damning critique of it. But the Greek and Roman public embraced it with vigour. Astrology grew in popularity, and people turned to astrologers for advice and information on all parts of their lives.

Nevertheless, the Babylonian astrologers had a rough time with the coming of Christianity, since early Christians were hostile to other gods and pagan religions. In Europe, astrology had become almost extinct by the early Middle Ages but was being kept alive in the Middle East by Islamic scholars. The Crusaders brought astrology back to Europe, and it became madly popular again.

The dawn of the age of science in the 1600s brought new thinking to astronomy and astrology, with the discovery of the elliptical solar system. The notion that the Sun, not Earth, was the centre of the solar system almost proved the end of astrology. By 1900, a French encyclopaedia was describing it as 'a vanishing cult', with 'no young devotees'.

Then came a revival. The catalyst was British astrologer RH Naylor who, after World War I, invented the daily newspaper astrology column. Soon there were similar columns in other papers and magazines, spreading around the world. People were beginning to find in astrology a form of self-reflection that was absent elsewhere in their lives.

The result is that 90% of all Americans under the age of 30 know their Sun sign, and there are more than 10,000 practising astrologers in the United States. Millions of dollars are spent annually in the US, Australia and Europe by people consulting astrologers. Ronald Reagan, the Emperor Caligula, Claudius, Ptolemy, St Augustine and Queen Elizabeth I have all looked to the stars for guidance.

Classy folk that they were, it turns out the Babylonians were on to a good thing . . .

The Science of Astrology

In some ways, astrology can be a lot to digest. There is a vast world of interpretation in a chart, where everything – planets, angles, constellations – has a meaning. Many people think astrology simply outlines twelve types of personality. You'll soon find the possibilities of astrology are as endless as human diversity.

As well, there is a very real universe above and below us. Most people feel better when they have the facts, and in astrology this means having some understanding of the cogs that operate the universe and, in particular, our galaxy. Once you understand the movements of the planets, you will be able to create in your mind an image of what it means to be a Capricorn. You'll see Venus marking a vigorous path between the Earth and the Sun. And then the jargon will become clear.

The Science of Astrology will introduce the concept of a star chart, that is, a map of the heavens at a single point in time. We will then dissect the star chart and show how each part relates to the moving sky. There are no instructions for interpreting a chart here, simply what is needed to understand the structure of a chart. The glossary at the back of the book explains all the terms used.

Remember, there's nothing stopping you from jumping ahead. If you know the details of your chart, don't feel you have to brush up on your knowledge of the universe.

So, let's take a peek at that Grand Dame, the universe . . .

Preparing the Way
Astrology vs Astronomy

This is not a book about astronomy. Astronomers study the physical structure of the universe. They don't care about meeting a handsome stranger, or whether they get on well with Aquarians. In fact, most astronomers have nothing to do with astrology. On the other hand, astrologers would be lost without astronomy. Astrologers need to know the exact position of the planets at any given time, and this requires the science of astronomy. Data such as the position of the planets from the perspective of Earth is contained in a publication called the *Ephemeris*. This data is used by astrologers to construct star charts.

The Astrological Chart

An astrological chart should be an accurate representation of a specific time and place. A chart representing New York at 9 a.m. on 6 January 1945 would be completely different from one representing Sydney at the same time. A chart should contain no inaccurate information and nothing should be altered for the sake of appearances.

Drawing a chart requires a good grasp of mathematics. A chart is a flat version of the universe taken from two different perspectives – one from space, looking down from above the North Pole, and the other from the point of view of the person on Earth. It might seem strange to reduce the solar system to two dimensions, but we'll see that this transformation works quite well.

We've noted that a chart represents a particular time and place. An example is the time and place of birth. This type of chart is a natal chart, or a birth chart. It relates to a specific individual. In the example below, you can see the name of the person in the top left-hand corner. You can also see the date, time and location of the birth.

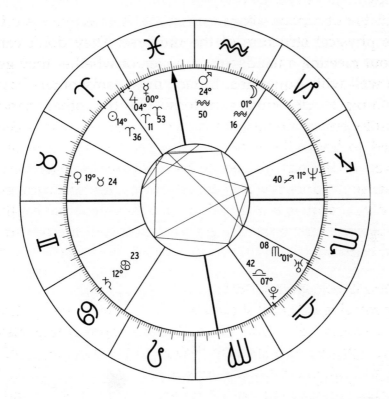

By the end of this section, you should have no trouble reading the astrological language of this chart. Then you'll be ready to deal with chart interpretation.

How to Get Your Own Natal Chart

It is beyond the scope of this book to help you create your own complete and accurate natal chart. However, there are a few ways to obtain your own chart. No matter what you do, you'll need two things: the location of your birth and the exact time of birth. The time of your birth should be accurate to within 15 minutes because certain parts of the sky can change completely in that time.

If you do not know your exact time of birth, but only your date of birth, you will be unable to discover many of the details of your chart. Mainly you will only know the signs of the planets (see the following chapter, The Planets and the Signs). Some astrologers are skilled enough to estimate your time of birth. This can only be done if they know you well, because they will go through a process of elimination to find a time that most reflects your personality. This is a rare skill, as it relies on years of experience, a great deal of intuition and a feel for personality.

Using the Internet, you needn't consult an astrologer at all. There are various websites that offer free charts. All you do is enter your details and your chart will be generated automatically. To get started, use your favourite search engine and run a search on the words: 'astrology', 'natal', 'chart' and 'free'. Some search engines will allow you to search for an exact phrase. If so, the phrase 'place of birth' will help weed out websites that only offer daily horoscopes.

If you ask an astrologer to create your natal chart, you will need to provide the time and place of your birth. Again, the time should be accurate to within 15 minutes or at least the nearest hour. Alternatively, the astrologer can do a sunrise chart, that assumes you were born at sunrise.

As a last resort, see the reference section at the end of this book for a selection of tables that will help you find many of the planets in your chart. These tables are relatively simple compared to the complex tables used by astrologers. They won't enable you to find out your whole chart, but there will be enough information to begin with.

The Planets and the Signs
The Ten Planets

The solar system consists of a star (the Sun) orbited by nine planets. Most of the solar system is more or less flat, and we can metaphorically think of it like a compact disc that has been left in the Sun for a while and buckled. The Sun is in the centre, Mercury is closest to the Sun, Pluto is way out on the edge and Earth is third from the Sun.

Most astrological charts will depict the solar system from above the North Pole. The following diagram shows the solar system from the side, but from a raised perspective so that we are looking down from above the northern hemisphere of Earth.

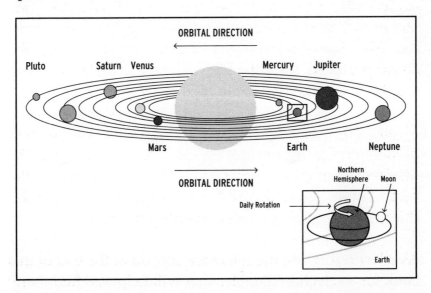

You can see from this diagram that the planets orbit the Sun in an anticlockwise direction (the same direction as Earth's rotation). Also, Earth's rotation, the Moon's orbit and the orbit of the nine planets are all on roughly the same plane.

Astrology is based on the positioning of ten planets, including the Sun and the Moon, but not including Earth. This is because astrology considers the position of the planets from the perspective of Earth, thus making Earth the centre of the universe (although we know in reality that it is not).

Thus, whenever this book refers to 'the planets', this includes the Sun and the Moon. And although in the context of astrology Earth is not a planet, it does have a symbol that is used for different purposes. Below are the glyphs (symbols) of the ten planets and Earth:

PLANET	GLYPH	PLANET	GLYPH
The Sun	☉	Jupiter	♃
The Moon	☽	Saturn	♄
Mercury	☿	Uranus	♅
Venus	♀	Neptune	♆
Mars	♂	Pluto	♇

Earth	⊕

The Twelve Signs

The word 'sign' is another term for 'star sign'. A sign is really just a constellation of stars. When you look up into the sky you'll see thousands of constellations, including the Saucepan and the Southern Cross. But if you're wondering how a Scorpio might get along with a Saucepan, you'll be disappointed to find that only twelve constellations are used in astrology. These are the constellations that sit directly in the path of the planets.

Earlier we likened the solar system to a slightly warped compact disc, since it is roughly flat. If we extend this disc to the surrounding stars, its edge will join up with the twelve constellations (star signs) of the zodiac. In the diagram below, we lay the solar system flat on its back and view it from above the Earth's North Pole. Around the rim of the disc are the twelve constellations that identify the twelve signs.

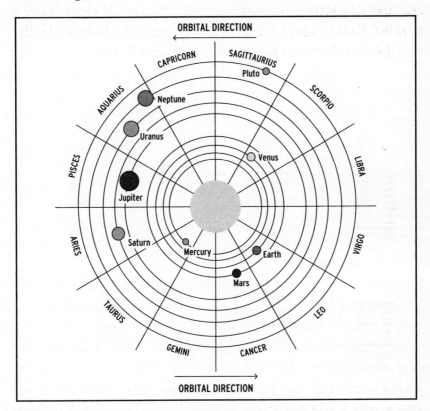

This diagram is clearly labelled with the names of each constellation/star sign. However, natal charts normally save space by using minimal words, so it is a good idea to become familiar with the glyphs used to represent each sign. These glyphs are shown in the following table, in their traditional order.

	SIGN	GLYPH		SIGN	GLYPH
1	Aries	♈	7	Libra	♎
2	Taurus	♉	8	Scorpio	♏
3	Gemini	♊	9	Sagittaurius	♐
4	Cancer	♋	10	Capricorn	♑
5	Leo	♌	11	Aquarius	♒
6	Virgo	♍	12	Pisces	♓

Planetary Positions
Measuring the Sky

Before continuing, we need to introduce a unit of measurement that is fundamental to astrology. This is 'degrees', commonly used for measuring circles. We measure the position of the planets as if they were positioned on the rim of a circle. First we divide the circle into 360 divisions, ie, 360 degrees. The bigger the slice of pie, the greater the number of degrees (°) made by the angle. For accuracy, each degree is further divided into 60 'minutes'. (Don't confuse these with the minutes on a clock.) So, $1^1/_2$ degrees = 1 degree and 30 minutes.

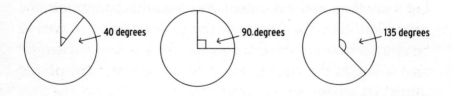

40 degrees   90.degrees   135 degrees

If we divide a circle into twelve pieces, each piece will measure 30°. Therefore, each star sign spans 30° of the sky.

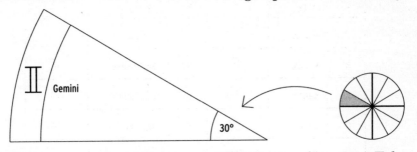

Degrees are measured in an anticlockwise direction. Take the next example of two hypothetical positions in the sign Gemini. First, we write the number of degrees. Then we write the glyph of the appropriate star sign (Gemini). And finally we write the number of minutes.

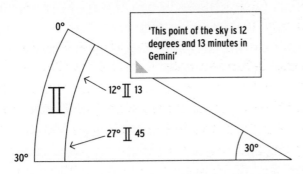

Now we are ready to measure the position of a planet.

How is a Planet 'in' a Sign?

In this book we'll often say things like 'Mars is in Gemini'. Let's say that, at the moment you read this paragraph, the constellation of Gemini is in the eastern sky. You would be able to look up at the section of sky known as 'Gemini' and see both the constellation of Gemini and the planet Mars. This has changed over the years. Please see Precession. Let's say that Mars is halfway across Gemini. We can now add some detail to our diagram of Gemini by marking the position of Mars.

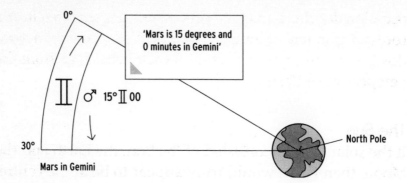

Mars in Gemini

The Sun Sign (the Sun 'in' a Sign)

When someone refers to your star sign they are actually referring to the position of the Sun at the time of your birth. This is more accurately referred to as your Sun sign. For example, if your star sign is Libra, then your Sun sign is Libra. This means that when you were born the Sun was 'in' Libra. Or, if someone tells you that your 'Sun is in Scorpio' then your star/Sun sign is Scorpio. All three terms refer to the same thing.

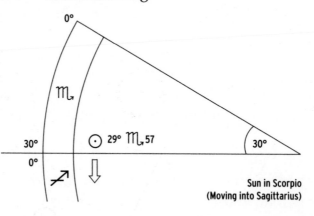

Sun in Scorpio
(Moving into Sagittarius)

Planets in Orbit

From the perspective of Earth, the movement of the planets in relation to each other and in relation to the stars is, for the most part, pedestrian. The general impression is that of an orderly procession, and for thousands of years people believed the planets revolved around Earth. But occasionally the planetary procession degenerates into a confusing game of musical chairs. Following is a run-down of some of the planets and their behaviour from the perspective of Earth.

The Sun

If the solar system consisted of the Sun, the Earth and the Moon, then Earth would truly appear to be at the centre. The Sun moves from sign to sign in a regular fashion, staying about one month in each sign. You can see from the diagrams below that Earth orbits the Sun in the same direction as the signs (ie, anticlockwise). This movement causes the Sun to appear to orbit Earth, also in an anticlockwise direction.

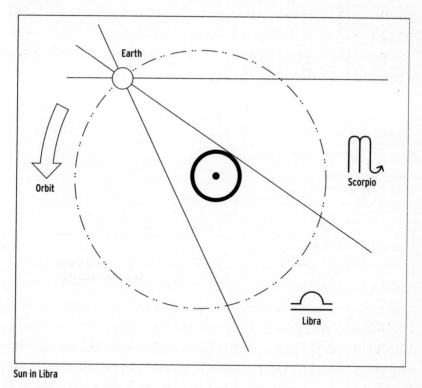

Sun in Libra

continues

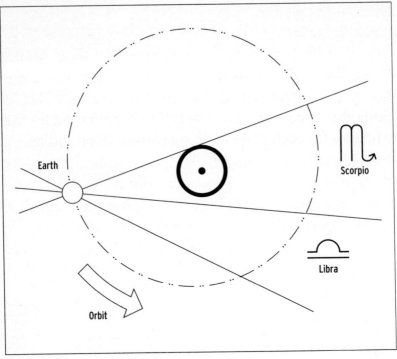

After 1 month the Sun moves into Scorpio

The Moon

The Moon orbits the Earth once a month. Its path is regular and passes through the signs in the same direction as the Sun. It spends about three to four days in each sign.

Mercury and Venus

These two planets are *always* closer to the Sun than Earth. In other words, it is impossible to have the Sun on one side of Earth and Venus or Mercury on the other side. You'll often see Venus preceding the Sun at dawn or following the Sun at dusk, and for this reason it is also known as the morning or evening star (although it is actually a planet). Because of their close orbits, Venus and Mercury are always near the Sun in a natal chart. And, like the Sun, they take one year to pass through all the signs.

Uranus, Neptune and Pluto

The main point to note about the orbits of these three outer planets is that, because they are so far from the Sun, they take a number of years to pass from one sign to the next. Consequently, whole generations of people can have these planets marking the same star sign. The following chart tables the time it takes for each planet to move through the zodiac.

PLANET	TIME TAKEN TO PASS THROUGH...	
	1 SIGN	FULL ZODIAC
Moon	2.5 days	28 days
Sun	1 month	1 year
Mercury	1 month	1 year
Venus	1 month	1 year
Mars	2 months	2 years
Jupiter	1 year	12 years
Saturn	2.5 years	30 years
Uranus	7.5 years	90 years[1]
Neptune	15 years	180 years
Pluto	30 years	360 years

Retrograde Motion

The general direction of the planets through the zodiac is Aries, Taurus and so on through to Pisces. This corresponds to the direction taken through the zodiac by the Sun. However, occasionally planets follow a reverse path, referred to as retrograde motion. From Earth, the planet appears to loop back and forth. In its reverse motion, it is said to be in 'retrograde' and is identified by the symbol: R

The following diagram illustrates the basic principle of retrograde motion. At first, Mars is seen to be in the sign Cancer (Position 1). As both Earth and Mars continue their orbit around the Sun, Mars appears to move in reverse, and when Earth reaches Position 2, Mars is seen in Gemini. As Earth moves on to Position 3, Mars makes up ground and again moves into Cancer.

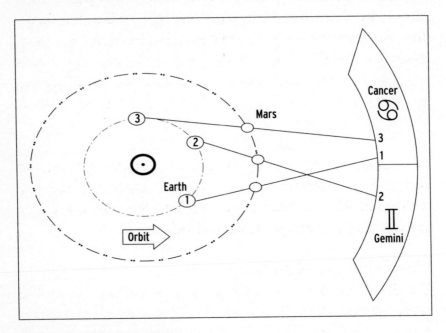

Demonstration of Retrograde Motion
Three points in time are marked 1, 2, 3.

For some astrologers, the retrograde motion of a planet will affect the way that the planet is interpreted in a chart. However, retrograde motion is more commonly used to determine short-term planetary movement. For example, the astrologer might note that two planets are close at the time of birth. They would then be interested in whether the planets were moving closer together or further apart. This relates more to aspects (see Planets Compared later in this section).

The Order of the Zodiac
Aries in the Spring

We now know that the Sun takes one year to pass through the zodiac. We also know that a year consists of four seasons. Consequently, the start of each season is always marked by the same star sign. This phenomenon has been a useful tool for humans. For example, it allowed people to predict the coming seasons and successfully plant crops simply by observing the procession of the zodiac. It is therefore no coincidence that the constellation Aries is recognised as the first sign of the zodiac, as it is the Sun's alignment with Aries that marks the beginning of spring in the northern hemisphere. New life on Earth is thus mirrored by a new cycle of the zodiac.

However, the beginning of Aries is not the first day of March as you might expect, but a seemingly unusual day around 21 March. Aries begins around this date for a very good technical reason, described below.

The Changing Seasons

The Earth rotates on its axis at an angle of 23.45° from the plane of the ecliptic, which is the apparent path of the Sun around the Earth. This idea is demonstrated in the following diagram, where we see Earth's orbit from the side, ie, the ecliptic. (In most of the diagrams in earlier chapters, we have viewed the solar system from above.)

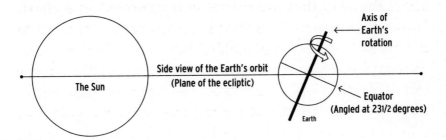

The Sun

Side view of the Earth's orbit
(Plane of the ecliptic)

Axis of
Earth's
rotation

Equator
(Angled at 231/2 degrees)

Earth

When the Earth is tilted away from the Sun, as in this diagram, it presents the southern hemisphere directly to the Sun. This is the case for six months of the year. The rotation of the Earth causes the Sun to appear to move east to west, not north to south, so there is no such thing as four seasons in one day.

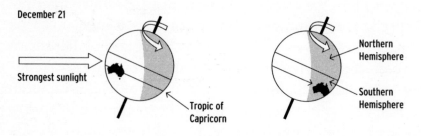

December 21

Strongest sunlight

Tropic of Capricorn

Northern Hemisphere

Southern Hemisphere

The above diagram shows that on 21 December the Sun is directly above the Tropic of Capricorn (so named because the Sun is in Capricorn). Six hours later, the Sun is still directly above the Tropic of Capricorn. This is as far south as the Sun will ever appear in the sky. For the next six months, as Earth orbits the Sun, the path of the Sun will move north. Six months later, on 21 June, Earth is on the opposite side of the Sun, and this is as far north as the Sun will go.

The following diagram illustrates how the Sun's position in the sky changes throughout the year. Note that Aries begins when the Sun is directly above the equator.

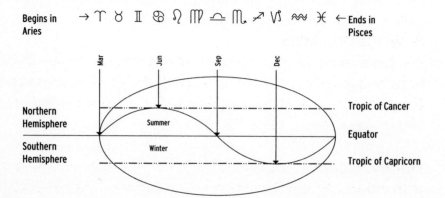

Begins in Aries

→ ♈ ♉ ♊ ♋ ♌ ♍ ♎ ♏ ♐ ♑ ♒ ♓ ← Ends in Pisces

Mar   Jun   Sep   Dec

Northern Hemisphere

Summer

Southern Hemisphere

Winter

Tropic of Cancer

Equator

Tropic of Capricorn

Therefore, on 21 September and 21 March night and day are equal, which is why each of these dates is known as an equinox. On these dates, the Sun is directly above the equator. The following diagram represents 21 March, which is the vernal or spring equinox in the northern hemisphere, and the natural starting point of the zodiac.

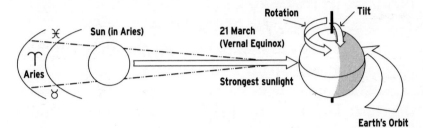

The Earth orbits the Sun each year with the North Pole constantly tilted towards the North Star. Also known as Polaris, this is the brightest star in the constellation Ursa Minor, and is slightly less than 1° from the North Pole.

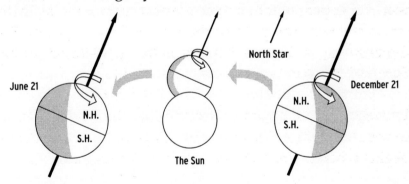

A Word on Dates

We have seen in this chapter that using Aries as the beginning of the zodiac is a logical choice. The ancient Babylonians linked the New Year with the spring planting and it was therefore tied closely with the vernal equinox.

However, most civilisations have marked the New Year with culturally significant events, rather than astrological events. Our modern practice of changing the calendar to the New Year on 1 January began with the Romans. In 153 BC they moved the first day of the year from 1 March, a date tied to the beginning of spring, to 1 January, when the civil year began and newly elected consuls assumed office.

Houses in the Sky
The Bare Bones of a Natal Chart

We are now ready to start piecing together the components of a natal chart. Usually a chart does not include any representation of Earth, as the Earth is always at the centre of the chart. However, the Earth is shown in the following diagrams to give you a clear understanding of why a chart looks the way it does.

You'll remember that an astrology chart is a representation of the sky from a point of view above the North Pole. So imagine yourself in deep space, looking down on Earth. In the following diagram, you can see a person on the equator. This represents a newborn baby, and the chart is a natal chart for this baby. If the baby looks to the left (anticlockwise), it will be looking east. This can be difficult to comprehend, because we are used to looking at maps from above the equator, not above the North Pole.

The second important element in the diagram is the backdrop of the constellations. There are twelve constellations, each spanning 30° of a circle that stretches out from the equator. So, directly to the baby's left is the eastern horizon. The Earth rotates in this direction and produces the following effect: the Sun, Moon, planets and constellations all 'rise' in the east about once a day.

Although this movement is caused by the Earth's rotation, in a chart the Earth is always fixed. Therefore, if this baby

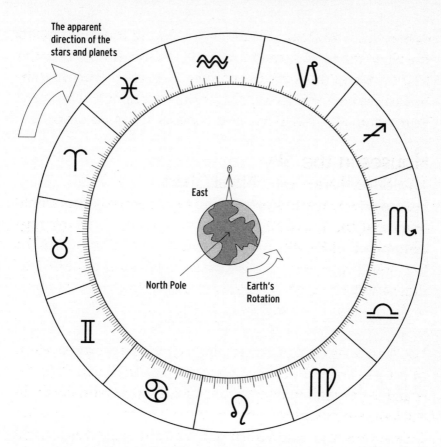

was born two hours later, the chart would change. The outer ring of constellations and planets would have turned clockwise 30°. But the point of sky directly above the baby's head would still correlate with the top of the chart. The baby is always on top of the world!

The Houses

A major part of a natal chart is the houses. To discuss these, we need to establish some basic terms.

The top of the chart is known as the midheaven (medium coeli, or MC). This is the sky above the newborn's head, and the point in the sky where the path of the Sun intersects the meridian line. Opposite this point, on the other side of the globe, is the subheaven (imum coeli, or IC). To the east (the *left* of the chart) is the exact point where the Sun rises and this is known as the ascendant. The descendant, opposite the ascendant, is the exact point where the Sun sets.

A cross is formed by the ascendant, descendant, MC and IC. Between each pair of spokes we place two additional spokes. The result is a division of the sky into twelve sections known as houses.

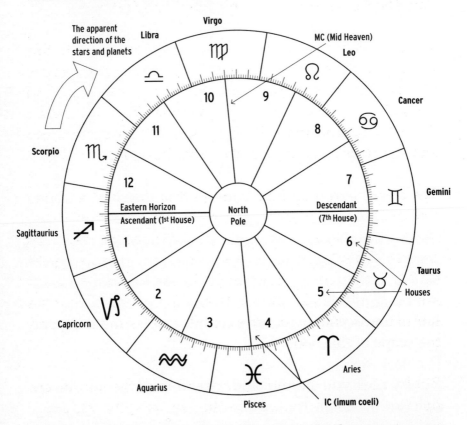

As you can see in the above diagram, the houses are not of equal size. This is caused by the latitude of the person's place of birth, and the latitude of the Sun in the sky. The house system shown here is the Placidus House System and it is the most popular in use. There are many other systems. Another popular one is the Equal House System, where the houses are divided equally.

The diagram shows the houses numbered from 1 to 12. The position of the First House is the section of the sky directly below the eastern horizon. Note that the houses do *not* rotate around the Earth. A common misconception regarding the houses is that the MC is equivalent to noon and so on. This is *not* so. The MC is *always* at the top of the chart (in the sky above the baby's head) regardless of the time of day. The Sun is in the MC only once a day (at noon).

The eastern horizon is marked by the ascendant, so in this diagram we can see that Sagittarius was rising at the time of birth. In this case we say that the 'ascendant is in Sagittarius' or that 'Sagittarius is rising'. Two hours after the birth, Sagittarius will have risen into the eastern sky and Capricorn will appear above the horizon.

The rising sign is an important part of the chart and one that can easily be wrong. Since a new star sign moves past the ascendant every two hours, the astrologer needs a very accurate time of birth. Even half an hour could make a great deal of difference to your chart. In the same way, the houses are easily affected by the location of birth. Calculating the line of the ascendant requires complex tables and is beyond the scope of this book.

But by now you should understand how the houses are determined. In the context of a chart reading, the astrologer will place great emphasis on the First House, because this determines your rising sign. The houses in which the planets reside are also important. But the houses that are empty of planets will have little impact on your reading and may not warrant a mention.

Combining the Planets, Signs and Houses

We have now discussed most of the physical elements that are represented in an astrological chart. The planets and the constellations move across the sky, above the equator, from east to west as the Earth rotates. The planets always have a corresponding sign and a corresponding house. Let's see how they look combined in a chart.

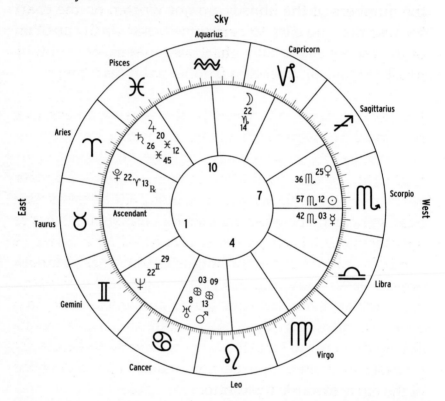

The chart consists of two spoked wheels. The outer wheel represents the twelve constellations, known as the signs of the zodiac. Each sign is allotted an equal portion of the sky, being 30° in a total of 360°. As we go forward in time, this outer wheel turns clockwise mimicking the way the constellations rise in the east and set in the west.

The inner wheel is also spoked. These spokes mark the divisions between the houses. The divisions are not always equal because they are determined by the position of the Sun in the sky. The left-hand spoke represents the eastern horizon. It marks the beginning of the First House.

The house numbers indicate the order in which the star signs will rise in the east in the hours after birth. The houses are numbered from 1 to 12 and they are fixed. Normally, the numbers of the houses are not written on the chart because they are easy to determine based on the position of the ascendant. In this chart we have numbered four houses to help you become familiar with the concept.

The very inner circle is normally reserved for aspects (see the following chapter, Planets Compared).

Within the houses are written the planets. Like the outer wheel (the signs), the planets also move clockwise as time passes. (Remember, when a planet is in retrograde it moves anticlockwise.) Each planet is identified by a series of symbols and numbers. The series order is: Planet | Degrees | Star Sign | Minutes. For example on this chart we can read 'Neptune 22 degrees, 29 minutes in Gemini', that is, $\Psi\ 22\mathrm{I\!I}\ 29$. For most uses, the value of the degrees is sufficient, the minutes being unnecessary. When you see the position of a planet, it is usually written from the outer edge of the circle towards the centre.

There are some other features worth noting in this chart. Tagged onto the end of the position of Pluto ($\female$) is the symbol for retrograde motion (R). Therefore, at the time this chart represents, Pluto was moving across the sky from west to east (anticlockwise around the chart).

Note also the positions of the Sun ($\odot$) and Mercury ($\female$). Both planets are in the sign Scorpio (M). However, Mercury is in the Sixth House, while the Sun is in the Seventh House. This is not unusual, but will help you to consider possible variations that can occur in a chart.

Planets Compared
Angles Between Planets

When we view two planets from the perspective of Earth, there will always be an angle formed between the two planets. Any angle between two points on a chart is referred to as an aspect and is the shortest distance between the two points. The following diagram shows three example angles, followed by an example from a chart.

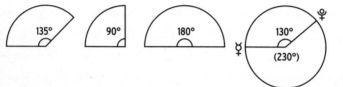

An aspect is derived from the smaller angle. That is, this aspect is 130°, not 230°.

Although every angle formed between two points is an aspect, only a handful of aspects are considered relevant to an astrological reading. Of these, usually only six are considered in a natal chart.

The following are some of the most common aspects. Keep in mind that the use of minor aspects and their symbols varies among astrologers. The columns 'Strength' and 'Nature' are related to chart interpretation, however they are included here because they dictate which aspects are commonly used. The full interpretative significance of aspects is discussed later in the Interpretation section (see the chapter, Aspects).

The orb represents the degree of accuracy needed to achieve a specific aspect. For example, a trine is 120° (orb 7°), which means that an angle of 126° is still considered a trine, although in this case it is a weak trine and will have less influence in a chart than a strong trine.

NAME	GLYPH	360÷	DEGREES	ORB	STRENGTH	NATURE
Conjunction	☌	1	360° (0°)	7°	Major	Neutral
Opposition	☍	2	180°	7°	Major	Tense
Quincunx	⚻	(5x30)	150°	2°	Major	Tense
Sesquiquadrate	⚼	(3x45)	135°	3°	Minor	Tense
Trine	△	3	120°	7°	Major	Harmonious
Square	□	4	90°	7°	Major	Tense
Quintile	Q	5	72°	3°	Minor	Harmonious
Sextile	✶	6	60°	5°	Major	Harmonious
Septile	✡	7	51°25	2°	Little Use	
Semi-Square	∠	8	45°	3°	Minor	Tense
Nonagen	N	9	40°	1°	Little Use	
Semi-Sextile	⚺	12	30°	2°	Minor	Harmonious

Many of the aspects represent the difference between two star signs. We can see from the following diagram that all the major aspects are of this type. There is also the semi-sextile which, although it is 30°, is not normally considered a major aspect.

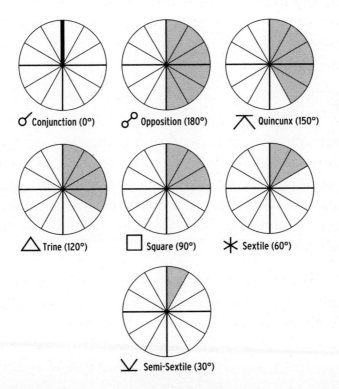

☌ Conjunction (0°)   ☍ Opposition (180°)   ⚻ Quincunx (150°)

△ Trine (120°)   □ Square (90°)   ✶ Sextile (60°)

⚺ Semi-Sextile (30°)

The major aspect angles (60°, 90°, 120°, 150° and 180°) are all multiples of 30. They are readily observed in a chart because each star sign is 30°. This is probably why they are seen to be more important. However, some astrologers argue for the strength of the quintile and the septile as well (shown in the table earlier).

The septile is interesting. If 360 is divided by any number between 1 and 10, the result will be a whole number. All except 7. So you could argue that a septile has a distinct significance.

Harmonic aspects are a recent development. Fundamentally, they allow for the division of 360 by any whole number. In practice, whole numbers up to 12 are in common use.

Calculating Aspects

With this knowledge of the aspects we can begin to look for them in a chart. By knowing the position of each planet we can calculate the exact angles they make with each other. With practice, aspects can be easily spotted. (Just remember that a degree has 60 minutes, so 00°59 + 00°02 = 01°01.) The following diagram shows how an aspect is calculated.

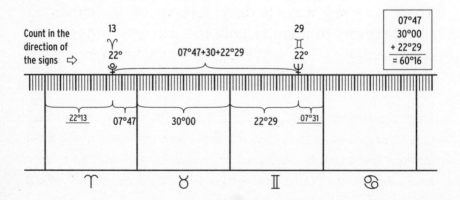

Once we find the total angle, we can ignore the minutes. In the previous diagram, the planets Pluto and Neptune form an aspect of 60°, which is a sextile. We can systematically work through all planetary combinations to find the possible aspects using the following table (this table applies to a specific chart, so a different chart would come up with a variation of this table). If an astrologer or a computer creates your natal chart, they will provide you with a list of aspects.

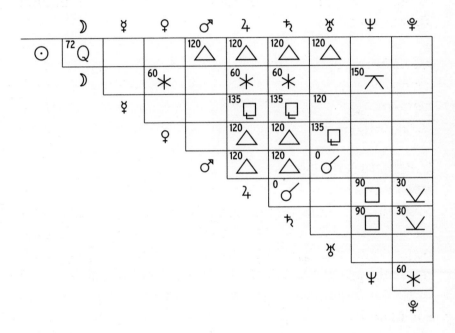

	☽	☿	♀	♂	♃	♄	♅	♆	♇
☉	72 Q			120 △	120 △	120 △	120 △		
☽		60 ✳		60 ✳	60 ✳			150 ⚻	
☿				135 □	135 □	120			
♀				120 △	120 △	135 □			
♂					120 △	120 △	0 ☌		
♃						0 ☌		90 □	30 V
♄								90 □	30 V
♅									
♆									60 ✳
♇									

There are a few ways to draw aspects into a chart. Some people prefer to identify only the strongest aspects (the most accurate), in which case there may be enough room for the associated symbol.

It is an advantage to use colour to distinguish between different types of aspects. In the following diagram we have left out the aspects that are traditionally considered minor, and used patterned lines for each type of aspect. Already

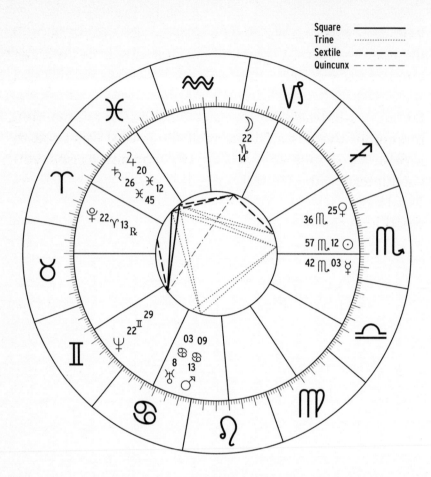

Square	————
Trine	··········
Sextile	– – – –
Quincunx	– · – · –

the centre of the chart is cluttered with lines. Using the table of aspect calculations can help sort out any confusion.

You might have noticed that a pattern has emerged in this chart. A triangle formed from eight trines is clearly visible. Such patterns are important in interpretation. Other distinct features of a chart might be a heavy bias of planets in one part of the chart, or a planet that forms the basis of most major aspects.

The Work is Over

Congratulations on taking the time to understand the science of astrology. Was it the steady patience of a Virgo that got you there? Or a burst of Arian obsession that will dissipate within a few pages? Unfortunately, if it's the latter, you may never find out!

Before you journey into the world of chart interpretation, remember there is a Glossary at the end of this book to refresh your memory or explain any new terms you encounter.

Good luck and have fun!

The Zodiac

This section will give you an understanding of the twelve signs of the zodiac and how they relate to the different planets and houses. It is concerned with learning all the elements that make up the interpretation of a chart. We are not concerned with the synthesis of that information into an interpretation just yet – that comes later in the section on Interpretation. But you will have a very good basis for interpreting a chart by the time we get there.

The Composition of the Twelve Signs covers the components of each sign, such as earth, air, water and fire, as well as other ingredients you might not be so familiar with. By learning these components, you are on the way to understanding each sign.

This chapter is followed by twelve chapters that cover each sign, its ruling planet and the house that it rules. Details about the planets and the houses can be found in the Interpretation section. There is a vibe about these twelve groupings that is easier to grasp when they are thought about together. Don't be too concerned with discerning the difference in meaning between the sign, the planet and its house – just learning the similarities is enough at this stage. The differences will become apparent when we tease apart the interpretation process later in the book.

An outline of the compatibility between each sign has been

included as the final chapter in this section – this is more for fun than for academic purposes. As you will soon discover, there is much more to a person than their Sun sign. You cannot expect that just because you are a Libra, that gorgeous Aquarian in your politics class will fall madly in love with you, or that Cancer boy will run a mile. Life, love and astrology are not that simple, but it is fun to take the basic traits of each sign and consider how they might interact.

And later you can find out the birth date and time of that good-looking Aquarian and draw up a chart comparing his compatibility with your own. But now we are really getting ahead of ourselves!

The Composition of the Twelve Signs

This chapter explains the basic components of the signs and how they can be remembered by three basic signatures: positive/negative; earth/air/fire/water; and cardinal/fixed/mutable. Each sign is a different combination of these three signatures, so by learning about these components, it is easier to piece together the character of each sign.

The Polarities

The twelve signs are split into two groups. We call these positive and negative, but they can also be known as masculine and feminine or yin and yang. They are called the polarities and they are the first step in dividing the signs. Their energy can be thought of like this:

✧ Positive – proactive, extroverted, masculine, yang energy

✧ Negative – passive, introverted, feminine, yin energy

The positive signs are Aries, Gemini, Leo, Libra, Sagittarius and Aquarius. The negative signs are Taurus, Cancer, Virgo, Scorpio, Capricorn and Pisces.

The Elements

The signs are split into a further four groupings called the elements. These are earth, water, air and fire. Certain characteristics are common for each of these elements:

✧ Fire – these signs have an explosive and energetic nature, and an intuitive decision-making process. They are enthusiastic and adventurous, but their energy can burn bright and furious, and then fade. They are impractical and become easily frustrated if things don't happen quickly enough. The three fire signs are Aries, Leo and Sagittarius.

✧ Earth – these signs have a steady and sensuous nature, and a perceptive decision-making process. They are reliable and efficient, but can lack imagination. They are practical and industrious and will get the job done. The three earth signs are Taurus, Virgo and Capricorn.

✧ Air – these signs have a thoughtful and communicative nature, and an intellectual decision-making process. They have clarity of thought and are good strategists. In general, they dislike commitment. The three air signs are Gemini, Libra and Aquarius.

✧ Water – these signs have a compassionate and sensitive nature, and an emotional decision-making process. They have wonderful imaginations and are of a more spiritual bent. They can be possessive of loved ones. The three water signs are Cancer, Scorpio and Pisces.

The Quadruplicities

The signs can be further defined by the way they use energy. These are called quadruplicities (singular: quadruplicity). They are also referred to as qualities or modalities. There are three modes and they relate to how the signs use their energy in the environment:

✧ Fixed quadruplicity – these signs keep their energy contained and tend to leave the environment as it is. They are conservative in their energy use and are strong on consistency. This quadruplicity dominates Taurus, Leo, Scorpio and Aquarius.

✧ Cardinal quadruplicity – these signs give out energy and like to assert their influence on the environment. They promote change, sometimes for its own sake. They are assertive and like to lead. This quadruplicity dominates Aries, Cancer, Libra and Capricorn.

✧ Mutable quadruplicity – these signs both give out and keep energy, making them unstable and the most open to flux in the environment. They are able to live with their environment as well as feel the need to control it. This can work well, but sometimes the two desires can be apparent at the same time. This quadruplicity dominates Gemini, Virgo, Sagittarius and Pisces.

The signs are further governed by their ruling planet. This is explored in the section on Interpretation (see the chapter The Planets). The following diagram shows how these three distinctions define each of the signs.

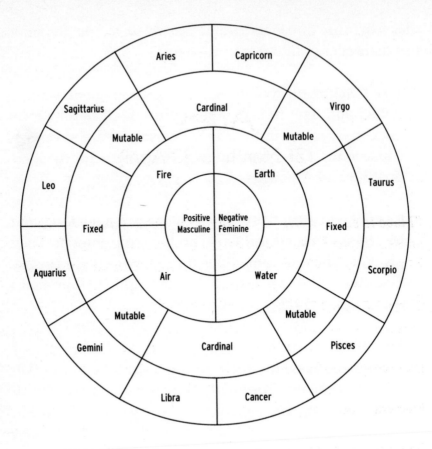

Aries
(21 March to 20 April)

"I love to see a young girl go out and grab the world by the lapels. Life's a bitch. You've got to go out and kick ass."
Maya Angelou (writer), Aries Sun sign, born 4 April 1928

Basic characteristics of the sign

Personal creed – *I am*

Positive/masculine sign

Element – Fire

Energy – Cardinal

Psychological type – Intuitive

Glyph – ♈ the ram's horns, possibly of Egyptian origin

Colour – Red

Body Part – Head

Gemstone – Diamond

Metal – Iron

Flowers – Thistle, honeysuckle, red poppy, geranium, hollyhock, ginger, clove, pennyroyal

Trees – Thorny varieties

Food – Plain and simple

People with an Aries Sun sign are generally:

✧ Open-minded

✧ Enthusiastic

✧ Individualistic

✧ Outspoken

✧ Alert

✧ Quick to act and speak

✧ Ambitious

✧ Candid

✧ Generous friends

✧ Adventurous

✧ Energetic

✧ Pioneering

✧ Courageous

✧ Confident

✧ Quick-witted

On the other hand, they can also be:

✧ Selfish

✧ Quick-tempered

✧ Impulsive

✧ Impatient

✧ Foolhardy

✧ Lacking in real direction

✧ Poor followers

Arians love:

✧ Action

✧ Coming first

✧ Challenges

✧ Championing causes

✧ Spontaneity

But they can't stand:

✧ Waiting around

✧ Humouring fools

✧ Admitting failure

✧ Tyranny

✧ Other people's advice

The Aries Character

The spring equinox falls on 21 March. It's the beginning of the new zodiacal year and Aries is the first flame. Desire, initiative, courage and action best describe Aries. The young ram is adventurous, ambitious, impulsive, enthusiastic and full of energy.

Aries is about learning the boundaries of individualism. Aries comes to every situation as though it is brand-new, and they need to burn their fingers to learn, and no one can tell them they're wrong. Aries' life lesson is to learn that doing things with others is more effective – but that comes later . . .

Arians love to be pioneers both in thought and action. They are very open to new ideas and are not afraid to try them out. Yet they can lose interest once the first excitement is gone. They welcome challenges, but can sometimes be undone by their own impatience, which will surface if they don't get quick results.

Aries make courageous leaders, with a genuine and gentle concern for those they command. But they are rather ordinary followers because they are usually convinced they have a much better way of doing things.

And they usually do have a better way. Aries spend a lot of time thinking about how quickest to get from A to B, and they can come up with some very laterally minded solutions. For this reason they can be obstinate about obeying directions. It is very important to explain the reasons for doing something carefully to an Aries. Particularly when they are children, an Aries is likely to heedlessly do it their way, if they think your way could be a waste of time.

Aries can be quite child-like in their enthusiasm for an idea, especially if it's one of their own, and this enthusiasm can be infectious. Aries believe all their ideas are original, and they are, at least to them. If it is true that people are reincarnated through the zodiac, from Aries through to Pisces as they develop their soul, this would make Aries a very new soul eager to explore all that the world has to offer.

Because of this, Aries are rarely cynical or world-weary. This refreshing approach makes them attractive to others, and it is what makes most of their egocentricities positively amusing!

And make no bones about it: they are egocentric. They have an immense amount of energy that can make them feel superior to other, more slothful, souls. This energy can also make them restless, headstrong, quick-tempered, easily offended and just a little bit aggressive. But Aries is the first flame and the heat doesn't last too long, so they rarely hold long-lasting grudges.

The Sun in Aries revels in self-expression. Arians would much rather speak than listen. Where others might fall silent for lack of things to say, the Aries will convince himself that he actually does have something to say – and then tell you about it.

Because of their independent spirit, they are often on the side of the battler in any given debate. They like to champion lost causes and losing battles because they have a strong belief in their own abilities to turn any situation around, and they are hopelessly optimistic.

With all this boundless energy and self-belief, Arians can easily be irritated by slowness or moderation. They can sometimes march straight over the sensibilities of others to get to where they are going.

This thoughtless behaviour can appear to be very selfish, but Arians need to allow their straightforward nature to flourish without getting caught up in resentment, negativity and self-pity. Though they may appear flippant when the conversation turns to more emotional issues, they are not insensitive to other people's problems, but just can't see the need to dwell on them. They can become irritated if they feel they are being swamped by other's issues; the Aries attitude is 'just get on with it' and they have very little time for those who are floundering emotionally.

"To look back is to relax one's vigil."
Bette Davis (actress), Aries Sun sign, born 5 April 1908

Aries is also irritated by nostalgia and sentimentality. Perhaps this is why many Arians have trouble recalling much of their childhood. They don't enjoy dwelling on the past, happy or sad, and prefer to live in the future.

A great challenge for those with a lot of Aries influence is to enjoy the journey, rather than treating life like a scorecard of experiences, with points to be racked up and compared. Aries can sometimes live life with so many half-attempted goals and ambitions that they never feel truly satisfied. In this way, they can benefit from a partner who will lean on them a little to actually finish things off and make them sit back and enjoy the reward.

The intensity of the Aries sexual urge can manifest itself in promiscuity and a conquistador approach to the opposite sex. Abundant enthusiasm for something new can also trick the gallant Aries into an early marriage.

A lackadaisical approach to contraception may have similar consequences.

This may not be so bad, as Arians make highly devoted parents. They connect with children in a wonderful way, because they remember what it is like to see the world with fresh eyes. An Aries parent will go to great lengths to protect the innocent wonder of their child.

Mentally, Arians pride themselves on being intellectual and objective, but their thinking can lack rigour. They are quick-witted but their thought processes can be a bit spotty. Their intuitive nature and lack of patience can make them jump ahead, and they can benefit from someone picking them up on their wild leaps of logic.

"I thought I'd begin by reading a poem by Shakespeare, but then I thought, why should I? He never reads any of mine."
Spike Milligan (comedian), Aries Sun sign, born 16 April 1918

If you are that someone, don't expect to be thanked for your patience. You may get some grudging thanks when the book/event/plan/debate has been successfully concluded, but don't expect a card or a little gift – that is not the Aries style.

Aries at Work

Arians are terrific in sales and with their enthusiasm could convince an Andean Indian to buy a snorkel, and perhaps even to upgrade to a full oxygen tank, wetsuit, flippers and night-vision goggles. However, the Arian can run out of steam at the vital moment.

If musically inclined, they make great songwriters, plus great jazz soloists because they can always come up with something new; this sort of unstructured approach suits them well. However, they usually make lousy pop singers because they can't maintain enthusiasm to rehearse properly, and so often forget the words to their own songs.

They usually have terrific people skills and have no trouble talking themselves into just about any job. For this reason they find it easy to chop and change at will and their restless minds wander quickly. Aries should be wary of becoming a jack-of-all-trades, and master of none. If they find out what they love doing early in life and focus on that, they can do whatever they put their mind to.

"Live all you can; it's a mistake not to. It doesn't so much matter what you do in particular, so long as you have your life. If you haven't had that what have you had?"
Henry James (writer), Aries Sun sign, born 15 April 1843

The great lessons Aries must learn is to discipline the qualities of their character to their advantage, not to their eternal frustration. They also must learn to know the difference between what can and can't be changed, and to find peace and harmony with their partner.

The Ultimate Renaissance Man
"Iron rusts from disuse; stagnant water loses its purity and in cold weather becomes frozen; even so does inaction sap the vigour of the mind."
Leonardo da Vinci (artist/inventor), Aries Sun sign, born 15 April 1452

Leonardo da Vinci is a great example of what focused Aries energy can achieve. His discoveries in art, science, botany, anatomy, geology, architecture, aerodynamics and engineering have remained unsurpassed. He was one of the most important artists of the Italian Renaissance (Latin for 'rebirth', a very important Arian concept), a period when the arts and sciences flourished.

This remarkably gifted and prolific man was self-made, and few artists owed so little to either circumstance or teachers. He brought his ingenious solutions to a breathtaking variety of topics.

Da Vinci invented bridges, guns and explosives; he painted works such as the 'Mona Lisa'; and he pioneered many techniques for making drawings look three-dimensional, all of which are in practice today.

Through his exploration of hydraulics Da Vinci discovered that the history of the Earth that could be seen in the layers of rock. He learned the effect of the Moon on the tides and foreshadowed modern conceptions of continent formation.

As an anatomist (he dissected nine bodies) he ascertained figures concerning the insertion of the muscles and their movements which specialists still admire for their accuracy. He devised the earliest theories concerning the muscular movements of the cardiac valves and studied the circulation of the blood and the action of the eye.

In mechanics he understood steam and its potential as a means of propulsion. He lay down the principles of aviation and, boldly adhering to the 'heavier than air' principle, he constructed the first artificial bird.

As if that wasn't enough, Da Vinci invented scissors, the parachute, the clock and an underwater diving suit. He divined the true nature of fossils. In botany, he formulated the laws of the alternation of leaves.

Not a bad life's work, even for an Aries.

Leonardo da Vinci's life also highlights the cardinal nature of Aries. For the Arian, a good idea is one worth exploiting, but Da Vinci's true mode of expression was creation, not manipulation or communication. Arians are the ideas-people of any organisation and are more than happy to let other people see the project through to completion.

Aries Health

Aries rules the head. Internally, it rules the brain and nerve centres, carotid arteries; and externally the cranium, jaw and facial bones. As a sign of this celestial association, many Aries are born with a birthmark on their head.

This means that Aries can be subject to all kinds of head complaints, such as sinusitis, headaches, toothache, gum afflictions and baldness. They can be prone to injuries to the head and face. Typical other Aries afflictions are: fainting; sunstroke and heatstroke; ear disorders, eye troubles; biliousness; facial blemishes, pimples, dyslexia, speech impediments, hypertension; anaemia; herpes; diabetes; brain disorders, meningitis, Alzheimer's disease, aphasia and stroke.

Aries should try to use their energy creatively and express themselves physically. If they expect others to provide them with stimulation they can become depressed and overweight. If ill, they should try eating bulgur wheat, oats and barley; eat more fish and less red meat; eat plenty of fresh salads, especially lettuce, tomatoes and spinach; and drink cooling juices like wheat grass, grape and apple. They should avoid heavily spiced foods and alcohol.

Aries are also prone to potassium deficiency (bananas are a great remedy for this). They should keep up the water intake during the day to maintain the Aries hot/cold balance.

When looking for music for meditation, the healing musical note for Aries is D sharp. Oils such as black pepper, clove, coriander, cumin, frankincense, ginger, neroli, pennyroyal, petitgrain, pine and woodruff are good for aromatherapy.

The Aries Partner

Fancy à la carte dinners are not the way to impress an Aries, as they usually regard food as more a necessity than a lavish gesture. Indulge his eclectic brain in a myriad of new experiences – take him salsa dancing, for a picnic at the zoo, to a smoky jazz club one night and to a Hare Krishna restaurant the next.

Keep the conversation lively, and engage him with a few witty anecdotes, but mostly let the flow revolve around him. It's usually a fine balance between being interesting and having your own opinions, and feeding his fire-eating ego.

Like a toddler, Aries mostly likes to play side-by-side rather than interacting and cooperating, and he will appreciate you having your own talents and hobbies rather than wanting him to be involved in everything you do.

When things get a little more smoochy, give your Aries a head massage or play with his hair and watch him melt like butter in your hands!

Gifts for your Aries

Aries don't value possessions that much and can appear to be quite monastic in their preferred environment, so don't go to too much effort or expense. You will only be hurt when you find that expensive ring that you spent a week's wages on lying carelessly next to the plug-hole in the bathroom. And don't expect her to be too distressed when you tell her where you found it – she'll just be happy that you did!

More bookish Aries will love books on philosophy and ideas. Practical gifts like a Swiss Army pocketknife will be appreciated, as Aries value functionality. Music CDs are a good idea, and don't be too worried that you might not pick her taste; she will enjoy the new experience of something a little off-beat.

Famous Aries Sun Signs

21 March 1946 – Timothy Dalton (actor)

21 March 1962 – Matthew Broderick (actor)

22 March 1923 – Marcel Marceau (mime artist)

23 March 1953 – Chaka Khan (singer)

24 March 1874 – Harry Houdini (magician)

24 March 1911 – Joseph Barbera (animator)

24 March 1930 – Steve McQueen (actor)

25 March 1934 – Gloria Steinem (publisher)

25 March 1942 – Aretha Franklin (singer)

25 March 1965 – Sarah Jessica Parker (actress)

26 March 1931 – Leonard Nimoy (actor)

26 March 1942 – Erica Jong (writer)

26 March 1944 – Diana Ross (singer)

27 March 1963 – Quentin Tarantino (film director)

28 March 1921 – Dirk Bogarde (actor)

29 March 1900 – John McEwan (Australian prime minister)

29 March 1916 – Eugene McCarthy (politician)

29 March 1943 – Eric Idle (comedian)

29 March 1964 – Elle McPherson (supermodel/businesswoman)

30 March 1853 – Vincent van Gogh (artist)

30 March 1937 – Warren Beatty (actor)

30 March 1945 – Eric Clapton (musician)

30 March 1957 – Debra Byrne (singer)

30 March 1962 – MC Hammer (singer)

30 March 1968 – Celine Dion (singer)

31 March 1934 – Richard Chamberlain (actor)

31 March 1948 – Rea Perlman (actress)

1 April 1815 – Otto von Bismarck (military commander)

1 April 1883 – Lon Chaney (actor)

2 April 1805 – Hans Christian Anderson (writer)

2 April 1914 – Sir Alec Guinness (actor)

2 April 1948 – Emmylou Harris (singer)

3 April 1783 – Washington Irving (writer)

3 April 1924 – Marlon Brando (actor)

3 April 1924 – Doris Day (actress)

4 April 1856 – Booker T Washington (educator)

4 April 1928 – Maya Angelou (writer)

4 April 1965 – Robert Downey Jnr (actor)

5 April 1900 – Spencer Tracy (actor)

5 April 1908 – Bette Davis (actress)

5 April 1916 – Gregory Peck (actor)

5 April 1937 – Colin Powell (military chief)

6 April 1866 – Butch Cassidy (outlaw)

7 April 1939 – Francis Ford Coppola (film director)

7 April 1964 – Russell Crowe (actor)

8 April 1938 – Kofi Annan (United Nations secretary)

9 April 1821 – Charles Baudelaire (poet)

9 April 1892 – Mary Pickford (actress)

10 April 1932 – Omar Sharif (actor)

10 April 1952 – Steven Seagal (actor)

12 April 1930 – Tiny Tim (entertainer)

12 April 1947 – David Letterman (TV host)

13 April 1743 – Thomas Jefferson (US president)

14 April 1934 – Loretta Lynn (singer)

14 April 1977 – Sarah Michelle Gellar (actress)

15 April 1452 – Leonardo da Vinci (artist/inventor)

15 April 1843 – Henry James (writer)

16 April 1889 – Charles Chaplin (actor/comedian)

16 April 1918 – Spike Milligan (comedian)

16 April 1921 – Peter Ustinov (actor)

17 April 1918 – William Holden (actor)

17 April 1975 – Victoria Beckham (singer)

18 April 1946 – Hayley Mills (actress)

19 April 1933 – Jayne Mansfield (actress)

19 April 1935 – Dudley Moore (actor/comedian)

20 April 1893 – Joan Miró (artist)

The First House

Aries is closely associated with the First House, which is usually referred to as the house of self. The principles of the First House are in keeping with the characteristics of Aries. The cusp of the First House is also the home of the ascendant, that is, the sign that was rising on the eastern horizon at the precise moment of your birth. Also known as the rising sign, the ascendant represents a person's image to the world. Along with your Sun and Moon signs, this is one of the most important influences on your chart. For more information on the First House see the chapter, The Houses, in the Interpretation section.

Mars

Aries is ruled by the planet Mars, and the principles of Mars are in keeping with the characteristics of Aries. For details on Mars and how to read it in a chart see the chapter, The Planets, in the Interpretation section.

Taurus
(21 April to 21 May)

"A good heart is the Sun and the Moon; or, rather, the Sun and not the Moon, for it shines bright and never changes."
William Shakespeare (playwright), Taurus Sun sign, born 23 April 1564

Basic characteristics of the sign

Personal creed – *I have*

Negative/feminine sign

Element – Earth

Energy – Fixed

Psychological type – Perceptive

Glyph – ♉ the bull's head, which has links with early Egyptian civilisations

Colour – Pastel shades, especially pink, and emerald green, brown, russet, turquoise

Body part – Throat, neck

Gemstone – Emerald

Metal – Copper

Flowers – Rose, poppy, foxglove, daisy, lily, daffodil, apple, magnolia

Trees – Apple, pear, ash

Food – Peaches, fruit puddings, home-cooked delights

People with a Taurus Sun sign are generally:

✧ Patient

✧ Reliable

✧ Warm-hearted

✧ Loving

✧ Persistent

✧ Placid

✧ Artistic

✧ Gentle

✧ Loyal

✧ Domestic

✧ Discriminating

✧ Sensual

On the other hand, they can also be:

✧ Jealous

✧ Possessive

✧ Resentful

✧ Inflexible

✧ Self-indulgent

✧ Greedy

✧ Unenterprising

Taureans love:

✧ Security

✧ Stability

✧ Practicality

✧ Consistency

✧ Sex

✧ Routine

✧ Fine food and good linen

✧ A good provider (either being one or having one)

But they can't stand:

✧ Risks

✧ Cheating

✧ Waste

✧ Change

✧ Uncertainty

✧ Cheap wine and a three-day growth

The Taurus Character

Taureans revel in gracious living and delicious excess. The second sign of the zodiac loves the prize, the big reward at the end. They are a tactile lot, and as children covet cuddles and kisses. They also probably had more than their fair share of comforters, like a favourite blanket or teddy, and most likely were difficult to wean.

"If all our happiness is bound up entirely in our personal circumstances it is difficult not to demand of life more than it has to give."
Bertrand Russell (philosopher), Taurus Sun sign, born 18 May 1872

The bed is the prized possession of most Bulls. They are luxuriant sleepers and will seek out a perfect sleeping position like Goldilocks. Once completely snuggled in, they will drift off into a deep repose and wake up exactly as they fell asleep. Most people's first big purchase will be a car or a stereo – the Taurean is more likely to buy a good double mattress.

And it will be the first well-considered purchase of many. Taureans love to own (usually expensive) things. This is not for an outward show of wealth or status, like their fellow earth sign the Capricorn, but more for the pleasure of the object itself.

"Wealth is not a hindrance, but rather a help towards attaining a proper standing in a chosen field of activity. I confess that as far as I am concerned, it has done me some service as it preserved my character from many a crookedness poverty might have exposed it to."
Henryk Sienkiewicz (writer), Taurus Sun sign, born 5 May 1846

Peek into a Taurean pantry and you are likely to be taken aback by its extravagance. No matter how dire the financial situation of the Bull, they will always find a few extra dollars for the very best extra virgin olive oil, or the delectably rich Belgian chocolate topping with more than a hint of Grand Marnier. A dinner party at a Taurean's house is a wonderfully sensual experience.

But never assume for a moment that your Taurean friend or lover is as straight as they come, for they will often have interests that border on the eccentric. Collecting snow domes, playing the zither, or translating the Bible from the original Hebrew are examples of some original Taurus hobbies. Furthermore, you would probably never suspect they had these skills, except for their annoying habit of making gifts of their favourite wares.

The Taurean nature is a kind one, and they can enjoy helping people out of sticky situations. They can sometimes be unassuming in this regard and may find themselves being taken advantage of. If this happens too often, watch out! And unfortunately, the final object of the Bull's wrath may have nothing to do with the original source of hurt or frustration. Taureans should learn to stand up for themselves, rather than letting resentment build. Taureans are slow to boil, but once they are enraged, be careful.

That bullish nature has more than once been called stubbornness, and it is true that Taureans, when they think they are right, can be very stubborn. But they also possess dogged determination to get the job done and they are one of the most reliable signs in the zodiac.

They are also very loyal. This can sometimes develop into possessiveness, and they should be aware that a life partner is not just a pretty addition to their homewares and manchester collection. However, they make wonderful, sensuous lovers and can turn any shack into a home, so the object of their affection is probably not going to mind a little of the green-eyed monster, as long as it is kept in hand.

Taureans are not explorers and pioneers like Aries; rather, they are the determined settler who builds houses and cultivates the soil. They have a tenacious and steady reserve of power which they put to thoughtful use. This makes for an irresistible and immovable force.

Taurus at Work

Taureans are methodical and thorough. These attributes combined make them excellent workers. For most Taureans, work is a means to an end, and they will not mind too much what they do, as long as it is close to home and they are adequately remunerated.

They often make pleasant workmates, who will turn the office into a nice place by burning essential oils and bringing in chocolate biscuits for a treat. The one-cup coffee plunger in the kitchen cupboard is probably a Taurean's.

Sometimes Taureans can find themselves stuck in jobs they despise because the money is too good or they fear the insecurity of finding another job. Maybe it is time to push the boundaries and do what you really want. If money isn't an issue (and unfortunately, for a Taurus, they always think that it is) most Taureans would love to be an art gallery curator, a florist or an antiques seller. Taureans have a wonderful talent for interior design and cooking, and could combine the two in running a lovely bed and breakfast in a picturesque valley in the country.

There are many exciting ways that Taureans could turn their marvellous home-making talents into quite a lucrative business, but they must be willing to make that jump out of their comfort zone. They have the perseverance and patience to make anything work, but just need the courage to go out and do it!

Viva Liberace
"You can have either the Resurrection or you can have Liberace. But you can't have both."
Liberace (entertainer), Taurus Sun sign, born 16 May 1919

Born to poor Polish-Italian immigrant parents, Wladziu 'Lee' Valentino Liberace was a child prodigy who, by the age of twenty, had performed with the Chicago Symphony Orchestra. In rags-to-riches style, he made a huge splash in Hollywood and Las Vegas. Liberace was a complicated man whose strongly held conservative views were at odds with his secret homosexual lifestyle. While successful and good-natured outwardly, privately he was known for his aggression and ambition.

Liberace's material excess was legendary; he surrounded himself with opulence. He had the hood of a Rolls Royce removed and attached to a VW Beetle so that his cape would have a sweet little limousine to ride in. Collecting porcelain dogs and enormous bejewelled rings were among his many eccentricities. He made a lot of money and chose to make a show of it. But Liberace didn't quite know where class began and where gauche left off.

He was said to have had many lovers who decreased in age as he grew older. According to those close to him, Liberace's private life was a constant, hedonistic orgy of sex, but he fought tooth and nail to prevent his homosexuality being exposed. When he was labelled as being gay by the *London Daily Mirror* in 1959, he sued and won.

It was his Bull-like refusal to admit to his homosexuality, or to maintain a dignified silence in the face of accusations, that brought Liberace a lot of pain in his last years. After discovering he had contracted AIDS, he became a recluse, and died on 4 February 1987.

Taurus Health

Taureans are usually solidly built with a heavy chest and torso, and thick legs. Taurus rules the throat, so vulnerable parts of the body are in this area, including the neck, shoulders and upper torso. Stiff necks, sore throats and earaches are common Taurean complaints.

Other Taurus afflictions include: adenoids, tonsillitis; anaemia; backache; colour blindness; abnormal breathing, croup, influenza, hayfever; ear disorders; knee problems; heart disease; haemorrhoids; painful and irregular menstruation; nasal polyps and mucus; eye troubles; cancer.

Taurus should avoid fattening, starchy and heating foods like meats and liquors, as they have a tendency towards gout and rheumatism. The Taurus with health problems might consider a short lemon juice and water fast (closely monitored by a physician) to offset toxic deposits leading to sore throats and earaches.

Moderation in food is the key word for this sign which tends to overindulge frequently. Yellow fruits like lemon, grapefruit, banana and melons and vegetables like carrots, celery, spinach, beans and peas will benefit Taureans.

When looking for music for meditation, the healing musical note for Taurus is A sharp. Oils such as apple, cardamom, honeysuckle, lilac, magnolia, oak moss, patchouli, plumeria, rose, thyme, tonka bean and ylang-ylang are particularly good for aromatherapy.

The Taurus Partner

Spoil your Taurus. No amount of money is too extravagant. Be sure to make some physical contact, touch her arm, look deeply into her eyes when you speak to her, ground her in your adoration. Physically and materially you must devote yourself to her.

She enjoys good manners and won't mind if you open the door for her or pull out the chair. Choose a good Italian restaurant for the first date (her favourite dessert is bound to be tiramisu). Do some homework as well, for she'll be impressed if you seem to know your way around a wine list. Feel free to order a good wine, after you know what she is eating, but don't order the dish for her. She is not that old-fashioned, and she always knows exactly what she wants to eat.

Dress nicely, smell good, clean your fingernails and use mouthwash. Flowers are a good idea, but only if you are picking her up from her place and she can arrange them before you go, as she won't gladly carry them around with her.

Gifts for your Taurus

Anything that is particularly sensual and pretty to look at will be appreciated, especially if it will contribute to his comfort. A soft wool rug in a luxurious colour (make sure it suits the decor), lambskin pillow undercovers or an electric blanket are nice ideas.

Scented body creams and luxury beauty items are also a good idea. Most earth signs love moisturisers and will be obsessive about moisturising one part of their body, be it lips, hands or elbows. Decadent foodstuffs are always a treat. Look for exotic treats like pears preserved in creme de menthe, baklava or halva.

Jewellery and lingerie will be genuinely appreciated, but don't think that you can skimp on quality. Your Taurus knows intimately the difference between white gold and platinum, llama and alpaca, cotton and linen, red and black caviar. It's his life's work and he cannot be fooled.

Famous Taurus Sun Signs

20 April 1889 – Adolf Hitler (dictator)

20 April 1941 – Ryan O'Neal (actor)

21 April 1816 – Charlotte Bronte (writer)

21 April 1926 – Queen Elizabeth II (British royalty)

22 April 1870 – Vladimir Lenin (Marxist)

22 April 1904 – Robert Oppenheimer (physicist)

22 April 1936 – Glen Campbell (entertainer)

22 April 1937 – Jack Nicholson (actor)

23 April 1519 – Catherine de Medici (French royalty)

23 April 1564 – William Shakespeare (playwright)

23 April 1891 – Sergei Prokofiev (composer)

23 April 1928 – Shirley Temple Black (actress)

23 April 1939 – Lee Majors (actor)

24 April 1934 – Shirley MacLaine (actress)

24 April 1942 – Barbra Streisand (singer)

25 April 1940 – Al Pacino (actor)

26 April 1933 – Carol Burnett (comedian)

27 April 1891 – Samuel Morse (inventor)

27 April 1922 – Jack Klugman (actor)

28 April 1937 – Saddam Hussein (Iraqi president)

29 April 1901 – Hirohito (Japanese royalty)

29 April 1970 – Uma Thurman (actress)

30 April 1933 – Willie Nelson (singer)

1 May 1769 – Duke of Wellington (militarist)

1 May 1945 – Rita Coolidge (singer)

2 May 1729 – Catherine the Great (Russian royalty)

2 May 1903 – Benjamin Spock (child specialist)

2 May 1903 – Bing Crosby (singer)

3 May 1919 – Pete Seeger (singer)

4 May 1929 – Audrey Hepburn (actress)

5 May 1818 – Karl Marx (revolutionary)

5 May 1846 – Henryk Sienkiewicz (writer)

5 May 1943 – Bob Woodward (journalist)

6 May 1758 – Robespierre (revolutionary)

6 May 1856 – Sigmund Freud (psychologist)

6 May 1895 – Rudolph Valentino (actor)

6 May 1915 – Orson Welles (actor/film director)

6 May 1937 – Rubin 'Hurricane' Carter (boxer)

6 May 1961 – George Clooney (actor)

7 May 1833 – Johannes Brahms (composer)

TAURUS

7 May 1901 – Gary Cooper (actor)

7 May 1908 – Eva Perón (actress)

8 May 1884 – Harry S Truman (US president)

9 May 1949 – Billy Joel (singer)

10 May 1899 – Fred Astaire (dancer)

11 May 1469 – Machiavelli (political writer)

11 May 1888 – Irving Berlin (composer)

11 May 1904 – Salvador Dali (artist)

12 May 1820 – Florence Nightingale (humanitarian)

12 May 1907 – Katharine Hepburn (actress)

13 May 1914 – Joe Lewis (boxer)

13 May 1931 – Jim Jones (cultist)

13 May 1939 – Harvey Keitel (actor)

13 May 1941 – Ritchie Valens (singer)

13 May 1950 – Stevie Wonder (singer)

14 May 1936 – Bobby Darin (singer)

14 May 1944 – George Lucas (filmmaker)

14 May 1952 – David Byrne (musician)

14 May 1969 – Cate Blanchett (actress)

15 May 1859 – Pierre Curie (scientist)

16 May 1905 – Henry Fonda (actor)

16 May 1919 – Liberace (entertainer)

17 May 1956 – Sugar Ray Leonard (boxer)

18 May 1872 – Bertrand Russell (philosopher)

18 May 1920 – Pope John Paul II (religious leader)

19 May 1890 – Ho Chi Minh (political leader)

20 May 1799 – Honoré Balzac (writer)

20 May 1908 – James Stewart (actor)

20 May 1946 – Cher (singer/actress)

21 May 1930 – Malcolm Fraser (Australian prime minister)

21 May 1960 – Robert Smith (singer)

The Second House

Taurus is closely associated with the Second House, and the principles of the Second House are in keeping with the characteristics of Taurus. The Second House reflects your attitudes about the material world, your philosophy towards money, possessions, finances and your earning and spending capacity. For more information on the Second House, see the chapter, The Houses, in the Interpretation section.

Venus

Taurus is ruled by the planet Venus, and the principles of Venus are in keeping with the characteristics of Taurus. For details on Venus and how to read it in a chart, see the chapter, The Planets, in the Interpretation section.

Gemini
(22 May to 22 June)

"The obstinacy of cleverness and reason is nothing to the obstinacy of folly and inanity."
Harriet Beecher Stowe (writer), Gemini Sun sign, born 14 June 1811

Basic characteristics of the sign
Personal creed – *I think*

Positive/masculine sign

Element – Air

Energy – Mutable

Psychological type – Thinking

Glyph – Ⅱ the two lines represent the two children, the two bright stars, Castor and Pollux of classical mythology

Colours – Yellow, blue

Body parts – Hands, breath

Metals – Mercury, alloy, mercury compounds

Gemstone – Agate

Flowers – Lavender, lilac, azalea, lily of the valley, myrtle, sweet pea

Trees – Nut-producing trees

Food – Salads, fruit, fish

People with a Gemini Sun sign are generally:

✧ Adaptable

✧ Intellectual

✧ Witty

✧ Logical

✧ Busy

✧ Spontaneous

✧ Good at writing and languages

✧ Lively

✧ Inquisitive

✧ Communicative

✧ Sociable

✧ Imaginative

✧ Persuasive

✧ Agile

✧ Positive

✧ Teasing

✧ Cheerful

On the other hand, they can also be:

✧ Nervous

✧ Tense

✧ Superficial

✧ Inconsistent

✧ Cunning

✧ Restless

✧ Two-faced

✧ Gossiping

✧ Unpunctual

✧ Make promises that can't be kept

✧ Irresponsible

✧ Exaggerating

✧ Over-optimistic

✧ Thinking in circles without a beginning, middle or end

✧ Cold

Geminis love:
✧ Variety

✧ Being occupied with many things simultaneously

✧ New people, new subjects, new ideas

✧ Flexible thinking

✧ Being knowledgeable and well-informed

✧ Flirting

✧ Fun

✧ Telling stories

But they can't stand:
✧ People with nothing interesting to say

✧ People without curiosity

✧ Overly emotional and irrational behaviour

✧ Possessiveness

✧ Jealousy

The Gemini Character
Geminis are considered the seekers of knowledge. They are curious, sociable, imaginative and have a strong desire to learn, to express themselves and to tell stories. Gemini is the sign of thinking, communicating and distributing information. The Gemini lifestyle is characterised by diversity, motion and collaboration with many different people. This

behaviour is all a means to an end, and the end that Geminis seek is the truth.

"Husbands are chiefly good as lovers when they are betraying their wives."
Marilyn Monroe (actress), Gemini Sun sign, born 1 June 1926

You probably met your Gemini friend at a party, looking completely at ease, playing the room with a glass of champagne in one hand and a cigarette in the other. She was flitting from group to group, leaving them laughing, and then moving on effortlessly to the next huddle.

It was a surprise, then, to discover she didn't actually know the host. She was there with a friend: 'He's over there,' she said, waving her hand airily in no particular direction. Her bright and expressive eyes remained locked on yours.

You think you might be falling in love. Who is this witty little lady? But before you know it, she is gone. The only thing left is the invigorating smell of lavender and her glass of champagne, left on the sideboard and barely touched. You realise it will take a little more than the ordinary to captivate the attention of this rare bird.

The Gemini Sun sign can often appear to be interested and interesting, but somehow emotionally detached. They are constant questioners and often dominate conversation, imparting information but often not of a very personal kind. They probably know your birth date, but you wouldn't know theirs. Hence, despite all their visibility, they can appear to be invisible.

Gemini is a yang sign, that is, a positive, masculine energy force, but the symbol of the Twins tells us there is more to the story. The Twins are both yin and yang, which we all possess to varying degrees, but which in Gemini is extremely pronounced.

Geminis love to see both sides of the argument. They are excellent debaters and can hold a contradictory view unflinchingly until they have won the argument. This is when they will exasperate you all over again by revealing that they actually agreed with you in the first place! They see no problem with changing their mind to suit the situation, and value the fluid motion of communication. This makes them lightning-quick thinkers.

"We make out of the quarrel with others, rhetoric, but of the quarrel with ourselves, poetry."
WB Yeats (poet), Gemini Sun sign, born 13 June 1865

This fluidity can also make them a bit wishy-washy and unable to stick at something for long. The Gemini can sometimes seem to lack a sense of style. This is because they can genuinely adapt to other people's tastes and see through their eyes.

Geminis can be wonderfully affirming in this way, and will find any angle to praise you. Most people agree that your giant fluoro statue of the Virgin Mary is a little off-colour, but the Gemini will earnestly argue that it is a powerful, yet cute, statement on religion in our commerce-driven society. He might even get a few people to agree with him!

But when it comes to decorating their own place, the Gemini can be downright indecisive, and will gather up an eclectic mix of Tuscan colours with Indian teak cabinetary and neo-Gothic light-fittings that almost, but not quite, work. They are not too concerned anyway, because they live primarily in their minds, and the comfort of their surroundings is not of utmost concern.

Geminis make fickle lovers. You can be in the middle of a passionate embrace when something catches their interest out of the corner of their eye. It might be a book on the desk, or a picture on the wall, but they will make a comment and expect you to answer in a logical, conversational manner. If you do manage to gurgle out an answer, the love-making will resume. For a Gemini, this is par for the course, but for others it can be a real candle-snuffer.

"A lover without indiscretion is no lover at all.
Circumspection and devotion are a contradiction in terms."
Thomas Hardy (writer), Gemini Sun sign, born 2 June 1840

Geminis use sex as they use most activities – to avoid boredom. Their penchant for variety and constant stimulation often finds Gemini with the strangest bedfellows. The greatest aphrodisiac for a Twin is a partner with a flashing wit. What the Gemini most craves is not the physical affection that comes from making love, but the verbal run up to it. Sometimes the flirting is much more satisfying for the Gemini than the consummation of lust. They love talking themselves into, and then back out of, bed with all sorts of people.

"I'm a very natural flirt, but I don't see it in a sexual way . . .
a lot of the time I'm like an overexcited puppy. I think I'm
being friendly with someone, they think I'm flirting with
them."
Kylie Minogue (singer), Gemini Sun sign, born 28 May 1968

The Gemini often appears to be living on their nerves. Young Geminis should avoid cigarettes, because it will become a nervous habit they will find exceedingly difficult to give up. Gemini rules the hands and Geminis find doing things with their hands very comforting. Couple this tendency with an edgy disposition, and cigarettes are dangerously attractive.

Harnessing their edgy energy is one of the lessons Gemini must learn. A mature Gemini will become a serious scholar, writer, researcher and therefore a great contributor. The immature Gemini is highly-strung, nervous and a gossip.

Gemini's anchor are words. They find a sense of safety in talking and exercising their excellent memories. They often have conversations in their heads. They also have a habit of absorbing information and instantly converting it into their own words in their minds. A Gemini will read, collate, simplify and imagine telling someone about it all at the same time. Some people are content to learn for their own sake. A Gemini learns for the joy of relaying the information on to others.

Geminis like to be able to verbalise everything. Of course, some emotions can't be put into words, and a Gemini will struggle with these, and eventually seem to lay them to one side. This filtering of emotions through the intellect can come across as calculating or aloof.

The Gemini eye for detail is breathtaking. Books being moved, a new clock, or a haircut will not go unnoticed. Geminis are often very good drivers for this reason, but you will wonder whether their minds are truly on the road when they point out a friend coming out of a shop that you have just flashed by, or spot a celebrity in a car two lanes away from you. Don't worry, the Twins can 'be' in two spots at once. You are in safe hands.

With all these abundant talents and charms, people are incredulous when they find out that the Gemini has very little faith in themself. Often it will be masked with an ironic wit or sarcasm. A Gemini would rather not do something at all and be thought of as unreliable, than do it badly and be thought of as incompetent or stupid.

This means Geminis are not good at pushing themselves into new projects. They have the verbal skills to mask any gaps in knowledge, and people can be enthralled by their insights, but their fear of looking stupid holds them back from making big breakthroughs. This is a huge pity, as the Gemini's flexible mind would be valuable in upper-management roles.

Gemini at Work

People enjoy working with Geminis for their cheery natures and funny one-liners. They can be an important lynchpin in the social fabric of the office and are also keepers of the office gossip.

With Mercury ruling, Geminis make wonderful salesmen or journalists, but they could also find themselves in more manual jobs like carpentry, lead-lighting, ceramics, jewellery or textiles, as they find working with their hands almost meditative. They also make very quick typists. They can be very expressive while talking, and their gesticulations can seem to take on a life of their own. They have a talent for magic tricks. With their ability to communicate, Geminis make engaging teachers, especially of high school students who find them nonpatronising and easy to relate to.

The Speedy Messenger

Tim Berners-Lee, born on 8 June 1955, the inventor of the World Wide Web, is an excellent example of a Gemini Sun sign. The Web has made communication across the world cheap and instantaneous, and continues to break down the barriers of distance.

Berners-Lee designed his Web software with the idea to organising material in a brain-like way, with links and inter-connections. He then developed a protocol by which information could be organised and delivered throughout the network. Mass communication had the potential for chaos, but Berners-Lee's system has left us communicating in a very ordered and truly Gemini way.

The Web is popular because it is potentially available to anyone. Berners-Lee chose not to licence his software (potentially losing him billions of dollars), because his main desire was to communicate, even with those who may not have bought his software. This has ensured the Web's success as the ultimate medium of communication and information.

It is a wonderful example of the Gemini desire to inform and communicate overriding even the desire to pocket wads of money.

Gemini Health
Gemini rules the hands and arms, and the lung area, so Geminis are subject to injury or infection in these areas (another reason why they should not smoke).

Constant mental activity and the weakness of the lungs means the Gemini requires oxygenating foods such as fresh fruits and vegetables. They will find extra benefit from orange-coloured foods such as oranges, pink grapefruit, peaches and apricots, which will loosen up the lungs and prevent mucus. They should drink plenty of water and carrot juice to keep the mucus moving. Geminis could consider cutting down on dairy products if this is causing an overproduction of mucus.

Lentils are an excellent Gemini legume, and Geminis generally like them because they are quick to prepare and eat, and very nutritious.

Geminis can have some trouble laying their busy head to rest, so they should avoid eating heavily before bedtime or having caffeine late in the day. While recuperating, meditating is excellent. A change of scenery is also beneficial. When meditating, pay careful attention to the breathing, which should be regular and deep.

Unfortunately, this double sign can mean that it is possible to suffer from two diseases at the same time. Common Gemini afflictions include anaemia; nervous disorders, stiff shoulders, diseases and injuries of the arms and fingers, leg pains; chest disorders, abnormal or shallow breathing, lack of proper oxygenation; hay fever, tuberculosis and pleurisy.

When choosing music for meditation, the Gemini healing musical note is A. Oils that are good to use in aromatherapy are benzoin, bergamot, mint, caraway, dill, lavender, lemon grass, lily of the valley, peppermint and sweet pea.

The Gemini Partner

You won't find a Gemini on the dance-floor or at the buffet; they will be at the bar, with every intention of buying a drink, just as soon as they talk to so-and-so. Geminis love a good chat and they love a sparkling mind even more, so just sidle up and say hello. They are one of the few signs to actually enjoy a good pick-up line, as long as it is funny or clever.

But that is as far as your proactive flirtation should go. When attempting to woo a Gemini, prepare to play woo-ee rather than woo-er. These guys know all the tricks in the book. In fact, they wrote the book, so don't try and beat them at their own game. They will be quite happy to take the lead.

Geminis love to be touched on the hands and arms and are especially sensitive in these areas. A Gemini woman will enjoy having her hand kissed in greeting, for it allows her to look coquettishly through her eyelashes and also show off her lovely fingers.

Going to see a film with coffee afterwards at a nice café is a good idea for a first date. Geminis will love having a common learning experience like a film to talk about.

Gifts for your Gemini

Books, music, videos or anything that will quench the Gemini desire for knowledge will be appreciated, as will theatre or concert tickets or an excursion to somewhere fun. Creativity and a sense of fun will impress more than expense and quality brand names, so think about something with a bit of novelty value; if it has a little story to go with it, all the better. They will love telling their friends about the funny gift you gave them.

Famous Gemini Sun Signs

22 May 1813 – Richard Wagner (composer)

22 May 1859 – Arthur Conan Doyle (writer)

22 May 1907 – Laurence Olivier (actor)

22 May 1959 – Morrissey (singer)

23 May 1974 – Jewel (singer)

24 May 1819 – Queen Victoria (British royalty)

24 May 1941 – Bob Dylan (singer)

25 May 1963 – Mike Myers (actor/comedian)

26 May 1867 – Mary Queen of Scots (Scottish royalty)

27 May 1878 – Isadora Duncan (dancer)

27 May 1923 – Henry Kissinger (statesman)

28 May 1944 – Gladys Knight (singer)

28 May 1968 – Kylie Minogue (singer)

29 May 1903 – Bob Hope (comedian)

29 May 1917 – John F Kennedy (US president)

30 May 1474 – Albrecht Dürer (artist)

30 May 1908 – Mel Blanc (cartoons voice)

31 May 1923 – Prince Rainier III (Monaco royalty)

31 May 1930 – Clint Eastwood (actor)

1 June 1926 – Andy Griffith (actor)

1 June 1926 – Marilyn Monroe (actress)

1 June 1934 – Pat Boone (singer)

2 June 1840 – Thomas Hardy (writer)

2 June 1965 – Steve and Mark Waugh (cricketers)

3 June 1925 – Tony Curtis (actor)

3 June 1926 – Allen Ginsberg (poet)

4 June 1975 – Angelina Jolie (actress)

5 June 1956 – Kenny G (musician)

6 June 1955 – Sandra Bernhard (comedian)

7 June 1848 – Paul Gauguin (artist)

7 June 1940 – Tom Jones (singer)

7 June 1952 – Liam Neeson (actor)

7 June 1958 – Prince (musician)

8 June 1933 – Joan Rivers (comedian)

8 June 1940 – Nancy Sinatra (singer)

8 June 1955 – Tim Berners-Lee (inventor)

9 June 1893 – Cole Porter (songwriter)

9 June 1963 – Johnny Depp (actor)

10 June 1922 – Judy Garland (actress/singer)

11 June 1910 – Jacques Yves Cousteau (ocean explorer)

11 June 1934 – Gene Wilder (actor)

12 June 1929 – Anne Frank (writer)

13 June 1865 – WB Yeats (poet)

14 June 1811 – Harriet Beecher Stowe (writer)

14 June 1946 – Donald Trump (entrepreneur)

14 June 1961 – Boy George (musician)

14 June 1969 – Steffi Graf (tennis champion)

15 June 1954 – Jim Belushi (actor)

17 June 1867 – Henry Lawson (poet)

17 June 1878 – MC Escher (artist)

17 June 1882 – Igor Stravinsky (composer)

17 June 1917 – Dean Martin (singer)

17 June 1946 – Barry Manilow (singer)

18 June 1942 – Paul McCartney (musician)

18 June 1952 – Isabella Rosselini (actress)

19 June 1896 – Wallis Simpson (almost royalty)

19 June 1947 – Salman Rushdie (writer)

20 June 1909 – Errol Flynn (actor)

20 June 1972 – Nicole Kidman (actress)

21 June 1905 – Jean-Paul Sartre (philosopher)

21 June 1921 – Jane Russell (actress)

21 June 1973 – Juliette Lewis (actress)

21 June 1982 – Prince William (British royalty)

22 June 1936 – Kris Kristofferson (singer/actor)

22 June 1949 – Meryl Streep (actress)

The Third House

Gemini is closely associated with the Third House, and the principles of the Third House are in keeping with the characteristics of Gemini. The Third House describes your relationship to your siblings, and your early schooling. For more information on the Third House, see the chapter, The Houses, in the Interpretation section.

Mercury

Gemini is ruled by the planet Mercury, and the principles of Mercury are in keeping with the characteristics of Gemini. For details on Mercury and how to read it in a chart, see the chapter, The Planets, in the Interpretation section.

Cancer
(23 June to 22 July)

"You can find the entire cosmos lurking in its least remarkable objects."
Wislawa Szymborska (poet), Cancer Sun sign, born 2 July 1923

Basic characteristics of the sign

Personal creed – *I feel*

Negative/feminine sign

Element – Water

Energy – Cardinal

Psychological type – Feeling

Glyph – ♋ represents the breasts, probably a Babylonian sign

Colours – White, cream, silver

Body part – Stomach

Metal – Silver

Gemstones – Pearl, moonstone

Flowers – Moonflower, white rose, lily, water lily (lotus), iris, white poppy, carnation, jasmine, southern magnolia, chamomile

Trees – None in particular

Food – Dairy foods, fish

People with a Cancer Sun sign are generally:

✧ Sensitive

✧ Caring

✧ Nurturing

✧ Feeling-oriented

✧ Loving

✧ Home-loving

✧ Protective

✧ Supportive

✧ Creative

✧ Charitable

✧ Productive

✧ Fecund

✧ Psychic when it comes to their children

On the other hand, they can also be:

✧ Crabby

✧ Moody

✧ Worriers

✧ Insecure

✧ Clingy

✧ Jealous

✧ Manipulative

✧ Undaring

✧ Dependant

✧ Possessive

✧ Touchy

✧ Indirect

✧ Fussy

✧ Martyrs to their children's whims

✧ Pursuant of other's dreams at the expense of their own

Cancers love:

✧ Holding on

✧ Nurturing

✧ Planning for the future

✧ Superannuation, security for their money

✧ Parenthood

✧ Home-making, cooking, tailoring

✧ Childcare

✧ Business

✧ Food

✧ Security

✧ Routine

✧ The predictable

But they can't stand:

✧ Spontaneity

✧ People intruding on their family's harmony

✧ Sarcastic jokes directed at them

✧ Tactless criticism

✧ Practical jokes

✧ Being away from home for too long

The Cancer Character

"Eschew the monumental. Shun the Epic. All the guys who can paint great big pictures can paint great small ones."
Ernest Hemingway (writer), born Cancer Sun sign, 21 July 1899

Cancers are the homemakers of the zodiac. People with a Cancer Sun sign single-handedly keep cookbook-sellers, homewares shops, plant nurseries and hardware stores in business.

Cancers are in their element at Christmas time – the table will groan with food, all the family has gathered round and the Christmas tree, always drooping with home-made decorations, will be the central focus. The story of Christmas itself is a very Cancerian one, with everyone heading home for the census, and Mary making a manger in a stable for her newborn baby.

Cancers are good with money. They enjoy the community of team sports and can be quite competitive in a fun way. They are always first up at a picnic, organising a game of cricket, and like both playing and watching sports.

Cancer's body part is their stomach and they do well when they listen to their gut feelings. When things are out of kilter, they will feel it in their stomach, and they often get constipated on long holidays, probably because they are away from home for too long.

The Cancer ability to make a home can superficially appear to be similar to the Taurean desire to nest, but they have completely different motivations. For a Taurus, making a home is about making a beautiful house to enjoy, whereas for Cancer a beautiful home is a by-product of their desire to make a harmonious nest for their loved ones.

"House ordering is my prayer, and when I have finished, my prayer is answered. And bending, stooping, scrubbing, purifies my body as prayer doesn't."
Jessamyn West (writer), Cancer Sun sign, born 18 July 1902

Cancers love communal activities and family traditions. They create them and uphold them with great vigour. They are great story-tellers, especially about the exploits of family members, and are often the keepers of the oral family history. A home run by a Cancer will have a sense of timelessness about it. People can leave for many years and return and find the radio playing the same station at the same time in the morning, showers taken and breakfast eaten, and a cup of tea and the paper before work all continuing to the same schedule. A Cancer parent will keep every little piece of cardboard painted by their offspring.

Cancers find a Zen-like serenity in the routine of everyday life. When this routine is thrown out, it can cause a great deal of stress for the Cancer, but like water, they will find their level. They have a knack for creating a home virtually anywhere. They have to, in order to feel safe.

"When indeed shall we learn that we are all related one to the other, that we are all members of one body?"
Helen Keller (diarist), Cancer Sun sign, born 27 June 1880

Cancers have a deep yearning to be a part of a big flourishing family. If this is not possible, they will try and create a family out of the people around them. They can make great flatmates for this reason. Celebrations are very important to the Cancer. If they have been born into a large family, they often choose partners who they think could benefit from being embraced by them. They just want to share the love, and their maternal hearts break when they see someone who could do with a bit of mothering.

Male Cancers are a real catch because they combine their inherent masculinity, and the unusually outward show of feminine energy in their Sun sign. Cancer is also a water sign, that is, an emotional sign, with cardinal or outputting active energy. This means that Cancers actively seek out places and people to nurture.

In the Cancer male, this manifests itself as an unusually sensitive side seeking to nourish others. Cancer males make patient and attentive fathers and empathetic husbands who love to involve themselves in the business of home-making. They have good taste in most things and are especially well-dressed. So well-dressed, in fact, that they trust their ironing to no one, not even their adoring partner. They like to woo with their cooking skills and come with more than the average amount of male domestic nous.

Cancer's planet is the Moon, and like the Moon which controls the tides, they are affected by moodiness. This can be hard to cope with, since they are usually in denial about their mood swings, or reluctant to admit to how much they affect those around them.

Cancers avoid confrontation and will not say anything they think will cause an argument, but that does not mean they hide their feelings well. Cancers wear their hearts on their sleeve, so you don't have to be the most perceptive person to know when they are upset with you.

They will let their feelings be known with a barbed or cutting comment, sometimes so well disguised that it will only hit its target. They are usually only aware of what they have said after it has come out of their mouth, but even then they might not admit to it.

Ironically, Cancers do not take criticism well, no matter how well-intended, and they can be terribly hurt by the slightest of insults. Like the Crab, the appearance is of an impervious shield able to deflect the worst insults, but underneath the soft flesh is taking quite a battering.

"After every war, someone has to tidy up."
Wislawa Szymborska (poet), Cancer Sun sign, born 2 July 1923

They also use their shells to retreat into at difficult moments. Cancers can be tenacious and strong-willed and like to get their own way. But if their kindness and gentleness doesn't do the trick, they're not above using emotional manipulation. If that still doesn't work, they'll just go back into their shell and sulk, or find a way to get back at the source of their pain. Crabs can be rather vindictive this way.

Cancers are very empathetic. They have an in-built radar to read what is happening with the emotions in the room and are very sensitive to when someone is off-balance. A Cancer will mirror that emotion. They are always the first to laugh or cry with you.

This intuitive approach can make them seem psychic, and they are especially good to have around when someone is in need, as they can verbalise feelings that the person can't express. Cancers are wonderful at breaking through the walls of other people's isolation.

As parents, they can scare their children witless by seeming to know exactly what they are doing at all times, especially when what they are doing is wrong. For the Cancer parent, it is simply years of tuning their ear to the mischievous silences. Cancers make great parents but usually have a tough time letting go of their children in the teenage years, which causes some friction, but at the end they will always be there with a clean, comforting home and open arms.

Cancer at Work

Cancers are lovely to have around the office as they nest wherever they go. They will be the ones burning the aromatherapy oils in the staff room, buying the birthday cakes and sending around the hat for retirements, keeping the communal areas clean and pleasant, and organising the Christmas party every year. They are indispensable to any harmonious workplace, but they can often find that their efforts, although noticed and appreciated, go unrewarded.

Cancers make wonderful teachers, paediatricians, gynae-cologists, midwives, nurses and doctors, social workers, counsellors, vets and zoo keepers and psychologists because of their magnanimous hearts. Other professions that might not be so obvious are human resources man-agement, catering, dairy farming, business and commerce, fishing, sailing and archaeology.

From little things, big things grow

"Think of your forefathers! Think of posterity!"
John Quincy Adams (US president), Cancer Sun sign, born 11 July 1767

Julius Caesar was one of the great Cancer Sun signs. He is probably best known for a very Cancer thing indeed – the manner of his birth, which was named after him and is now known as a caesarean section.

Caesar used his Cancer skills of negotiation and ability to create family bonds to convince Crassus, Pompey and the Roman Senate to name him as the third consul. This coali-tion of three equal rulers later became known as the First Triumvirate. When Caesar's year-long term as consul ended, he led an army that captured most of Western

Europe. His successes on the battlefield made him the most popular man in Rome.

In 49 BC, the Senate ordered Caesar to return to Rome, but to leave his army behind. His orders clearly told him not to bring his army across the Rubicon River. Caesar knew that if he obeyed the Senate and disbanded his army, his career would be over; but if he marched his troops across the river, the Senate would order Pompey and his army to retaliate. 'The die is cast,' he is supposed to have said, as he made the decision to cross.

Caesar succeeded, and the Roman people elected him emperor of Rome. Today when people say they are 'crossing the Rubicon', they refer to a significant decision that cannot be undone.

Caesar once said, 'In war, events of importance are the result of trivial causes.' He understood it was important to look after the small things and let the bigger picture take care of itself. He also knew that the genesis of great events often came from humbler beginnings closer to the home and hearth.

Caesar used his power to make many changes in Rome, often without approval from the Senate. He instituted the Julian calendar of $365 \frac{1}{4}$ days, which is closely related to the calendar we use today. The cancer month of July is named in his honour. A year after his election as emperor, the Roman people elected him 'dictator for life'.

He also used his power to protect his family, saying: 'I feel that members of my family should never be suspected of breaking the law'. It is unclear if he actually believed his family to be above suspicion, or was simply acting out of familial love.

The Roman senators were outraged at the extent of Caesar's power and popularity. On 15 March 44 BC, Caesar was stabbed to death by a mob of sixty senators.

Cancer Health

The crab is Cancer's astrological symbol so, when threatened, people with Cancer prominent in their chart tend to withdraw into solitude. When upset, they use food as consolation, which in turn can result in obesity, food allergies and intestinal upsets.

Externally, Cancer rules the breasts, and Cancer women often have lovely breasts and they go out of their way either to enhance them or hide them.

Cancer also rules the elbows, the stomach, digestive organs and womb. People with Cancer active in their charts are subject to coughs, indigestion, gas, gallstones, general problems with the stomach, liver and intestines, plus emotional disorders such as depression, hypochondria and hysteria. Other typical Cancer afflictions are: anaemia, weak and/or impure blood; biliousness, dyspepsia; oedema, swollen feet, lymphstasis, obesity; backache; stomach ulcer, jaundice and liver torpidity; and mammary infections.

Cancers should consider avoiding meat, breads and beer, which ferment in the stomach. They should be on guard against candida and avoid yeast-producing foods such as refined sugar, pastry and meats with antibiotics. Fish is a much better food for Cancers.

Cancers will benefit from drinking plenty of water upon rising and at bedtime. Grapes and buckwheat are great and fresh cabbage juice is good for the stomach, offsetting ulcers and irritations. Fresh sauerkraut benefits the intestines. The cabbage group overall benefits those with the Sun in Cancer (cabbage, kale, broccoli, mustard greens, watercress and cauliflower).

There is also a possibility of potassium deficiency, particularly if you crave salt. This can be offset by drinking fresh fruit and vegetable juices and eating bananas.

When choosing meditation music, the healing musical note for Cancer is E. Chamomile, cardamom, jasmine, lemon, lily, myrrh, palmarosa, plumeria, rose, sandalwood and yarrow are the most suitable oils to use in aromatherapy.

The Cancer Partner
"A woman's chastity consists, like an onion, of a series of coats."
Nathaniel Hawthorne, Cancer Sun sign, born 4 July 1804

Your average Cancer is usually unpretentious in her tastes and can be downright uncomfortable if she thinks she may have to put on any airs and graces, so keep your first date fairly low-key. If you can cook, invite her over to your place and whip up some good tucker, something with strong gutsy tastes, and comfort foods like mashed potatoes or dumplings on the side.

Cancers are old-fashioned romantics and will enjoy all the trappings of flowers, chocolates and love poems, and will give you more than your share in return. Make sure your Cancer knows you are enjoying their attentions, because they can become despondent if they think their efforts aren't appreciated.

Cancers can be self-protective, and don't like to leave themselves open to hurt by jumping into bed too soon. Still, they will want you to meet the family quite soon, and if you know what is good for you, you will go along.

Don't fear that visiting her parents is barely a step away from walking down the aisle. The Cancer woman simply wants you to meet her family, just as she wants you to meet her friends and her cat – because they are a living, breathing part of her life that she cherishes. If you are going to get to know her, even in the most perfunctory way, you are going to get to know her family.

And whatever you do, be nice and don't make jokes about them when you are back on mutual ground – she won't find them funny.

Gifts for your Cancer

Cancer's cupboards are usually overflowing with crockery and homewares, but they will gladly accept more, especially large serving platters, because they love feeding the hoards. Cancers can sometimes have a deep-seated feeling that they are being taken advantage of, or that they are overworked or undervalued. If this is your Cancer, a pampering present like perfume or a voucher for relaxation massage is a thoughtful idea.

A well-chosen card with some thoughtful words is obligatory for a present for your Cancer. Cancers live and breathe by the saying 'it's the thought that counts', and will be put out if those thoughts are not expressed. This can be a bit presumptuous, because they are experts at expressing their own thoughts and don't know how difficult it can be for other people, but a little imagination can go a long way.

Famous Cancer Sun Signs

23 June 1894 – Edward VIII (British royalty)

24 June 1944 – Jeff Beck (guitarist)

25 June 1903 – George Orwell (writer)

25 June 1945 – Carly Simon (singer)

25 June 1963 – George Michael (singer)

25 June 1970 – Chris O'Donnell (actor)

26 June 1956 – Chris Isaak (singer)

26 June 1963 – Harriet Wheeler (singer)

27 June 1880 – Helen Keller (diarist)

28 June 1491 – Henry VIII (British royalty)

28 June 1926 – Mel Brooks (movie director)

28 June 1948 – Kathy Bates (actress)

28 June 1966 – John Cusack (actor)

29 June 1900 – Antoine de Saint-Exupery (writer)

29 June 1919 – Slim Pickens (actor)

29 June 1940 – Ken Done (artist)

30 June 1966 – Mike Tyson (boxer)

1 July 1916 – Olivia De Havilland (actress)

1 July 1945 – Deborah Harry (singer)

1 July 1952 – Dan Aykroyd (actor)

1 July 1961 – Carl Lewis (athlete)

1 July 1961 – Princess Diana (British royalty)

1 July 1967 – Pamela Anderson (actress)

1 July 1977 – Liv Tyler (actress)

2 July 1877 – Hermann Hesse (writer)

2 July 1923 – Wislawa Szymborska (poet)

3 July 1883 – Franz Kafka (writer)

3 July 1937 – Tom Stoppard (playwright)

3 July 1962 – Tom Cruise (actor)

4 July 1804 – Nathaniel Hawthorne (writer)

4 July 1927 – Neil Simon (playwright)

5 July 1810 – PT Barnum (entertainer)

5 July 1889 – Jean Cocteau (writer/artist)

6 July 1933 – Dalai Lama XIV (religious leader)

6 July 1946 – Sylvester Stallone (actor)

CANCER

7 July 1922 – Pierre Cardin (fashion designer)

7 July 1940 – Ringo Starr (musician)

7 July 1947 – Camilla Parker Bowles (almost royalty)

7 July 1956 – Tom Hanks (actor)

8 July 1882 – Percy Grainger (composer)

8 July 1885 – John Curtin (Australian prime minister)

8 July 1958 – Kevin Bacon (actor)

9 July 1947 – OJ Simpson (footballer)

9 July 1951 – Angelica Huston (actress)

10 July 1920 – David Brinkley (journalist)

10 July 1947 – Arlo Guthrie (singer)

11 July 1767 – John Quincy Adams (US president)

11 July 1916 – Gough Whitlam (Australian prime minister)

11 July 1934 – Georgio Armani (fashion designer)

11 July 1953 – Leon Spinks (boxer)

12 July 100 BC – Julius Caesar (Roman emperor)

12 July 1817 – Henry Thoreau (writer)

12 July 1937 – Bill Cosby (comedian)

13 July 1927 – Slim Dusty (singer)

13 July 1942 – Harrison Ford (actor)

15 July 1946 – Linda Ronstadt (singer)

16 July 1911 – Ginger Rogers (dancer/actress)

17 July 1917 – Phyllis Diller (comedian)

17 July 1935 – Donald Sutherland (actor)

18 July 1902 – Jessamyn West (writer)

18 July 1921 – John Glenn (astronaut)

20 July 1938 – Diana Rigg (actress)

21 July 1899 – Ernest Hemingway (writer)

21 July 1948 – Cat Stevens (singer)

21 July 1952 – Robin Williams (comedian)

22 July 1939 – Terrence Stamp (actor)

The Fourth House

Cancer is closely associated with the Fourth House, and the principles of the Fourth House are in keeping with the characteristics of Cancer. The key concerns of the Fourth House are the home, the home circumstances, the family and caring for somebody. For more information on the Fourth House, see the chapter, The Houses, in the Interpretation section.

The Moon

Cancer is ruled by the Moon, and the principles of the Moon are in keeping with the characteristics of Cancer. For details on the Moon and how to read it in a chart, see the chapter, The Planets, in the Interpretation section.

Leo
(23 July to 23 August)

"Drama is life with the dull bits cut out."
Alfred Hitchcock (film director), Leo Sun sign, born
13 August 1899

Basic characteristics of the sign

Personal creed – *I will*

Positive/masculine sign

Element – Fire

Quality – Fixed

Psychological type – Intuitive

Glyph – ♌ probably originated in ancient Egypt from the
constellation and represents the lion's tail

Colours – Gold, scarlet

Body parts – Heart, upper back

Gemstone – Ruby

Flowers – Marigold, sunflower

Trees – Citrus, walnut, olive

Food – Honey, cereal, most meats, rice

People with a Leo Sun sign are generally:

✧ Generous

✧ Self-assured

✧ Warm-hearted

✧ Creative

✧ Witty

✧ Enthusiastic

✧ Broad-minded

✧ Flamboyant

✧ Verbose

✧ Vivacious

✧ Faithful

✧ Loving

✧ Ambitious

✧ Dominant

✧ Gracious

✧ Courageous

✧ Strong-willed

✧ Independent

✧ Popular

✧ Natural leaders

✧ Dramatic

✧ Uncomplicated

✧ Daring

✧ Intelligent

✧ Religious

On the other hand, they can also be:

✧ Pompous

✧ Spendthrifts

✧ Proud

✧ Self-centred

✧ Patronising

✧ Bossy

✧ Overbearing

- ✧ Dogmatic

- ✧ Opinionated

- ✧ Ruthless

- ✧ Jealous

- ✧ Tricksters

- ✧ Backstabbers

- ✧ Liars

- ✧ Egotistical

- ✧ Fanatical in religious beliefs

Leos love:

- ✧ Luxury

- ✧ Power

- ✧ Sex

- ✧ Money

- ✧ The spotlight

- ✧ Gambling

- ✧ Pleasure

- ✧ Overindulgence

✧ Acclaim

✧ Making a wonderful impression

✧ Being desirable and attractive

✧ Feeling pampered

✧ Being the boss

But they can't stand:

✧ Apathy

✧ Being ignored

✧ Criticism

✧ Nagging

✧ Competition

✧ Lying/deceit

✧ Laziness

✧ Introspection

The Leo Character

When the Babylonians were first looking up into the sky, their bellies full of wine and their heart full of song, the Sun was considered the brightest star in the universe. Of course, we now know that the Sun is one star in a galaxy of many in a universe of many galaxies. But no one told Leo that.

Leo is the only sign to have the Sun as its astrological

planet. Leos continue to think the universe revolves around them . . . in a good way, of course. Two key words for Leos are magnanimity and bonhomie.

Leo's moniker is the lion, the flamboyant King of the Beasts, and Leo's colours are regal gold and scarlet. In the zodiac, Leo is opposite Aquarius and their personalities could not be more opposite. Aquarius is about keeping it real, where Leo just likes to spend the reals. Or any other currency for that matter: reals, pesos, pounds or dollars. Leo is not fussed.

It is helpful to think about Leo in terms of the Sun and its place in our lives. The Sun has energy that is vibrant, healing, emboldening, enriching and relaxed with its place in the scheme of things. It's also hot, just as Leos can be hot-headed, hot-blooded and hot-tempered.

Centre of the universe or not, the Sun is vital to our existence. It is this sort of power Leos thrive on, enabling them to be all-powerful, yet gracious and giving. Leos love to be in power, but they don't like to look like they broke their nails getting there. They are the sign of old money, and the monarchy is the perfect place for them, where they can impress with both their status and their philanthropic generosity.

The lesson we can learn from Leo is that it is a fine thing to love what you are, because only once you have learnt to be happy in your own skin can you use the force of your personality to help others see their own beauty. Superficially Leo may appear to be very egotistical, but in fact Leo cannot live just for themselves. They have to be leading others into their own glory in order to feel fulfilled because the prime desire of the Sun, after all, is to encourage life.

"A woman can look both moral and exciting – if she also looks as if it was quite a struggle."
Edna Ferber (writer), Leo Sun sign, born 15 August 1885

Leos make great mates who are always up for a bit of fun. They are embarrassingly generous, but you should never turn down a gift, no matter how extravagant, because their pride will be hurt. Leos don't take a blow to their pride very lightly.

They usually possess a belly-trembling chuckle that can break into gales of laughter if really tickled. Their sense of humour is fresh and simple, with an eye for the ridiculous. They are more likely to enjoy a Jim Carrey movie than a political satire, and their favourite Seinfeld character is more likely to be the clownish Kramer than the decidedly dry Jerry. That aside, they can see the funny side in most situations and are willing listeners to funny stories. They'll make mental notes so they might appropriate the story for their own use later on. Just don't take the floor for too long. You will soon know if you are stealing Leo's limelight.

Leos have an eye for the decadent and will shell out for the most outrageous things, even if it is rent week. A night out at the pub can be an expensive exercise for the magnanimous Lion. And all he wants in return is your unfettered approval and adoring silence as he tells you another of his usually very funny but sometimes exaggerated stories. Not a bad deal, really.

The legendary Leo ego extends to their friends (as a fixed sign, they see their friends as an extension of themselves), and you are, of course, almost as wonderful as they are. They can be very affirming and supportive of any endeavour you might set out on and they believe in you as much as they believe in themselves. If needs be, they will pull you up by the strength of their convictions.

They stick around too; the Leo you met in kindergarten will be the Leo you sit with on the porch of the Sunset and Dusk Retirement Village. Leos are constants.

The only exception to this loyalty is when they find love. Leos tend to fall truly, madly and deeply in love, and you might find yourself bumped down the list a peg. But once that mad rush of endorphins settles into blissful companionship, you will be back on the speed-dial.

"What really flatters a man is that you think him worth flattering."
George Bernard Shaw (writer), Leo Sun sign, born 26 July 1856

Fixed fire is like a campfire needs to be stoked and tended to keep it roaring. Leos are the same in love. They need constant appreciation and adoration, and the warmth of the fire will be reflected back to you. When a Leo has found the perfect partner she gives herself over completely. There is nothing more awe-inspiring than the Lion's ability to make themselves completely vulnerable to their partner. Sometimes, meeting a Leo's high standards can be daunting, but all you really have to do is be faithful and funny, and appeal to that tremendous Leo vanity. Just say 'Darling, you're wonderful' every fifteen minutes, and your pussycat will purr happily for the whole of your life together.

Leos can be flirtatious, but it is just their way of reassuring themselves that they've still 'got it'. They are completely loyal as partners and never take flirting any further, unless there are serious problems in the relationship. Then they are looking in other places for the affirmation that they crave.

"I believe that it's better to be looked over than it is to be overlooked."
Mae West (actress), Leo Sun sign, born 17 August 1893

They can also become overly critical of their partner's physical appearance, or of how they hold themselves in social situations. Leos need to be reminded that their partner is a whole person, not an extension of themselves, and that others will not judge Leo on whether their partner has matched his socks or not.

Leos think and act bigger than others would normally dare. The audacity of their schemes sometimes daunts their followers, but their practicality and ability to go straight to the heart of any problem is reassuring. Leos thrive on adversity.

When Leo is working for good, they are strongly idealistic, humane and altruistic. They have powerful intelligence and are of a broad philosophical, sometimes religious, turn of mind. Those who are devout may become very obstinate in upholding traditional beliefs and will cling tenaciously, but with complete sincerity, to practices and doctrines that more liberal thinkers regard as absurdly out-of-date.

If you happen to strike a negative Leo, you can find yourself confronted with someone very unpleasant, who displays bombastic arrogance, autocratic pride and haughtiness, all tied up with a mean, mean temper. If jealous, they are not above using cunning, lies, trickery and plagiarism to discredit another. Add to this a passion for luxury, a lust for power and sex, and emotional indulgence, and you are left with one highly unattractive human being. Fortunately, it is very rare that a Leo indulges in all of these vices.

Leo at Work

Leos gravitate to all that shimmers and will often find themselves in theatre, cabaret or cinema. Leos just love the stage. They also excel in creative careers, and will be designers, painters, and film and television directors. And half the pubs, clubs and cabaret spots in the world are run by Lions. In fact, you'll find Leos anywhere that glitters, be it gold or not!

"Take care of the luxuries and the necessities will take care of themselves."
Dorothy Parker (writer), Leo Sun sign, born 22 August 1893

Even if your Leo has an office job, they will be sure to find themselves seeking out local theatre groups, or ballroom dancing in their spare time.

Leos are charismatic leaders who know how to get things done. They are courageous decision-makers and masterful at delegating, as they know how to charm people into doing the work for them. This isn't to say that the Lion won't be doing his share, it's just that he will make sure all the drudge work will fall to someone else.

Larger than Life

Cecil Blount DeMille was Hollywood royalty. In many ways, DeMille epitomises all that is Leo-like about Hollywood – he possessed oodles of self-confidence, ambition, passion, artistry and a hungry desire for everything that was big, big, big.

Born on 12 August 1881 to the son of a clergyman and a school principal, DeMille ran away from military school to try and enlist in the Spanish-American War, but was turned down for being too young. Impatient to get his show on the road, he decided to join his older brother William on the stage, and he enrolled at the New York Academy of Dramatic Arts in 1900. William was a mentor to him for the next 12 years as he trod the boards of Broadway and collaborated with him in writing several successful plays.

In 1913 DeMille made his most breathtaking move. With an eye on the fledgling film industry as the way of the future, he formed the Jesse L Lasky Feature Play Company with vaudeville musician Jesse L and glove salesman Samuel Goldfish (later Goldwyn). They moved to Hollywood (then merely a dusty outpost), rented an old barn and made their first feature film, *The Squaw Man*. It was a huge hit.

In the days before the cult of the auteur, it was the stars alone that sold a movie to its audience. Many directors would sacrifice a huge slice of their budget to secure a leading man or woman. However, DeMille had other ideas about how to sell a picture and he consistently used no-name actors and bred them to be stars.

With more money to play with, he spent the bulk of his budget on big sets, lavish costumes and breathtaking stunts. Consequently it was the DeMille name that sold the movie. With cat-like stealth and judgement, he made his name the top of the billing.

On set, DeMille always made an entrance. Dressed in jodphurs, boots and carrying a riding crop, his walk was described as 'Germanic swagger'. He was the consummate autocrat and he demanded complete obedience and loyalty from his mostly female staff. 'You are here to please me. Nothing else on earth matters,' he famously said to his crew. He was rarely disappointed.

Other directors such as DW Griffith were more critically acclaimed in their day, but it was the DeMille touch for giving the people what they wanted in the most lavish eye-candy way that has defined the early post-sound era in movies. This ensured that DeMille's name was synonymous with 'epic'. His obsession with realism was such that he was known to use real bullets, but he was never boring or earnest. DeMille made real bigger than real, and movies larger than life.

Historical and biblical subjects were grist for DeMille – *The Sign of the Cross*, *The King of Kings*, *Samson and Delilah* and *Cleopatra* are among his most famous films. It is for the momentous *Ten Commandments* (1923, followed by an even more overblown remake in 1956) that he is most remembered. This film saw him come to blows with his studio, Paramount – 'What do they want me to do? Stop now and release it as The Five Commandments?' he asked.

Leo Health

Leo rules the spine, the back and the heart. The heart is associated with warm emotions, the back with courage. Leos display both these qualities. They have robust constitutions, supple spines and good coordination. They are usually excellent dancers and athletes.

Leos often push themselves so hard that they suffer strain from overexertion and nerves. Their upper back tires more easily than other parts of their bodies. They are also subject to pains and pressure around the heart. When startled, a

Leo's heart will seem to jump into his or her throat. They can usually feel their pulses beat inside their heads.

Leo's ruler, the Sun, also influences the spleen and the body's vitality. The sign of Leo is characterised by growth, vitality and good health. As a rule, Leos live healthy lives, however, they must learn to slow down in later years to avoid the risk of heart attack. Leos are noted for their longevity.

Common Leo ailments include pain in the back and lungs, heart disease, palpitations; sickness in the ribs and sides, convulsions, violent burning fevers traditionally including the plague, pestilence, jaundice, anaemia, spinal disorders, backache; baldness; and eye troubles.

Leo's cell salt is magnesium phosphate, which keeps the motor nerves in top condition, so foods that contain this element are important. Whole wheat and rye products, almonds, walnuts, sunflower seeds, figs, lemons, apples, peaches, coconut, rice, seafood, beets, asparagus, cos lettuce and egg yolk all contain traces of magnesium phosphate. Foods that are rich in iron and aid the circulation are recommended for Leos, including beef, lamb, poultry, liver, fresh fruit, salad greens, cheese, whole milk, yoghurt, spinach, raisins and dates.

When choosing music for meditation, the healing note for Leos is E. Good oils for aromatherapy are bay, basil, cinnamon, frankincense, ginger, juniper, lime, nasturtium, neroli, orange, petitgrain and rosemary.

The Leo Partner

If you are planning to woo a Leo, it is prudent to first take out a small loan at a low interest rate. Leos love to pounce quickly and you could find yourself involved in a flurry of theatre and dinner dates snowballing to an early but lavish white wedding.

Make the first date something to remember. Low-key is not in the Leo vocabulary. See a musical, but use whatever influence you have to wrangle backstage passes to meet the actors; go to the tennis, but make sure you watch it from a corporate box. Leos love big dramatic statements and the effort you have gone to will make them feel more special. Don't worry about appearing to be a name-dropper, Leos are the King of the Pride when it comes to big-noting, and they won't bat an eyelid.

Gifts for your Leo

Leos are extravagant gift-givers so make sure you get in first with a wonderful present. They can't stand cheap and nasty imitations, so always buy the high-quality original, or settle for something else.

Leos love anything that shows them off to their best advantage so you might consider a voucher for a session of glamour photography. They will love being made up and fussed over, and the resulting photos will take pride of place on their wall. Another idea is to take a favourite photo and have it cropped and blown up and elegantly framed – the bigger the better. Send it with a nice little card telling her to hang it on the wall for her future grandchildren, so they will know what a beautiful young woman she was. She will be tickled pink.

A video camera is an expensive idea that is sure to be a big hit. They will love directing the action from behind the lens as well as hamming it up in front. Make sure you include a tripod, so they can set it up and film their own commentary.

Gold is always appreciated, and rubies and amber are Leo gemstones. Board games with lots of dramatics and interaction, like Pictionary and Charades, are always a lot of fun. (You might want to let them win the first few games though.)

Famous Leo Sun Signs

23 July 1961 – Woody Harrelson (actor)

24 July 1895 – Robert Graves (poet)

24 July 1897 – Amelia Earhart (pilot)

24 July 1900 – Zelda Fitzgerald (jazz age figure)

24 July 1970 – Jennifer Lopez (singer/actress)

26 July 1856 – George Bernard Shaw (writer)

26 July 1875 – Carl Jung (psychologist)

26 July 1894 – Aldous Huxley (writer)

26 July 1939 – John Howard (Australian prime minister)

26 July 1943 – Mick Jagger (musician)

26 July 1956 – Dorothy Hamill (Olympic ice-skater)

27 July 1948 – Betty Thomas (actress/film director)

28 July 1929 – Jacqueline Kennedy (US first lady)

29 July 1934 – Stanton Friedman (physicist)

LEO

29 July 1938 – Benito Mussolini (dictator)

30 July 1818 – Emily Bronte (writer)

30 July 1863 – Henry Ford (industrialist)

30 July 1947 – Arnold Schwarzenegger (actor)

31 July 1946 – Wesley Snipes (actor)

1 August 1936 – Yves St Laurent (fashion designer)

1 August 1942 – Jerry Garcia (musician)

2 August 1932 – Peter O'Toole (actor)

3 August 1940 – Martin Sheen (actor)

4 August 1792 – Percy Bissche Shelley (poet)

4 August 1900 – Queen Mother (British royalty)

4 August 1904 – Witold Gombrowicz (writer)

5 August 1806 – John Huston (film director)

5 August 1927 – Andy Warhol (artist)

5 August 1930 – Neil Armstrong (astronaut)

5 August 1945 – Loni Anderson (actress)

6 August 1809 – Alfred Tennyson (poet)

6 August 1881 – Ian Fleming (writer)

6 August 1911 – Lucille Ball (actress)

7 August 1876 – Mata Hari (secret agent)

8 August 1937 – Dustin Hoffman (actor)

9 August 1963 – Whitney Huston (singer)

10 August 1874 – Herbert Hoover (US president)

11 August 1953 – Hulk Hogan (wrestler)

12 August 1881 – Cecil B DeMille (film director)

12 August 1939 – George Hamilton (actor)

13 August 1899 – Alfred Hitchcock (film director)

13 August 1927 – Fidel Castro (political leader)

14 August 1969 – Magic Johnson (basketballer)

15 August 1769 – Napoleon Bonaparte (French emperor)

15 August 1885 – Edna Ferber (writer)

15 August 1950 – Princess Anne (British royalty)

16 August 1960 – Timothy Hutton (actor)

17 August 1786 – Davey Crockett (frontiersman)

17 August 1893 – Mae West (actress)

17 August 1943 – Robert De Niro (actor)

18 August 1922 – Shelley Winters (actress)

18 August 1933 – Roman Polanski (film director)

18 August 1936 – Robert Redford (actor)

18 August 1952 – Patrick Swayze (actor)

18 August 1969 – Christian Slater (actor)

19 August 1946 – Bill Clinton (US president)

20 August 1948 – Robert Plant (musician)

21 August 1938 – Kenny Rogers (singer)

21 August 1962 – Matthew Broderick (actor)

22 August 1893 – Dorothy Parker (writer)

22 August 1904 – Deng Xiaoping (political leader)

23 August 1970 – River Phoenix (actor)

The Fifth House

Leo is closely associated with the Fifth House, and the principles of the Fifth House are in keeping with the characteristics of Leo. The Fifth House is about your creativity and how you express it, about leisure time, and also influences your attitude towards children. For more information on the Fifth House, see the chapter, The Houses, in the Interpretation section.

The Sun

Leo is ruled by the Sun, and the principles of the Sun are in keeping with the characteristics of Leo. For details on the Sun and how to read it in a chart, see the chapter, The Planets, in the Interpretation section.

Virgo
(24 August to 22 September)

"To insist on purity is to baptise instinct, to humanise art, and to deify personality."
Guillaume Apollinaire (poet), Virgo Sun sign, born 26 August 1880

Basic characteristics of the sign
Personal creed – *I analyse*

Negative/feminine sign

Element – Earth

Energy – Mutable

Psychological type – Perceptive

Glyph – ♍ Represents the female genitalia

Colours – Yellow, green, blue, brown, cream, grey

Body part – Lower back

Gemstones – Peridot, opal, agate, sardonyx

Metal – Mercury

Flowers – Narcissus, vervain and herbs, bright small flowers like
the buttercup

Trees – Nut-producing varieties

Food – Root vegetables such as potatoes and yams

People with a Virgo Sun sign are generally:

✧ Detailed

✧ Precise

✧ Fanatically tidy

✧ Skilled communicators

✧ Devoted

✧ Hardworking

✧ Observant

✧ Shrewd

✧ Loving

✧ Nurturing

On the other hand, they can also be:

✧ Cold

✧ Critical

✧ Reserved

✧ Self-serving

✧ Jealous

✧ Fearful

✧ Distrustful

✧ So meticulous they lose sight of larger issues

✧ Critical of anything outside of their own beliefs

✧ Phobic about hygiene and sanitation

Virgoans love:

✧ Feeling secure

✧ Personal cleanliness

✧ Routines

✧ Loyalty

✧ Being pampered when feeling down

✧ Equality

✧ Subtle displays of romance

✧ Dedication

✧ Being active

✧ Perfection

✧ Attention to detail

✧ Stimulating employment

✧ Conventions and rules

But they can't stand:
✧ Tardiness

✧ Vulgarity

✧ Loud displays of affection

✧ Personal untidiness

✧ Hypocrisy

✧ Weakness

✧ Complaining

✧ Idleness

✧ Forming new relationships

✧ Being wrested away from the grindstone

The Virgo Character
Virgo is all about synthesising knowledge for the greater good rather than personal gain, and about the altruistic goal of serving others. But some days Virgoans may wonder if they're here just to tidy up the mess that Leo left behind (lovely Leo, such a laugh, but such an untidy house guest!).

Virgoans love to tidy, there is no doubt about that. They usually have a favourite form of tidying that they are experts at. Some find solace in ironing, others enjoy filing or bookkeeping, others find the peak of serenity in the sweep, sweep, sweep of a soft-bristled broom.

The symbol of the Virgin that represents Virgo doesn't quite tell the full story. It is not purity of the body which the Virgo seeks, it is purity, full-stop. Virgoans love to make order in the chaos. This includes putting order into the chaos of other people's lives. They are very good at giving excellent advice as they have an uncluttered thought process that enables them to see cause and effect from a distance.

Virgoans can see the big picture, but they love to revel in the minutiae. If they are feeling off-balance or unconfident, they will often retreat into the detail and let someone else deal with the consequences. The Virgo mind is enormously patient and will pick over at a pace that ensures no mistakes are made. They make great subeditors and software writers because they can keep their mind on track for great lengths of time.

This can also make them a little pedantic and loath to make rash decisions, even when deadlines loom perilously. Once occupied with a problem, the Virgo mind refuses to be interrupted until it has reached a considered conclusion.

With their ruling planet being Mercury, Virgoans are communicators, but in a much more subtle way than Gemini. Virgoans seek to synthesise the information they receive, not simply convey it in its raw form like changeable Gemini. Virgo likes to take all the facts and draw conclusions from them.

The Virgo is anchored to the ground, enjoying the winds of change, but ultimately staying true to the one line. The Gemini is likely to change their mind several times, but Virgo already has a position from which to defend their turf. Do not enter into a debate with a Virgo lightly.

It is the critic in the Virgo that is their inner tormentor. Virgoans have a keen eye for earthly flaws. They almost automatically notice the imperfection in everything, including themselves. It is very natural for a Virgo to be incessantly critical about everything they do. The mildest criticism will carry a lot of sting for a Virgo child, who is already a developing a 'to do' list about themself.

The same is true of older Virgoans. Try to find a gentle way to suggest change as they don't need to be pushed too far before they plunge deep into self-flagellation. This criticism carries over to others, but Virgoans usually convey their suggestions tactfully.

"The learner always begins by finding fault, but the scholar sees the positive merit in everything."
Georg Hegel (philosopher), Virgo Sun sign, born 27 August 1770

Caring and serving others is what they do best. They will attend to your needs, but try to be aware of their intense desire for sacred space. They are the loners of the zodiac, so give your Virgo a space that you don't enter, so they can pick every speck of lint off the floor if they want.

Your Virgo will surely have a very tidy mind. Virgoans always know where they put everything, and they very rarely lose anything. If they do happen to make a mistake or be a little absent-minded, they will beat themselves up about it. They find comfort in having everything under control in their minds, and can't understand it when their mind appears to betray them.

Virgoans are painfully aware of their shortcomings and they have the art of self-concealment down pat, hiding their apprehension about themselves and their sympathy for others under a mantle of matter-of-factness. They are still waters that run deep. Yet in their unassuming and agreeable fashion, they can be sensible, discreet, well-spoken, wise and witty.

When a Virgo falls in love, it is a love not given lightly. As a mutable earth sign, the movement of the Virgo's mind is controlled, filtered through the senses and ultimately grounded. They may allow their mind to wander a little into romance, but they are too practical to embark on anything that is not a relatively safe bet. They can't stand public displays of affection or overt grandstanding. Do not propose to your Virgo by employing a sky-writer or buying advertising space on a billboard – you are guaranteed a terse rejection.

"Life is pain and the enjoyment of love is an anaesthetic."
Cesare Pavese (writer), Virgo Sun sign, born 9 September 1908

But when their heart is captured, all the feelings and passion that Virgo has been keeping under lock and key are lavished upon the loved one. They are devoted, loyal and nurturing, great conversationalists and masterful at tender moments. Virgoans do most things with reserve, but once in love, they will care for you and cherish you with frightening abandon. They will go out of their way to make the union work and will spare no sacrifice in keeping it alive.

This makes them very vulnerable, especially when that cool, analytical approach convinces others that there is only a heart of steel beating away in their chest. Fortunately, Virgo's excellent judge of character will see them usually falling in love with the right person. They also have high expectations of their loved ones. They adore strength, especially the dignified and quiet kind.

Virgo at Work
"Be wiser than other people, if you can; but do not tell them so."
Lord Chesterfield (statesman/writer), Virgo Sun sign, born 22 September 1694

Virgo's memory is amazing and they like to file away the most trivial facts. They make great writers and teachers, as they always seem to have the answer for the curliest of questions. They combine mental ingenuity with the ability to produce a clear analysis of the most complicated problems. They also see the shades of grey in any given issue.

They can be a little pernickety about detail and may slow down projects by being too exact. They are unlikely to be leaders, but when they rise to the top they are hard-working bosses who pull their sleeves up and get into it. No three-hour lunches for this lot, they will work as one with the team. Virgoans in leadership positions have to learn to delegate, even if that means letting someone do a job that won't be up to their exacting standards.

A Mission to Serve
"We cannot all do great things, but we can do small things with great love."
Mother Teresa (humanitarian), Virgo Sun sign, born 27 August 1910

Mother Teresa is an excellent example of Virgo leadership. Born in Skopje in present-day Macedonia, she received her calling as a teenager and told a childhood friend, 'I have decided before the Lady of Letnica to go in missions and to dedicate myself completely to God and to serving souls.' It was this concept of serving that dictated the path of her life.

At age 18, she joined the Irish Sisters of Loreto, who sent her to St Mary's High School in Calcutta to teach geography, history and catechism. She later became the school's principal, and mastered both Hindi and Bengali.

On 10 September 1946, while travelling on a train to be treated for tuberculosis, Mother Teresa received what she described as her 'call within a call' to help the poorest. She left teaching and began working in the slums of Calcutta.

In 1950 she founded the Missionaries of Charity, whose work was to provide 'free service to the poor and the unwanted, irrespective of caste, creed, nationality or race'. In 1952 she established a home for the dying destitute, and soon after she opened her first orphanage.

In 1979 Mother Teresa received the Nobel Peace Prize 'for work undertaken in the struggle to overcome poverty and distress, which also constitute a threat to peace'. After being told of the honour, her simple response was: 'I am unworthy.'

Her order had grown to 1800 nuns and 120,000 lay workers, operating almost 200 centres and homes. By the end of the 20th century, this number had more than doubled.

Mother Teresa never became simply a figurehead for the Missionaries of Charity. She worked with the poor every day of her working life until March 1996, when she stepped down due to ill health. She died on 5 September 1997 in Calcutta, after suffering cardiac arrest. She was 87.

Virgo Health

Mercurial energy makes Virgoans great worriers; when this worry is turned on themselves it can be quite destructive. For instance, Virgoans usually take a puritanical approach to their health, only eating simple foods and engaging in exercise. If they let their regime slip, they can become preoccupied with their health and tend to hypochondria. Foolish fears and apprehensions can lead Virgoans into early invalidism. These individuals are also susceptible to suggestion in health matters and should choose their doctor carefully. Normally, however, Virgoans have a unique resistance to disease once the mind is disciplined.

The main health problem of Virgoans is digestion. They should chew food thoroughly, eat at regular intervals and not drink cold liquids with meals. Virgoans should not eat too many raw foods, and vegetables should be lightly steamed to aid digestion.

Greens such as spinach, lettuce, green beans, as well as brown rice, bulgur wheat, millet and lentils will stabilise blood sugar. Water should be drunk at room temperature, as cold drinks will weaken the digestive powers. Virgoans tend to suffer from potassium deficiency, so foods such as celery, tomatoes, apples and bananas benefit them.

Virgo rules the abdominal region, large and small intestines and spleen. Common afflictions include food allergies, catarrh of the bowels, poor assimilation of food, colitis, diarrhoea, constipation; hypochondria, chronic disease; peritonitis, cancer; dysentery; hypoglycaemia and diabetes.

When choosing music for meditation, the Virgo healing musical note is C sharp. Oils that are good to use in aromatherapy are caraway, clary sage, costmary, cypress, dill, fennel, lemon balm, honeysuckle, oak moss and patchouli. Lavender is also good to soothe anxious minds.

The Virgo Partner

"She plucked from my lapel the invisible strand of lint (the universal act of woman to proclaim ownership)."
O Henry (writer), Virgo Sun sign, born 11 September 1862

Virgoans will be drawn out by your warmth and enjoy a thoughtful compliment, but will be repelled by overt shows of physical affection or gushiness.

Keep your first date simple. See a film or a show with coffee afterwards, because Virgoans can be a little shy but are never lost for words when given something to critique. If the spark is there, you could find yourself talking till dawn, ranging over current affairs, music, politics, religion and the meaning of life.

Don't assume that because your Virgo is the embodiment of stylish understatement that you will be expected to be the same. Virgoans are often quite attracted to the outlandish or the quirky. Above all, they treasure scrupulous honesty, so be yourself and no one else.

Gifts for your Virgo

Virgoans have green fingers, so presents such as gardening tools could be a good idea, or a bonsai might put them on the path to a healthy hobby. Bonsais require a lot of care and attention and a judicious pruning every now and then, skills that Virgoans excel in.

Their colour preferences are all shades of blue, dark brown and beige. If you are looking for clothes, be sure to err on the generous size rather than mistakenly get them something too tight-fitting. They don't like revealing any more flesh than is prudent.

They usually like reading nonfiction, so biographies and reference books are good ideas. A magazine subscription is in the same vein. A good filofax or digital notebook is sure to be put to rigorous use. Lavender soap, bath salts or perfume will soothe that worried mind.

Virgoans are meticulous people and appreciate it if you pay attention to the detail, so make sure the gift is perfectly wrapped, and the card is signed with something personal and fitting.

Famous Virgo Sun Signs

24 August 1958 – Steve Guttenberg (actor)

25 August 1918 – Leonard Bernstein (conductor)

25 August 1930 – Sean Connery (actor)

25 August 1954 – Elvis Costello (singer)

25 August 1961 – Billy Ray Cyrus (singer)

25 August 1970 – Claudia Schiffer (supermodel)

26 August 1819 – Prince Albert (British royalty)

26 August 1880 – Guillaume Apollinaire (poet)

27 August 1770 – Georg Hegel (philosopher)

27 August 1908 – Lyndon B Johnson (US president)

27 August 1910 – Mother Teresa (humanitarian)

27 August 1939 – Pee Wee Herman (comedian)

28 August 1965 – Shania Twain (singer)

29 August 1862 – Andrew Fisher (Australian prime minister)

29 August 1915 – Ingrid Bergman (actress)

29 August 1958 – Michael Jackson (singer)

30 August 1972 – Cameron Diaz (actress)

31 August 1945 – Van Morrison (singer)

31 August 1949 – Richard Gere (actor)

1 September 1875 – Edgar Rice Burroughs (writer)

1 September 1939 – Lily Tomlin (comedian)

1 September 1957 – Gloria Estefan (singer)

2 September 1952 – Jimmy Connors (tennis player)

2 September 1964 – Keanu Reeves (actor)

3 September 1965 – Charlie Sheen (actor)

3 September 1969 – Shane Warne (cricketer)

4 September 1530 – Ivan the Terrible (Russian royalty)

5 September 1847 – Jesse James (outlaw)

5 September 1912 – John Cage (composer)

5 September 1940 – Raquel Welch (actress)

5 September 1946 – Freddie Mercury (singer)

7 September 1900 – Taylor Caldwell (writer)

7 September 1936 – Buddy Holly (singer)

8 September 1925 – Peter Sellers (actor)

8 September 1979 – Pink (singer)

9 September 1908 – Cesare Pavese (writer)

9 September 1911 – John Gorton (Australian prime minister)

9 September 1941 – Otis Redding (musician)

9 September 1951 – Michael Keaton (actor)

9 September 1952 – Angela Cartwright (writer)

9 September 1960 – Hugh Grant (actor)

9 September 1966 – Adam Sandler (actor)

10 September 1929 – Arnold Palmer (golfer)

11 September 1862 – O Henry (writer)

11 September 1885 – DH Lawrence (writer)

11 September 1965 – Moby (musician)

11 September 1967 – Harry Connick Jnr (singer)

12 September 1940 – Linda Gray (actress)

13 September 1916 – Roald Dahl (writer)

13 September 1944 – Jacqueline Bissett (actress)

14 September 1947 – Sam Neill (actor)

15 September 1879 – Joseph Lyons (Australian prime minister)

15 September 1880 – Agatha Christie (writer)

15 September 1922 – Jackie Cooper (actor)

16 September 1638 – Louis XIV (French royalty)

16 September 1924 – Lauren Bacall (actress)

16 September 1956 – David Copperfield (magician)

17 September 1935 – Ken Kesey (writer)

18 September 1876 – James Scullin (Australian prime minister)

18 September 1905 – Greta Garbo (actress)

19 September 1928 – Mickey Mouse (cartoon character)

19 September 1941 – Cass Elliot (singer)

19 September 1948 – Jeremy Irons (actor)

19 September 1949 – Twiggy (model)

20 September 1878 – Upton Sinclair (writer)

20 September 1934 – Sophia Loren (actress)

21 September 1866 – HG Wells (writer)

21 September 1934 – Leonard Cohen (singer)

21 September 1947 – Stephen King (writer)

21 September 1950 – Bill Murray (actor)

21 September 1968 – Ricki Lake (talk show host)

21 September 1972 – Liam Gallagher (musician)

22 September 1694 – Lord Chesterfield (statesman/writer)

22 September 1885 – Ben Chifley (Australian prime minister)

22 September 1957 – Nick Cave (singer)

22 September 1960 – Joan Jett (singer)

The Sixth House

Virgo is closely associated with the Sixth House, and the principles of the Sixth House are in keeping with the characteristics of Virgo. The Sixth House shows how you work, as opposed to your career. For more information on the Sixth House, see the chapter, The Houses, in the Interpretation section.

Mercury

Virgo is ruled by the planet Mercury, and the principles of Mercury are in keeping with the characteristics of Virgo. For details on Virgo and how to read it in a chart, see the chapter, The Planets, in the Interpretation section.

Libra
(23 September to 23 October)

"Light is meaningful only in relation to darkness, and truth presupposes error. It is these mingled opposites which people our life, which make it pungent, intoxicating. We only exist in terms of this conflict, in the zone where black and white clash."
Louis Aragon (poet), Libra Sun sign, born 3 October 1897

Basic characteristics of the sign

Personal creed – *I balance*

Positive/masculine sign

Element – Air

Energy – Cardinal

Psychological type – Thinking

Glyph – ♎ the scales were probably devised from their use in weighing harvests; the glyph is thought to look like a yoke

Colours – Greens, blues

Body part – Kidneys

Gemstone – Sapphire

Flowers – Bluebells, large roses

Trees – Ash, apple

Food – Cereals, most fruits and spices

People with a Libra Sun sign are generally:

✧ Objective

✧ Intellectual

✧ Independent

✧ Valuing of others

✧ Principled

✧ Treat everyone as equals

✧ Respectful

✧ Civilised

✧ Tasteful

✧ Charming

✧ Good-looking

✧ Artistic

✧ Well-balanced

✧ Perceptive

✧ Observant

✧ Compromising

✧ Romantics

✧ Committed in marriage

On the other hand, they can also be:
✧ Opinionated

✧ Promiscuous

✧ Gullible

✧ Inclined to give in to keep the peace

Librans love:
✧ Beauty

✧ Love

✧ Communicating

✧ Making people happy

✧ Elegance

✧ Morality

✧ Designer clothes

✧ Expensive things

But they can't stand:
✧ Conflict

✧ Distasteful things

✧ Unprincipled behaviour

The Libra Character

Libra is typified by the scales. The first day of Libra falls at the time of the equinox, when day equals night, and it is in this state that Libra feels most at ease.

Equilibrium is what Libra seeks, but the symbol of the scales can be misleading. Your initial impression might be that Libra is perfectly even-handed and even-tempered, seeing everything as perfectly balanced.

But Libra is much more of a meddler than that! Scales are not perfectly weighted all the time, and can be in a state of flux. Libra will always try and pull the scales back. If you have an opinion about something Libra will look at you kindly, and tell you in perfectly even tones why that argument may not be perfectly so. And then she will tell you in the same even tones why you are, in fact, perfectly correct.

"So far as we are human, what we do must be either evil or good: so far as we do evil or good, we are human: and it is better, in a paradoxical way, to do evil than to do nothing: at least we exist."
TS Eliot (poet), Libra Sun sign, born 26 September 1888

Libra just wants you to see that there are two sides to every-thing, not change your opinion or create a fuss (in fact, she probably values your opinion more than you do). She will then smooth things over by telling you exactly what you want to hear.

You can never be truly sure what a Libran really thinks. Until they have made up their mind they can be quite gullible. Once they have weighed up the evidence and come to a conclusion, their mind is set in concrete.

Librans love people and they love to be near people and have their own brood. They tend also to gather a large circle of friends and, unlike Cancer, Librans consider friends and family of equal importance.

The Libran's home is a place of love and laughter, with people coming and going, stopping for tea and a chat. They don't crave the serenity of solitary pursuits – not for them the quiet game of chess or the lonely fishing spot. They love to talk and communicate. However, because they have such a highly developed sense of morality, they do not allow themselves to be connected to anyone or anything they consider distasteful.

If a Libran finds out something about someone they consider distasteful, within their family or among close friends, then they will quietly pretend it has not happened or does not exist. The offending person will not even know Libra has judged them, but they will never be accepted in the same way in Libra's mind. Even close friends and family won't know when this has occurred.

"The trouble with writing a book about yourself is that you can't fool around. If you write about someone else, you can stretch the truth from here to Finland. If you write about yourself the slightest deviation makes you realise instantly that there may be honour among thieves, but you are just a dirty liar."
Groucho Marx (comedian), Libra Sun sign, born 2 October 1890

Libran energy tends to seek good relations with the energy of all other signs. So they are inclined to bend the truth a little in the cause of harmony. Mostly it would be far better to tell it as it is, suffer a little temporary pain and get on with life. But Librans can't always do this because they hate conflict and just want everybody to be happy.

"All truth is simple . . . is that not doubly a lie?"
Friedrich Nietzsche (philosopher), Libra Sun sign, born 15 October 1844

There is an old adage about an owl, which Libra would do well to ponder in a rare quiet moment:

> A wise old owl sat in an oak,
> The more he heard the less he spoke,
> The more he spoke the less he heard,
> Too bad a Libran is not like that old bird!

The Libran is a great story-teller and is never happier than when sitting at the kitchen table with a cup of tea, coffee or wine, and talking. But don't be deceived. While talking, Libra is also observing and you are likely to be the subject matter for another of those compelling stories. Never fear, if you are related, or if you are a friend, the story will be kind. It's others who may be slandered!

Libra is cardinal air (mental assertiveness) with Venus (planet of love and beauty), so it is always concerned with relationships. Librans combine a flirtatious nature with a genuine desire to learn all about you, so they are danger-ous in love indeed. Romance and relationships are where they really excel and where they learn their lessons in life. Libra is enamoured by the thrill of the chase and that first flush of new love to the point of obsession, and once in a relationship it becomes his life's work. Though there is still an aspect of Libra that likes to remain independent.

"It is better to be unfaithful than to be faithful without wanting to be."
Brigitte Bardot (actress/animal rights activist), Libra Sun sign, born 28 September 1934

Generally Librans are beautiful people with a sense of style and serenity about them. Just about any advertisement about air freshener tries to portray the Libran ideal – beautiful light-filled house, tasteful throw pillows, gorgeous children and sexy mum, classical music in the background. Librans look like they have it all, and that is how they want it to be.

But sometimes life isn't smooth, and they can look very ruffled in bad weather. If something is weighing down an aspect of their life, they will be pulling hard on the other end of the scales trying to balance this discrepancy.

They can be quite erratic in their efforts to communicate their hurt and desire for a compromise solution. If the other party is unwilling or unable help achieve this balance, Libra will become very frustrated. When this hurt stems from childhood and family, that hurt and frustration can be magnified a thousandfold.

Generally though, the Libran navigates a smooth path through life.

They raise children with a heart-through-the-mind approach. This can be very effective if the mind has last say, but it can cause problems if the Libran leans more to what their heart says. Librans are not particularly good at enforcing boundaries for their children; they can't bear to chide anyone, let alone the little person they love so much! So they tend to let the child set the bed time, nap time, snack time and so on. When the child begins exploring their world, the worrying Libra will find this very difficult. They may find themselves running around after their child, arms outstretched, like a human gatekeeper to the big bad world. The child may become out of control, and poor old Libra will be at their wit's end.

Libra at Work

Librans make wonderful diplomats and do well in the fields of psychology and social work, where an understanding of the contradictory nature of the human mind is an advantage. They are good to have around the meeting table because they make a genuine effort to understand all points of view, and are often better at crystallising other's arguments than the people themselves. Coupled with a strong sense of justice, they do well in the fields of law and mediation.

Librans dislike coarse, dirty work. They are usually modestly content, and if their surroundings are pleasant they don't feel the need to march up the ladder. Their eye for beauty makes them decent antique dealers, fashion designers, artists, composers and interior decorators.

"May we never confuse honest dissent with disloyal subversion."
Dwight D Eisenhower (US president), Libra Sun sign, born 14 October 1890

They are wonderful at publicity and event management. Some work philanthropically with great self-discipline and significant results. Libra has a well-developed sense of social justice. They support causes that value human dignity. They treat their employees and their servants with respect. They are civilised and elegant.

All You Need is Love . . .

Libran John Lennon embodied many of the contradictions of this sign. He is also a good example of what happens when the scales are in a state of flux.

Lennon was a spokesperson for his generation; witty, liberal, with an irreverent twist, he articulated the feelings of young people in the 1960s and early 1970s in a very Libran way – heart through mind, emotion intellectualised.

When he was murdered in 1980, his death signified for many people the end of an era. Conservative politics had come to hold sway in England and the US; drugs and excess had turned peace and love into disco and punk. Lennon's death marked the end of the optimism that had characterised the baby-boomer generation.

Lennon's true genius was to make people love him. Born on 9 October 1940, he was separated from his parents as an infant and raised by an aunt in middle-class England. He had behavioural problems all through school, but found balm for the soul in rock'n'roll.

Throughout his career, Lennon made many comments on life and the state of the universe. One notable comment was given in a 1966 interview with friend and journalist Maureen Cleave, where he stated in relation to the Beatles: 'Christianity will go. It will vanish and shrink. I needn't argue that; I'm right and I will be proved right. We're more popular than Jesus now.'

This quote made headlines, and in typically Libran fashion, Lennon immediately tried to restore the balance by defending his remarks, saying he was merely musing on his perceptions of the Bible-belt South with a friend. For all his braggadocio and witty banter, John Lennon just dearly wanted to be loved.

Lennon met Yoko Ono, a person whom he considered balanced him and made him whole. Their relationship was characterised by their equanimity and their romantic idealism of living and working together, 24 hours a day. As with most Librans, the loved one became Lennon's life's work.

After the Beatles broke up, the 1970s were not a great period for Lennon. He spent the first half of the decade fighting the US Immigration Department for his green card and drinking heavily. Sadly, Lennon was an unusually violent man in his personal life. His emphasis on universal love and peace was driven not only by his overwhelming need to balance the scales, but also to intellectualise his personal problems on a world scale.

He spent the second half of the seventies in seclusion. He and Yoko separated, reunited in 1980 and produced a new album together, released that November.

On the evening of 8 December 1980, Lennon was hailed by Mark David Chapman, a fan to whom he'd given an autograph earlier that day. Chapman shot him five times with a .38 revolver. Lennon was rushed to hospital but pronounced dead on arrival from a massive loss of blood. Chapman claimed it was Lennon's remarks on Jesus in 1966 that drove him to his act.

"We know that the nature of genius is to provide idiots with ideas twenty years later."
Louis Aragon (poet), Libra Sun sign, born 3 October 1897

Libra Health

Librans are prone to kidney weakness and should be careful of uric acid produced by eating animal flesh. They should try to drink copious quantities of water and indulge in cranberry juice (only if they do not have cystitis, as cranberry juice can worsen symptoms). Cereals, beans, corn, almonds and eggs are good Libran proteins.

Fresh vegetable juices like cabbage, celery and cucumber will keep their kidneys clean and functioning. A delicious kidney-cleansing combination is apple, lemon, beetroot and ginger. This is the sign of balance, so Librans should avoid sugar and refined foods and intoxicating drinks. Recuperation comes through mental relaxation and a change in scenery.

Some Librans avoid physical activity and are addicted to luxuries and creature comforts. They also tend to be fond of sugary foods which may result in adrenal fatigue and hypoglycaemia.

Libra rules the kidneys and skin, urinary organs and the anus, and the lumbar vertebrae. Some typical Libran afflictions are lumbago, kidney disease, uraemia, polyuria, renal calculi and oedema.

When choosing music for meditation, Libra's healing note is D. Good oils to use in aromatherapy are chamomile, daffodil, dill, eucalyptus, fennel, geranium, peppermint, pine, spearmint, palmarosa and vanilla.

The Libra Partner

If you happen to fall under the spell of Libra, don't surrender too quickly. Let them flirt with you for a while. Even if they push towards a relationship, imagine that it's just the scales tipping to compensate for your cooler attitude. Libra has so much fun pursuing relationships that they will love you for dragging out the anticipation.

First dates should be fairly conservative and tasteful. When choosing a restaurant, don't go for anything remotely tacky. When she says dinner and a show, she means that nice little Italian place and *Les Miserables*, not a theme restaurant with an all-you-can eat buffet.

Don't go anywhere too modern, with concrete floors and clattering coffee machines. Libra is very sensitive to the beauty of her surroundings and will be much more relaxed with dim lighting and gentle music.

Gifts for your Libra

Whatever you buy a Libran, make sure you give them the receipt as well so they can take it back. It's not that they don't appreciate your gift, it is just that they have their own sense of style that is hard to pick. Even they find it hard to pick. So she will go back to the store with the pepper grinder you gave her, receipt in hand, spend fifteen minutes looking through all the other pepper grinders, weighing up their pros and cons, and end up leaving the shop with the grinder you bought in the first place. But she will be satisfied that the right decision has been made.

Libran colours are green and blue. For gardening Librans (they love to be out in the green beauty) a coffee-table gardening book would be appreciated. Self-indulgent luxuries go down well, and a well-chosen antique will be accepted with great joy.

Famous Libra Sun Signs

23 September 1920 – Mickey Rooney (actor)

23 September 1943 – Julio Iglesias (singer)

24 September 1896 – F Scott Fitzgerald (writer)

24 September 1942 – Linda McCartney (photographer/musician)

25 September 1897 – William Faulkner (writer)

25 September 1944 – Michael Douglas (actor)

25 September 1952 – Christopher Reeve (actor)

26 September 1888 – TS Eliot (poet)

26 September 1898 – George Gershwin (composer)

26 September 1948 – Olivia Newton-John (singer)

26 September 1956 – Linda Hamilton (actress)

27 September 1920 – William Conrad (writer)

28 September 1902 – Ed Sullivan (TV host)

28 September 1909 – Al Capp (cartoonist)

28 September 1916 – Peter Finch (actor)

28 September 1934 – Brigitte Bardot (actress/animal rights activist)

29 September 1935 – Jerry Lee Lewis (singer)

29 September 1948 – Bryant Gumbel (TV host)

30 September 1924 – Truman Capote (writer)

1 October 1920 – Walter Matthau (actor)

1 October 1928 – George Peppard (actor)

1 October 1935 – Julie Andrews (actress)

2 October 1869 – Mahatma Gandhi (pacifist/political leader)

2 October 1890 – Groucho Marx (comedian)

2 October 1951 – Sting (musician)

3 October 1897 – Louis Aragon (poet)

3 October 1900 – Thomas Wolfe (writer)

3 October 1909 – Chubby Checker (singer)

3 October 1925 – Gore Vidal (writer)

4 October 1923 – Charlton Heston (actor)

4 October 1946 – Susan Sarandon (actress)

5 October 1951 – Bob Geldolf (singer/activist)

6 October 1908 – Carol Lombard (actress)

7 October 1931 – Bishop Desmond Tutu (religious leader)

7 October 1951 – John Mellencamp (singer)

8 October 1941 – Jesse Jackson (political activist)

8 October 1949 – Sigourney Weaver (actress)

9 October 1940 – John Lennon (musician)

10 October 1813 – Giuseppe Verdi (composer)

10 October 1955 – David Lee Roth (musician)

11 October 1884 – Eleanor Roosevelt (US first lady)

12 October 1875 – Aleister Crowley (occultist)

12 October 1935 – Luciano Pavarotti (opera singer)

13 October 1925 – Lenny Bruce (comedian)

13 October 1925 – Margaret Thatcher (British prime minister)

13 October 1941 – Paul Simon (singer)

14 October 1888 – Katherine Mansfield (writer)

14 October 1890 – Dwight D Eisenhower (US president)

14 October 1896 – Lillian Gish (actress)

14 October 1894 – ee cummings (poet)

14 October 1928 – Roger Moore (actor)

15 October 1844 – Friedrich Nietzsche (philosopher)

16 October 1854 – Oscar Wilde (writer)

16 October 1925 – Angela Lansbury (actress)

17 October 1915 – Arthur Miller (writer)

17 October 1919 – Rita Hayworth (actress)

17 October 1920 – Montgomery Clift (actor)

17 October 1938 – Evel Knievel (dare devil)

18 October 1956 – Martina Navratilova (tennis player)

19 October 1931 – John Le Carre (writer)

19 October 1932 – Robert Reed (actor)

19 October 1945 – John Lithgow (actor)

20 October 1854 – Arthur Rimbaud (poet)

20 October 1859 – John Dewey (educator)

20 October 1882 – Bela Lugosi (actor)

21 October 1833 – Alfred Nobel (chemist)

21 October 1956 – Carrie Fisher (actress)

22 October 1811 – Franz Liszt (composer)

22 October 1917 – Margot Fontaine (dancer)

22 October 1922 – Timothy Leary (professor/drugs experimenter)

22 October 1952 – Jeff Goldblum (actor)

23 October 1844 – Sarah Bernhardt (actress)

23 October 1925 – Johnny Carson (TV host)

The Seventh House

Libra is closely associated with the Seventh House, and the principles of the Seventh House are in keeping with the characteristics of Libra. The Seventh House is concerned with your relationships with others. For more information on the Seventh House see the chapter, The Houses, in the Interpretation section.

Venus

Libra is ruled by the planet Venus, and the principles of Venus are in keeping with the characteristics of Libra. For details on Venus and how to read it in a chart see the chapter, The Planets, in the Interpretation section.

Scorpio
(24 October to 22 November)

"Out in the garden where the air is sweet with the breath of roses, with sighs of jasmine and of lily, a lovely daughter of the house, under the shielding murmur of the limes, caught in a starry Nocturne, whispers to some sad youth the tender sorrows of the summer night."
Ignace Paderewski (composer/statesman), Scorpio Sun sign, born 6 November 1860

Basic characteristics of the sign

Personal creed – *I create*

Negative/feminine sign

Element – Water

Energy – Fixed

Psychological type – Feeling

Glyph – ♏ symbolises a serpent's coil and is linked to the male genitalia

Colour – Deep red

Body part – The genitalia

Gemstone – Opal

Flowers – Dark red flowers such as geraniums

Trees – Thorn-bearing varieties

Food – Foods with strong flavours

People with a Scorpio Sun sign are generally:

✧ Strong-willed

✧ Stubborn

✧ Complex

✧ Able to get things done when nobody else can

✧ Deeply emotional

✧ Lusty

✧ Perceptive

✧ Searching for inner values

✧ Capable of genius

✧ Extravagant in their tastes

✧ Not interested in money

✧ Intense

✧ Have hypnotic qualities

✧ Industrious in private pursuits

✧ Thoughtful

✧ Reserved

✧ Sensitive

✧ Able to reason with imagination

✧ Passionate lovers

✧ Loyal

✧ Supportive

✧ Protective

✧ Humble

On the other hand, they can also be:

✧ Demanding

✧ Possessive

✧ Jealous

✧ Unforgiving of faults

✧ Quick to a powerful rage

✧ Grudge-holders

✧ Creators of life enemies

✧ Obsessive, especially with sex

✧ Angry

✧ Suspicious

✧ Secretive

✧ Self-pitying

✧ Self-justifying

Scorpios love:

✧ Sex

✧ Religion

✧ Loyalty in a partner

✧ Mystery

✧ Secrets

✧ Privacy

✧ Trust

✧ Sensuality/passion

✧ Strength

✧ Knowing where they stand

✧ Acknowledgment

✧ Honesty/integrity

But they can't stand:

✧ Surprises

✧ Lying and deceit

✧ Apathy

✧ Being analysed/questioned

✧ Being 'understood'

✧ Excessive compliments

✧ Insincerity

✧ Being embarrassed

✧ Passivity

The Scorpio Character

Scorpio's constellation is impressive in that it actually resemblances its sign, the Scorpio, whereas other constellations are obscure. Probably for this reason, the scorpion is often used to explain the concepts of Scorpio, with a sting in its tail. Scorpio also has two other symbols (it is the only sign with three), the eagle and the phoenix, and these have some interesting connotations.

All three signs are able to conquer their difficult environments with a combination of stealth and intelligence. The phoenix is the Greek name for a mythological bird offered in sacrifice to Ra, God of the Sun, in the ancient Egypt. This bird was similar to an eagle, and possessed golden-red feathers like flames.

Only one phoenix could exist at a time and, according to the legend, it could live anywhere from 500 to 1000 years. At the end of its life, the phoenix built its own mortuary pyre and was consumed by fire. From the ashes, the phoenix was reborn. This cycle was repeated over and over, so that the phoenix was the symbolic representation of the death and rebirth of the Sun.

"Do you not see how necessary a world of pains and troubles is: to school an intelligence and make it a soul?"
John Keats (poet), Scorpio Sun sign, born 31 October 1795

Scorpio is very much concerned with death, birth and rebirth. It is a period of darkness and introspection after the social interaction of Libra. The difference between Libra and her neighbour Scorpio is quite radical. Probably the most pertinent difference is their attitudes to truth. For Libra, the truth is changeable; for Scorpio, the truth is a given, and it is their life's mission to seek it out. They would never bend the truth to placate someone, but will tell the story as they see it, good or bad, because the truth cannot be tampered with.

"You mustn't always believe what I say. Questions tempt you to tell lies, particularly when there is no answer."
Pablo Picasso (artist), Scorpio Sun sign, born 25 October 1881

Scorpios are people of deep faith, whether they are Christian, atheist or something more exotic. They think emotionally and deeply about the meaning of life and this can lead them into the priesthood or a similar vocational profession.

Their natural suspicion can make for torrid relationships. People generally expect to be trusted and can find this behaviour insulting, and this can drive many a good prospect away. Scorpio can see this as a confirmation of their suspicions which only makes them more vigilant next time. Scorpios require solid security without feeling their partner is a doormat. This is a precarious balance that has to be learned by both partners over time. The longer a relationship lasts with a Scorpio the more secure it tends to become.

Scorpios carry the deceits of the past with a hurt as fresh as if it was yesterday. Many an ill-mannered Scorpio has bored a first date to tears with vitriolic stories of his ex-lover. This can turn into full-blown self-pity, and Scorpio can become his own worst enemy.

"We make a ladder of our vices, if we trample those same vices underfoot."
Saint Augustine (theologian), Scorpio Sun sign, born 13 November 354

Yet though they can be jealous and possessive, you will not find a more passionate sign in the zodiac.

The Scorpio ego can also be the most resilient in the zodiac. You can neither insult nor compliment a Scorpio to ill or great effect, as Scorpios know their strengths and weaknesses.

To the mere mortals of the other eleven signs, the Scorpio character sounds so sexy and complex and mysterious, and that's exactly how Scorpio likes it. They are firm believers that familiarity breeds contempt, and they will go out of their way to keep a pocket of themselves veiled in mystery.

They are often called the loners of the zodiac. In fact, they hate being alone, and this misinterpretation of their desire to protect themselves as aloofness is the most heartbreaking part of being a Scorpio. They are a deeply emotional water sign with a great need and desire to partner. You may not be able to insult them, but you can easily break their heart once it has been given to you. The Scorpio is a deeply compassionate sign that can suffer from intense feelings of loneliness.

Scorpio is fixed water, that is, controlled emotion. They tend to dominate in any relationship as this control makes them feel safe. To the world they like to portray themselves as the subservient partner, but they are very much in control, and are not above blackmail and manipulation to keep it that way.

Scorpio at Work

Scorpios are drawn to the religious and austere professions. Many ministers, priests and nuns have a great deal of Scorpio influence in their chart. However, they can also use these professions to cloak their deeply passionate and sexual natures which they sometimes find disturbing. Passion and anger can be all-too-comfortable bedfellows with guilt and self-loathing – watch that you don't curl that sting back on yourself.

It comes as no surprise then that you will find many a Scorpio at the other end of the scale, brandishing a whip and hot wax. Scorpios are night people (although they love their sleep as well) and they are often found working the bar at the seedier end of town.

Science is the modern religion and is a field where Scorpio can find many challenges. Psychology is a field that often interests the Scorp. Human nature intrigues them, though they can be abrasive counsellors and psychologists. They also have an uncanny knack for remembering everything you have ever said to them, word for word, and they are not afraid to repeat it back to you when you appear to be inconsistent! Scorpios also make great parents – they are fiercely protective of their offspring and will go to any length to do their best by them.

Lady Lazarus

Probably the life that most embodies the passion and pathos of the Scorpio is that of the poet Sylvia Plath. Sex and death were her life's work, and her poems are still favoured reading by those going through a period of introspection.

Dying
is an art, like everything else.
I do it exceptionally well.
from 'Lady Lazarus'

Born in Massachusetts on 27 October 1932, Plath was a popular, straight A student, whose first poem was published by the age of nine. She had a constant drive for perfection that earned her the high-school nickname 'The High Priestess of Suffering'.

Plath used her writing to explore the taboo topic of death. In her work, she views death not merely as an escape, but as her chance to be reborn. The very Scorpion imagery of the phoenix comes up more than once in her poetry.

Out of the ash
I rise with my red hair
And I eat men like air.
from 'Lady Lazarus'

And her epitaph read: 'Even amidst fierce flames – the golden lotus can be planted.'

After she won a scholarship to Cambridge, England, Plath met her future husband, the poet Ted Hughes. Plath described him as 'that big, dark, hunky boy, the only one there huge enough for me'. He kissed her 'bang smash on the mouth' and ripped off her headband and earrings, before she bit him on the cheek until he bled. This flavour of sex and violence tainted their relationship from the beginning. After a brief courtship, Plath and Hughes married in June 1956.

After finishing her studies at Cambridge, they returned to the US, where Plath worked as a lecturer and then as a receptionist at a psychiatric clinic. Here she did most of the research for her book *The Bell Jar*, which explores, among other themes, mental illness. She worked days, visited a therapist during the afternoon, and spent her evenings diligently writing.

The couple returned to England in December 1959. Plath gave birth to their first child, Frieda, in 1960, but miscarried the following year. This event was the catalyst for a dark period of her life.

A second child, Nicholas, was born in 1962 and the family moved to countryside Devon. Feeling isolated, Sylvia wrote and cared for her children. In July that year, she discovered Hughes was having an affair with a German woman with movie star looks, Assia Wevill. They separated in September and later divorced.

Not at all eager to begin life on her own, Plath reluctantly packed her bags and moved with her two children to an apartment in London. Ill with chronic flu, she would work on *The Bell Jar* from 4 a.m. until the children woke. The book was submitted under the pseudonym of Victoria Lucas; it was published in January 1963, but the critics were unimpressed.

Extremely depressed over the break-up of her marriage and lack of success, Plath felt she could no longer go on. In the final days of the coldest winter Britain had seen in sixty years, she penned her last works. On 11 February 1963, she put her children to bed upstairs, opened their window to the night air, and stuffed towels to cover the crack under the door.

She made a plate of bread and butter for her sleeping children for the morning, placed it on the kitchen table with glasses of milk, and put her head in a gas oven.

The Bell Jar was published in the US in 1971 under Plath's real name. It became wildly popular and earned her a place in literary history. Plath received a posthumous Pulitzer Prize in 1981 for this work.

Scorpio Health

Scorpios should avoid fatty, rich and intoxicating food and drinks. Scorpios benefit from a vegetarian diet. Stabilising foods like brown rice, millet, wheat grass, spinach, lettuce, celery and cucumbers are good. Others are cherries, oranges, lemons, asparagus and rhubarb. The influence of Mars requires that Scorpios drink plenty of water and vegetable juices, and avoid salt.

Scorpio rules the nose, the pubic area and genital organs. Internally, it rules the gonads, haemoglobin, bladder and prostate. It has influence over the vocal cords and larynx.

This sign also has influence over the liver, uterus, menstruation, sweat glands and the endocrine glands in general.

Typical Scorpio afflictions are anaemia in women; adenoids, sore throats, hay fever; profuse menstruation, painful and irregular menstruation, ovarian disturbances; diarrhoea, haemorrhoids; hypersensitivity; bladder problems and infections; obesity, diabetes; heart disease; genital infections; and renal calculi.

When choosing music for meditation, keep in mind that the healing note for Scorpio is C. Oils that are good to use in aromatherapy are black pepper, cardamom, coffee, ginger, hyacinth, hops, pennyroyal, pine, thyme, tuberose and woodruff.

The Scorpio Partner

If you go to a party together, you need to master the art of letting your Scorpio go and reeling him in. Scorpios generally feel a bit on edge in a social situation with a partner, as they can see too much danger in flirtatious situations. They are very quick to jealousy but they don't want you to stick to them like a lap dog.

Make sure you have a proprietary hand on the small of their back when you are introducing them to people. Meet their eyes across the room, and if you see they need a drink, get them one.

Break away from the group to go up behind them and whisper in their ear that they look fantastic. You will have the hairs on the back of their neck standing up in excitement.

Gifts for your Scorpio

Scorpios are intense and passionate with a love of mystery and secrets. They get as much pleasure wondering what's inside the box as they do opening it.

They love to investigate – think about mysteriously giving them only a clue to the present. For instance, if you are planning on surprising them with a 'romantic' weekend for their birthday, wrap up a carry-on luggage bag, packed with nothing but a black lacy lingerie. Their eyes will sparkle with delight as they put two and two together. It's at that moment you can take the plane tickets out of your top pocket.

Giving the gift in secret will titillate them even more. If you have bought a bracelet for her, wait until you are at a party. Pull her away mysteriously during the evening to some-where secluded to give her your gift. After a passionate embrace, make a show of going back into the party as if nothing has happened.

Some Scorpios like to flirt with the occult so they might like a crystal ball, Tarot cards, Rune stones or a book on white magic. Scorpios also love water and they like to swim, so a new swimsuit might be a good idea. Exotic perfumes, satin sheets and or something a little kinky will tease their sensual tastes.

Famous Scorpio Sun Signs

24 October 1947 – Kevin Kline (actor)

25 October 1881 – Pablo Picasso (artist)

25 October 1941 – Helen Reddy (singer)

26 October 1947 – Hillary Rodham Clinton (senator/US first lady)

26 October 1947 – Jaclyn Smith (actress)

27 October 1857 – Theodore Roosevelt (US president)

27 October 1914 – Dylan Thomas (poet)

27 October 1932 – Sylvia Plath (poet)

28 October 1939 – John Cleese (actor)

28 October 1955 – Bill Gates (computer entrepreneur)

29 October 1947 – Richard Dreyfuss (actor)

29 October 1971 – Winona Ryder (actress)

30 October 1885 – Ezra Pound (poet)

31 October 1795 – John Keats (poet)

1 November 1942 – Larry Flint (publisher)

2 November 1755 – Marie-Antoinette (French royalty)

2 November 1913 – Burt Lancaster (actor)

3 November 1922 – Charles Bronson (actor)

3 November 1952 – Roseanne Arnold (comedian)

4 November 1879 – Will Rogers (actor)

4 November 1916 – Walter Cronkite (news anchor)

4 November 1937 – Loretta Swit (actress)

5 November 1913 – Vivien Leigh (actress)

5 November 1941 – Art Garfunkel (singer)

6 November 1860 – Ignace Paderewski (composer/statesman)

6 November 1946 – Sally Field (actress)

7 November 1867 – Marie Curie (scientist)

7 November 1879 – Leon Trotsky (revolutionary)

7 November 1913 – Albert Camus (writer)

7 November 1926 – Joan Sutherland (opera singer)

7 November 1943 – Joni Mitchell (singer)

9 November 1934 – Carl Sagan (scientist)

10 November 1925 – Richard Burton (actor)

11 November 1821 – Fyodor Dostoevsky (writer)

11 November 1922 – Kurt Vonnegut (writer)

11 November 1962 – Demi Moore (actress)

12 November 1840 – Auguste Rodin (sculptor)

12 November 1929 – Grace Kelly (actress/royalty)

12 November 1945 – Neil Young (singer)

13 November 354 – Saint Augustine (theologian)

13 November 1949 – Whoopi Goldberg (comedian)

14 November 1908 – Joseph McCarthy (politician)

14 November 1935 – King Hussein (Jordan royalty)

14 November 1948 – Prince Charles (British royalty)

17 November 1925 – Rock Hudson (actor)

17 November 1938 – Gordon Lightfoot (singer)

17 November 1942 – Martin Scorsese (film director)

17 November 1943 – Lauren Hutton (actress)

17 November 1944 – Danny De Vito (actor)

19 November 1483 – Martin Luther (religious leader)

19 November 1917 – Indira Gandhi (political leader)

19 November 1938 – Ted Turner (media magnate)

19 November 1962 – Jodie Foster (actress)

20 November 1925 – Robert Kennedy (US attorney-general)

20 November 1956 – Bo Derek (actress)

21 November 1694 – Voltaire (writer)

21 November 1946 – Goldie Hawn (actress)

22 November 1890 – Charles de Gaulle (political leader)

The Eighth House

Scorpio is closely associated with the Eighth House, and the principles of the Eighth House are in keeping with the characteristics of Scorpio. The Eighth House is the house of sex, procreation and one's sexual tastes. For more information on the Eighth House see the chapter, The Houses, in the Interpretation section.

Mars and Pluto

Scorpio is ruled by Mars and Pluto, and the principles of both planets are in keeping with the characteristics of Scorpio. Until Pluto was discovered in 1930, Mars ruled Scorpio alone, but now Pluto is considered the stronger ruler. Pluto's influence on Scorpio is more obvious, but it still useful to read about Mars. For details on Mars and Pluto and how to read them in a chart see the chapter, The Planets, in the Interpretation section.

Sagittarius
(23 November to 21 December)

"Friday I tasted life. It was a vast morsel. A Circus passed the house – still I feel the red in my mind though the drums are out. The Lawn is full of south and the odors tangle, and I hear to-day for the first time the river in the tree."
Emily Dickinson (poet), Sagittarius Sun sign, born 10 December 1830

Basic characteristics of the sign
Personal creed – *I see*

Positive/masculine sign

Element – Fire

Energy – Mutable

Psychological type – Intuitive

Glyph – ♐ represents the arrow of the centaur

Colours – Purple, deep blue

Body part – The thighs

Gemstones – Topaz, lapis lazuli, blue quartz, azurite, labradorite

Flowers – Carnations, rush, hyssop

Trees – Oak, fig, ash, birch

Food – Currants and the onion family

People with a Sagittarius Sun sign are generally:

✧ Loyal

✧ Impulsive

✧ Independent

✧ Lucky

✧ Talkative

✧ Outgoing

✧ Broad-minded

✧ Straightforward

✧ Enthusiastic

✧ Idealistic

✧ Ambitious

✧ Optimistic

✧ Honest

✧ Passionate

✧ Charming

✧ Funny

✧ Far-sighted

✧ Adventurous

✧ Nonpossessive

On the other hand, they can also be:

✧ Impatient

✧ Impetuous

✧ Aggressive

✧ Irrational

✧ Selfish

✧ Unpunctual

✧ Prone to exaggeration

✧ Flighty

✧ Sarcastic

✧ Unreliable

✧ Dogmatic

✧ Judgmental

✧ Careless with possessions and money

Sagittarians love:

✧ Freedom

✧ Intellectual compatibility

✧ Taking risks

✧ Socialising

✧ Philosophical and political debate

✧ Becoming involved with causes and demonstrations

✧ Feeling trusted

✧ An active partner

✧ Daydreaming

✧ Literature

✧ Theatre

✧ Family

✧ Friends

✧ Travel

✧ Music and dance

But they can't stand:

✧ Jealousy

✧ Possessiveness

✧ Routine

✧ Being doubted

✧ Having to explain themselves

✧ Control

✧ Apathy/laziness

✧ Duplicity

✧ Shallow people

✧ Inward-looking institutions

✧ Clubs

✧ Convention

✧ Housework

The Sagittarian Character

In Sagittarius, we reconcile the spiritual level discovered in Scorpio with the external world. Sagittarius searches for the magic moment where universal principles are glimpsed through personal experience.

Sagittarius is linked to the legend of the centaur, Chiron. The two sides of the centaur are the freedom-loving creature and the divine healer. Chiron is half-man, half-horse, portraying the conflict between the philosophical mind and the carnal instinct, an arrow aiming at the stars.

Sagittarians radiate energy and vitality and possess alert minds. They crave experience. They love to travel (though some don't know when to stop) and once they have stepped out, their itchy feet will have them planning the next trip. When they are at home, they quench their thirst for experience by reading avidly.

"I don't respond well to mellow, you know what I mean,
I-I have a tendency to . . . if I get too mellow, I-I ripen and
then rot."
Woody Allen (comedian/film director), Sagittarius Sun sign, born 1 December 1935

Sagittarians are explorers both of the world and of the mind. Though they love to experience new people, places and cultures, they are also happy to sit at home in front of an open fire, glass of red on the hearth, exploring ideas with good friends. They generally love to find out about people and explore philosophy with strangers. Sagittarians have been known to take several hours buying a litre of milk after picking up a conversation on the bus or at the milk bar.

They are an engaging mix of teacher and student. Their mutable energy is about giving and taking, but their fire element puts them more on the giving side. This makes them quite similar to Gemini (their polar opposite on the zodiac) but whereas Gemini likes to order and communicate information, Sagittarius is much more engaged with its spiritual and philosophical framework.

Jupiter is the planet of luck and many Sagittarians experience more than their share. They are not gamblers as such, but they always seem to fall on their feet. They bounce up with a look of wonder that they got out of that one, and a cheerful skip and a wee trip over as they get on their way (Sagittarians are notoriously clumsy).

They are often portrayed as the cheerful clowns of the zodiac, a bit awkward and tactless but so positive and well-meaning you could hardly be upset about it. Sagittarians find that comedy comes easily to them and many become comedians. Their comedy usually comes from it not being funny so much, as being breathtakingly true.

"The only rules comedy can tolerate are those of taste, and the only limitations those of libel."
James Thurber (writer), Sagittarius Sun sign, born 8 December 1894

And this is the crux of it. Sagittarians are audacious in their truth-telling. They will say the most astounding things so flippantly, because they believe that's what everyone else was thinking anyway. Sagittarians think loftily most of the time, about interrelationships rather than the nitty-gritty. This can make social mores and protocol seem insignificant to them. So they just charge on through and say what they think should be said anyway. This is what makes having a Sag around so shocking, frustrating, but most of the time, exhilarating.

Sagittarians speak the truth unconsciously, but they do have trouble when restricting themselves while telling a story. If they are not getting the reaction they were expecting they can exaggerate, sometimes to a ludicrous extent, in order to emphasise a point.

"A little inaccuracy sometimes saves tons of explanation."
Saki (writer), Sagittarius Sun sign, born 18 December 1870

But generally they worship the truth. If your Sagittarian teenager comes home and announces that he tried marijuana and didn't like it, just be relieved he didn't like it, because Sags will try anything once but always tell the truth. There is nothing that will frustrate your boy more than if he has been honest with you, and you still suspect him of being duplicitous.

"A fanatic is one who can't change his mind and won't change the subject."
Winston Churchill (political leader), Sagittarius Sun sign, born 30 November 1874

Sagittarians love to talk and argue. They have sharp and inquiring minds and love to examine new ideas and use friends and family as sounding boards. This may appear argumentative, but to the Archer an opposite point of view is simply a challenge and an excuse to throw more ideas around – no resolution is required.

Sagittarians have been known to read a dictionary if there was no other reading matter available. The Sagittarian is always on the lookout for a new book to read. She will never willingly walk past a garage sale or a school fete without spending an hour browsing through the discarded books and returning home armed with a plastic bag full of reading matter. She will select anything that piques her wide-ranging interests at the time.

The benign and regal aspects of Jupiter are reflected in Sagittarius. Optimism, confidence and a positive attitude are great characteristics, but can change to imperiousness, impatience and recklessness. Sagittarians have to be reminded that their actions make waves, positive or negative.

Sagittarians are ardent, sincere and straightforward in love, normally conventional and in control of their sexual natures. If their loyalty is not returned, they may revenge themselves upon the opposite sex by becoming promiscuous. Sagittarian women find it difficult to express physical affection and may run the risk of being thought frigid or off-hand.

Because they are always exploring, it is important that the relationship has a grounding force. That is why Sagittarians often choose a quieter, more inwardly thinking person, who can bring the peace that the Sagittarian mind craves but is incapable of providing.

Sagittarius at Work

Sagittarians have enormous faith in their own abilities, but will often bite off more than they can chew. They often have difficulty finishing things because they never leave enough time. They tend to try to do too many things at once rather than do one thing well.

They are good researchers, and read widely. Being able to synthesise many different streams of thought into one coherent piece makes them shine in the areas of science, the arts, religion and philosophy. They will fight for what they believe to be right, sometimes to the point of being dogmatic or judgmental.

They not only join Book Clubs, they run them. A Sagittarian dreams of a job where they can be paid for reading books. But it would be no good. Books usually demand quiet places, libraries and so forth, and Sagittarians are anything but quiet. Library books also need to be put in some sort of order, and Sags are no good at that either. The queue at the counter would get longer and longer as the Sagittarian found himself getting caught up reading the cover blurbs, and expounding enthusiastically about a latest novel.

The Wind Beneath Her Wings

"I never know how much of what I say is true."
Bette Midler (entertainer), Sagittarius Sun sign, born 1 December 1945

Sagittarian Bette Midler is an excellent example of how invigorating all that positive, fiery energy can be. Born in Honolulu, Hawaii, as a member of the only Jewish family in a Polynesian neighbourhood, the Divine Miss M loved to sing and dance from an early age. She worked briefly in a pineapple cannery, then moved to New York in the 1960s. There she landed a role in the chorus of Broadway's long-running hit *Fiddler on the Roof* and eventually gained a lead role.

Midler set the record at Radio City Music Hall, selling 30 shows and playing to 176,220 people. Her nightclub act was (and still is) a heady mixture of comedy, show tunes, pop hits, and boundless energy and enthusiasm. Bawdy and brassy, she told dirty jokes and belted out songs in Manhattan's Continental Baths in 1971, becoming a cult figure on the local gay scene. Her appearances led to a successful pop career. She was signed to Atlantic Records and released *The Divine Miss M* (1972), which went gold. The album *Bette Midler* (1973) was similarly successful.

"I wouldn't say I invented tacky, but I definitely brought it to its present high popularity."
Bette Midler (entertainer), Sagittarius Sun sign, born 1 December 1945

Success fell away during the rest of the 1970s, but for 1979's *The Rose*, which gave Midler her first starring movie role, she received an Oscar nomination, and won a Grammy for the title song. In 1980 Midler's concert film, *Divine Madness*, was released, plus her best-selling book, *A View from a Broad*.

With success in the Disney comedies *Down and Out in Beverly Hills* (1986) and *Ruthless People* (1986), Midler channelled funds into a production company of her own. Her version of 'Wind Beneath My Wings' from the film *Beaches* (1988) really put her back on the map. It rejuvenated her singing career, and 1990's *Some People's Lives* became a million-selling album, with 'From a Distance' becoming a major hit.

After a few near misses in the early 1990s, Midler joined Goldie Hawn and Diane Keaton to round out the cast of cast-off wives in the revenge comedy *The First Wives Club* (1996). She recently performed 'Wind Beneath My Wings' at the Memorial Service for the firefighters killed in the 11 September attacks on New York. Perhaps this will see a new uphill run for this irreverent but tenacious entertainer.

Sagittarius Health

Sagittarius rules the hips, gluteal muscles, thighs, and has considerable influence over the muscles in general.

Sagittarians should avoid stimulants and intoxicants. This is a fiery, hot and choleric sign, so Sagittarians are better suited to a vegetarian diet. Cooling fruits such as citrus, bananas and berries are beneficial. Nerve-building foods likes oats, wheat and barley are important. They should drink plenty of water since their hot constitution can dehydrate them quickly. Salt, which damages the bones and blood, should be avoided. Other beneficial foods are asparagus, corn, endive, cucumber, red cabbage and apples.

Typical Sagittarius afflictions are disorders of the arms, hip joints, sciatica, spinal disorders, rheumatism; nervous disorders, hypersensitivity; baldness; heart disease; bronchitis, tuberculosis; abnormal breathing patterns; and eye disorders.

When choosing music for meditation, the Sagittarius healing musical note is G sharp. Oils that are good to use in aromatherapy are bergamot, calendula, clove, lemon balm, mace, nutmeg, oak moss, rosemary and saffron.

The Sagittarius Partner
"It takes two flints to make a fire."
Louisa May Alcott (writer), Sagittarius Sun sign, born 29 November 1832

Intrigue them, surprise them, tantalise them, worry them, just don't ever bore them. You could take Sagittarius just about anywhere for your first date as long as it is just the tiniest bit exotic. McDonald's and a blockbuster movie are not going to do the trick. But a Ninja film and duck soup on formica tables in a cafe in Chinatown will charm her. If it is a new experience she will love it whether or not she liked the movie, and she will love debating the merits of Ninja films with you late into the night.

Later on, take her away as often as you can afford it. It doesn't have to be an overnight trip but springing a surprise flight to the capital city for dinner and a show and a night on the town will delight her. A trip to the coast to fossick about in antique stores, or an afternoon at the wineries in the hills will have her glowing. Check out river cruises that might take you to the nearest port for fish and chips – such exotic pleasures can be surprisingly affordable.

Gifts for your Sagittarian

Sagittarians love to give presents as an expression of their warm personality. They usually agonise for weeks over what to buy, and almost always spend an embarrassing amount of money – money is not that important to the Sag, and after all, what price a friend or loved one? Jupiter is the giver of wealth and is associated with prosperity, laughter and happiness, so it's not surprising that Sagittarians are at their best when gifts are being exchanged, like at Christmas.

Sadly, these gifts are not always on the mark, but they would be mortified if they thought they had got it wrong, so be gentle.

When buying for your Sag, remember they usually feel comforted by their colours indigo and royal purple. Displays of honesty are very important to them, so it really is the thought that counts. If the giver forgets to write a card, then the gift is as good as flawed.

Books always go down well, especially if you have read it so they can discuss it with you later. Clothes are often a nice idea, as they usually can't stand shopping for themselves, and have a very laissez-faire sense of style that will accommodate most things.

Anything that will give them a new experience is accepted with joy: a shiatsu massage (massages are good for Sags as they are generally not physically demonstrative), a hot-air balloon ride, a night out at a cocktail bar trying everything on the menu (they can hold their drink), tickets to a show or enrolment at a course of life drawing/salsa dancing/theology classes.

Famous Sagittarius Sun Signs

23 November 1893 – Harpo Marx (comedian)

24 November 1864 – Henri Toulouse-Lautrec (artist)

25 November 1960 – John F Kennedy Jr (US president's son)

26 November 1938 – Tina Turner (singer)

27 November 1940 – Bruce Lee (martial arts exponent)

27 November 1942 – Jimi Hendrix (guitarist)

28 November 1757 – William Blake (poet/artist)

28 November 1820 – Friedrich Engels (political philosopher)

28 November 1829 – Arthur Rubenstein (conductor)

29 November 1832 – Louisa May Alcott (writer)

30 November 1835 – Mark Twain (writer)

30 November 1874 – Winston Churchill (political leader)

30 November 1955 – Billy Idol (musician)

1 December 1935 – Woody Allen (comedian/film director)

1 December 1945 – Bette Midler (entertainer)

2 December 1863 – Charles Ringling (circus entrepreneur)

2 December 1859 – Georges Seurat (artist)

2 December 1946 – Gianni Versace (fashion designer)

2 December 1968 – Lucy Liu (actress)

2 December 1973 – Monica Seles (tennis champion)

2 December 1978 – Nelly Furtado (singer)

2 December 1981 – Britney Spears (singer)

3 December 1857 – Joseph Conrad (writer)

3 December 1930 – Jean-Luc Godard (film director)

4 December 1795 – Thomas Carlyle (writer)

4 December 1866 – Wassily Kandinsky (artist)

4 December 1892 – Francisco Franco (dictator)

4 December 1964 – Marisa Tomei (actress)

5 December 1901 – Walt Disney (animator/film producer)

6 December 1956 – Peter Buck (singer)

7 December 1888 – Joyce Cary (writer)

7 December 1932 – Ellen Burstyn (actress)

8 December 1886 – Diego Rivera (artist)

8 December 1894 – James Thurber (writer)

8 December 1925 – Sammy Davis Jr (entertainer)

SAGITTARIUS

8 December 1939 – James Galway (musician)

8 December 1944 – Jim Morrison (musician)

8 December 1953 – Kim Basinger (actress)

8 December 1967 – Sinead O'Connor (singer)

9 December 1916 – Kirk Douglas (actor)

9 December 1953 – John Malkovich (actor)

9 December 1957 – Donny Osmond (singer)

10 December 1830 – Emily Dickinson (poet)

11 December 1843 – Robert Koch (bacteriologist)

11 December 1918 – Alexander Solzhenitsyn (writer)

11 December 1950 – Christina Onassis (heiress)

12 December 1915 – Frank Sinatra (singer)

13 December 1821 – Gustave Flaubert (writer)

13 December 1925 – Dick Van Dyke (actor)

14 December 1946 – Patty Duke (actress)

16 December 1770 – Ludwig van Beethoven (composer)

16 December 1775 – Jane Austen (writer)

16 December 1899 – Noël Coward (playwright)

16 December 1901 – Margaret Mead (anthropologist)

16 December 1917 – Arthur C Clarke (writer)

17 December 1958 – Mike Mills (musician)

18 December 1870 – Saki (writer)

18 December 1879 – Paul Klee (artist)

18 December 1916 – Betty Grable (actress)

18 December 1943 – Keith Richards (musician)

18 December 1946 – Steven Spielberg (film director)

18 December 1963 – Brad Pitt (actor)

18 December 1978 – Katie Holmes (actress)

18 December 1980 – Christina Aguilera (singer)

19 December 1608 – John Milton (poet)

19 December 1910 – Jean Genet (writer)

19 December 1972 – Alyssa Milano (actress)

20 December 1946 – Uri Geller (spoon bender)

21 December 1879 – Joseph Stalin (communist leader)

21 December 1912 – Lady Bird Johnson (US first lady)

21 December 1935 – Phil Donahue (talk show host)

21 December 1937 – Jane Fonda (actress)

21 December 1940 – Frank Zappa (musician)

21 December 1948 – Samuel L Jackson (actor)

21 December 1957 – Ray Romano (comedian)

21 December 1966 – Kiefer Sutherland (actor)

The Ninth House

Sagittarius is closely associated with the Ninth House, and the principles of the Ninth House are in keeping with the characteristics of Sagittarius. The Ninth House describes our philosophy on life, our religious and moral beliefs, and activities that expand our horizons, such as travel and higher education.

For more information on the Ninth House see the chapter, The Houses, in the Interpretation section.

Jupiter

Sagittarius is ruled by the planet Jupiter, and the principles of Jupiter are in keeping with the characteristics of Sagittarius. For details on Jupiter and how to read it in a chart see the chapter, The Planets, in the Interpretation section.

Capricorn
(22 December to 20 January)

"The only thing necessary for the triumph of evil is for good men to do nothing."
Edmund Burke (political theorist), Capricorn Sun sign, born 12 January 1729

Basic characteristics of the sign

Personal creed – *I use*

Negative/feminine sign

Element – Earth

Energy – Cardinal

Psychological type – Perceptive

Glyph – ♑ said to represent a goat's head and a fish tail

Colours – Dark colours, especially dark browns and navy

Body part – The knees

Gemstone – Amethyst

Flowers – Pansy, ivy

Trees – Pine, willow

Food – Starchy foods, meat

People with a Capricorn Sun sign are generally:

✦ Loyal

✦ Ambitious

✦ Dedicated

✦ Focused

✦ Honest

✦ Disciplined

✦ Deliberate

✦ Logical

✦ Patient

✦ Kind

✦ Supportive

✦ Serious

✦ Dependable

✦ Tolerant

✦ Attentive

✧ Practical

✧ Prudent

✧ Humorous

✧ Reserved

On the other hand, they can also be:

✧ Anxious

✧ Stubborn

✧ Retaliatory

✧ Suspicious

✧ Severe

✧ Possessive

✧ Controlling

✧ Cold

✧ Calculating

✧ Pessimistic

✧ Fatalistic

✧ Miserly

Capricorns love:
✧ Loyalty

✧ Security

✧ Financial stability

✧ Ambitious mates

✧ Feeling committed

✧ Making long-term relationship plans

✧ Dependability

✧ Perseverance

But they can't stand:
✧ Flightiness

✧ Bossiness

✧ Crudeness/coarseness

✧ Dominance

✧ Game-playing

✧ Ego displays

✧ Extravagance

✧ Being challenged by a lover

✧ Indecisiveness

The Capricorn Character

Capricorns seem to grow young, rather than old. They are born thirty, and spend their youth and early twenties growing their body into its rightful age.

To be truthful, they would love to have skipped all those tiresome early years, having to be friends with immature brats and having no control over their destiny. The teenage years are especially painful for a Capricorn – rebellion holds no sway with her; she just wants to get out of school, so she can start earning a wage and take some control over her life.

"No one is so old as to think he cannot live one more year."
Cicero (orator/writer), Capricorn Sun sign, born 3 January 106 BC

The Capricorn woman is beautiful indeed. She combines strength, grace and an iron will with the uncanny ability to convince anyone to do anything she wants, and they'll end up thinking it was their idea in the first place. A Capricorn woman can be found in the boardroom, sinking ships and building towers and generally making her mark on the world. But she could just as easily be found in the home, tending the hearth. In this situation she could even be mistaken for a Cancer, until you dare hurt one of her children – a Cancer mother would swiftly ferry them away from harm, but a Capricorn mother is just as likely to come at you with a World War II Howitzer!

Underneath that dependable, dry, buttoned-down exterior beats the heart of the warmest furnace. Capricorns have the most caring nature, it's just that they don't think they should show it in company. After all, it's hard work having such a principled planet like Saturn ruling your roost.

Capricorn males can suffer from this especially. Capricorn women are women first, so they are allowed to show a few emotions and get a few hugs as a matter of course (although she will often stiffen as though she is hating it). The Capricorn male isn't going to score any hugs unless he is in a committed relationship and even then he is the last to give them away. That isn't to say he doesn't enjoy them, in fact, sometimes he craves physical affection, but he just doesn't know how to ask in a proper manner.

Capricorns are also often said to hate compliments, and certainly if you paid one, they often pretend it didn't happen, or swiftly nod their head in thanks and get on with the conversation.

"Flattery corrupts both the receiver and the giver."
Edmund Burke (political theorist), Capricorn Sun sign, born 12 January 1729

But really he is pleased as punch inside, and will replay that comment in his head all day. It will be the last thing he thinks about that night. And, watch him deal with you at the office the next day – he might even self-consciously tousle your hair, or let you have one of his world-famous, melt-your-heart smiles, reserved only for the best of occasions and, in this case, reserved only for you.

For these reasons, Capricorn is the most intriguing romantic prospect in the zodiac. Scorpio's aloofness seems like an act compared to Capricorn's genuine, earthy sensuality, trapped beneath the Saturn desire to do and say the correct thing.

That is not to say that you will suddenly be able to find the key to unlock the frivolity of your Capricorn. Many a fire sign has tried, but failed to tease Capricorn out of their shell. It must be done with love and understanding. Hint that you know there is more to him than meets the eye. Tell him that you plan to discover what stokes the furnace burning beneath that conservative exterior. And, little by little, he will let a modicum of warmth escape.

You are never going to get a Capricorn to suddenly take a midnight skinny dip, as that is obviously not the proper thing to do, but with commitment, you will be able to get him to relax his guard a little with you – but only with you. And isn't that a much more exciting prospect than having a partner whose charms are plainly obvious to the world?

Just never tell a Capricorn in frustration that they are boring. It is the most hurtful thing you can say, not least because there is the tiniest ring of truth to it. They don't mean to bore you, they just can't understand why playing by the rules can't be fun too! A rush of adrenalin is ecstasy to some, but adrenalin only makes Capricorn anxious.

And you must have patience as well. As they mature, Capricorns start to get that spark of playfulness, and begin to dally with irreverence, as they grow more comfortable with themselves and their place in the world. Sometimes the catalyst to discovering their lost childhood can be the arrival of their children. This can be magical to watch.

You won't necessarily find him up to his elbows in mud pies when he gets home in the evening. He will most certainly maintain the role of father in charge, sitting at the head of the table and demanding respect, but that's what makes it so glorious when he loosens up a little for the children. It won't matter that Mum has accompanied them on every whizzy-dizzy they ever went on, Daddy will still be remembered the most fondly for that time he took them on the roller-coaster.

"Ambition can creep as well as soar."
Edmund Burke (political theorist), Capricorn Sun sign, born 12 January 1729

The three most important Capricorn goals are security, respect and authority. Everything else falls in line with them. Capricorn women are often portrayed as career-minded feminists aiming for the sky with no time for a partner and children. This is not true. They are ambitious, with a burning need for respect and authority, but this is not mutually exclusive of their desire for emotional security with a family. In the old days, it was called marrying up – a Capricorn woman is ambitious in her partnering as well.

"To be completely woman you need a master, and in him a compass for your life."
Marlene Dietrich (actress), Capricorn Sun sign, born 27 December 1901

Capricorn at Work

As the third Earth sign, Capricorn represents the principals of hard work, perseverance, integrity and determination. Earth signs are tenacious, and have stable reserves of energy. The symbol of the Goat is often used to explain the particular brand of Capricorn tenacity, climbing ever higher, not stopping to take in the view until they reach the top of that mountain. The Goat's ambition to be at the top is not the megalomaniac ambition that can push Leo or Taurus; it's simply a desire for the serenity of the peak.

Capricorn women need to be accomplished and it is only the modern Capricorn who has the benefit of an education to suit her needs, and opportunities in the business world that previously remained closed to her. In the old days, a Capricorn woman would have been characterised by her ability to marry well and to manage the family affairs with grace and discretion.

And these accomplishments can come in many guises. Capricorn women will not necessarily only go into business. You will find them in all sorts of jobs, even very artistic professions (their innate sense of taste and balance is well-known).

Some of the best real-estate agents are Capricorns, as it combines several of their great talents – long hours and stamina, an eye for style, and a natural love of property, investment and capital gains. They are gifted at 'spin' rather than the hard-sell, and they can be very persuasive in their subtlety.

Capricorns also make great social workers. They are very logical and can turn an emotional fuddle into a whiteboard of pros and cons, distilled down into a handy little 'to do' list. Capricorns love to clean up a mess, and there is nothing more satisfying for them than to sort someone's life out for them and see the joy of someone so relieved and motivated to get out of their muddle.

The Power of Passive Resistance

"Darkness cannot drive out darkness; only light can do that. Hate cannot drive out hate; only love can do that."
Martin Luther King Jr (civil rights leader), Capricorn Sun sign, born 15 January 1929

Martin Luther King was a great proponent for change for the African-American people in the USA, but rather than rail against the system from the outside, as his compatriot Taurus Sun sign Malcolm X advocated, he preached passive resistance from within the status quo.

And it worked. King made inroads into the consciousness of Middle America by gathering people together to protest in peace, but in great numbers. His strategy was based upon Mahatma Gandhi's campaign for justice for the Indian people known as 'Satyagraha' or 'Soul Force'. Gandhi believed that, if given the choice, his oppressors would choose good over evil; it was just a matter of forcing them to choose.

Martin Luther King brought this proven theory to his people, the African-Americans, who in the 1950s and 60s still suffered under the law of segregation. As a religious minister, King used his position to inspire people to come together in the cause against racism. His group organised protests where African-Americans would go to a white café and sit down at the counter en masse. For a fleeting time, police force was applied, but this 'passive resistance' soon toppled segregation laws across the South.

It was by highlighting the ludicrous injustice of the laws of segregation that King began to turn the tide for African-Americans. Until that time, white moderates had agreed that racism should not be entrenched in law, but they had been apathetic in doing anything about it. Meanwhile, King had to explain to his children that they could not go to an amusement park because it was for white children only, and see another generation of bitterness be born.

King's skills as an orator are world-renowned and the scratchy recording of his speech entitled 'I have a dream', delivered to 250,000 protesters outside Washington in 1963, is still extraordinarily moving. Martin Luther King is a wonderful example of a man ambitious for his people, a man not restricted by the status quo as Capricorns are often portrayed as being, but rather being able to use his innate understanding of how the system worked for the greater good of society. King knew that the laws of segregation were unconstitutional and that they would never hold up in the Supreme Court. He was proven correct.

After some unsuccessful protests in the northern US, and with the intervention of FBI director J Edgar Hoover undermining King's leadership, racial violence escalated. King criticised US intervention in the Vietnam war, but with this stand, he lost the support of many white liberals. His relations with Lyndon Johnson's presidency were at a low point when he was assassinated on 4 April 1968. After his death, King remained a controversial symbol of the civil rights struggle, revered by many for his stand on non-violence and condemned by others for his militancy.

"I would remind you that extremism in the defence of liberty is no vice! And let me remind you also that moderation in the pursuit of justice is no virtue!"
Barry Goldwater (politician), Capricorn Sun sign, born 1 January 1909

Capricorn Health
Capricorns are a cold sign that need heat-producing foods like meat. The iron in meat is also very useful for them. They should guard and protect themselves in cold weather. They also need magnesium to calm their nerves and relax their muscles. Hot soups and spicy foods will benefit them, especially during winter months. They should drink fresh, green vegetable juices regularly to prevent toxic deposits and calcifications. Capricorn is also a dry sign, so they

should drink copious quantities of water. Rye, almonds, eggs, fish, coconuts, kale, leeks and onions are foods that benefit Capricorn.

Capricorn rules the knees, hair and skin, mucous, nerves and portions of the stomach.

Capricorns are reluctant to yield to disease and they tend towards longevity, but once sick they can become hypochondriacal. Worry can result in health problems if they do not relieve their stress through proper exercise or meditation. Routine massage and foot reflexology benefit them considerably.

Typical Capricorn afflictions include: colds, poor metabolism, obesity; constipation, weakened digestion; weak vision; knee problems, rheumatism; chest disorders; disorders of the skin with pustular formations and eruptions. Accidents for this sign are broken bones, sprains, dislocations and hurts from the knees and below.

When choosing music for meditation, the healing note for Capricorn is F sharp. Oils good for aromatherapy are cypress, honeysuckle, lilac, mimosa, myrrh, patchouli, tonka, tulip and vetiver.

The Capricorn Partner

"Gentleman: A man who buys two of the same morning paper from the doorman of his favourite nightclub when he leaves with his girl."
Marlene Dietrich (actress), Capricorn Sun sign, born 27 December 1901

Dress well, for goodness sake, and check that your nails are clean. Capricorn is not on the look-out for a great beauty, but he does look for taste and grooming. If you are arranging the restaurant, choose somewhere with an established reputation, and an even better wine list. Capricorn won't quibble about the prices but he knows good service, so you don't want to risk a new restaurant.

He will love talking about his work and family, but you may wonder after a while if he wants to know anything about you. Of course he does, he just doesn't want to be impertinent about how he asks. Sometimes Capricorn is so uptight about manners that he can seem quite rude. Gently introduce yourself into the conversation and you will see his interest pick up. Be sure to put in a few points about your breeding, for example that your grandfather fought in World War II. Leave out that your Dad dodged the draft by engaging in the longest-running arts degree ever recorded by the university, at least for now.

Take mental notes on the hobbies of his mother and sisters. Down the track you can please him no end by taking his mother out for shopping and coffee. He probably still lives with her, so you are going to get to know her pretty well anyway.

Gifts for your Capricorn

Practical, sturdy, lasts forever. Go all-out on the quality of a gift but don't buy brand names, unless you want to hear snorts of derision.

They like homewares and tools, but they also like to be treated as though they have interests other than the practical. It may seem strange, but Capricorn will not hesitate to buy herself whatever she needs, but she will never buy those things that she might whimsically wish for. Capricorn does not put a high enough price on her own happiness, so it is up to her friends and loved ones to litter her life with frivolity.

Capricorns love a gift that has taken a lot of time and patience to make. Their colour preferences are indigo, dark brown and black. But whatever you buy, the key word is quality.

Famous Capricorn Sun Signs

24 December 1503 – Michel de Nostradamus (astrologer)

24 December 1905 – Howard Hughes (recluse)

24 December 1905 – Ava Gardner (actress)

25 December 1870 – Helena Rubenstein (founder cosmetics empire)

25 December 1887 – Conrad Hilton (founder hotel empire)

25 December 1949 – Sissy Spacek (actress)

25 December 1954 – Annie Lennox (singer)

26 December 1891 – Henry Miller (writer)

26 December 1893 – Mao Tse Tung (political leader)

27 December 1822 – Louis Pasteur (scientist)

27 December 1901 – Marlene Dietrich (actress)

28 December 1954 – Denzel Washington (actor)

29 December 1938 – Jon Voight (actor)

30 December 1865 – Rudyard Kipling (writer)

30 December 1946 – Patti Smith (musician/poet)

30 December 1959 – Tracey Ullman (actress)

31 December 1869 – Henri Matisse (artist)

31 December 1886 – Elizabeth Arden (founder cosmetics empire)

31 December 1943 – John Denver (singer)

31 December 1959 – Val Kilmer (actor)

1 January 1895 – J Edgar Hoover (director FBI)

1 January 1909 – Barry Goldwater (politician)

1 January 1920 – JD Salinger (writer)

2 January 1873 – Therese de Lisieux (saint)

2 January 1920 – Isaac Asimov (writer)

3 January 106 BC – Cicero (orator/writer)

3 January 1892 – JRR Tolkien (writer)

3 January 1956 – Mel Gibson (actor)

4 January 1643 – Isaac Newton (scientist)

4 January 1960 – Michael Stipe (singer)

5 January 1918 – Jean Dixon (psychic)

5 January 1946 – Diane Keaton (actress)

5 January 1969 – Marilyn Manson (singer)

6 January 1412 – Joan of Arc (saint)

6 January 1572 – Johannes Kepler (astronomer)

6 January 1883 – Kahlil Gibran (writer)

7 January 1844 – Bernadette of Lourdes (saint)

7 January 1912 – Charles Addams (cartoonist)

8 January 1935 – Elvis Presley (singer/actor)

8 January 1937 – Shirley Bassey (singer)

8 January 1942 – Stephen Hawking (physicist)

8 January 1947 – David Bowie (musician)

9 January 1908 – Simone de Beauvoir (writer)

9 January 1913 – Richard Nixon (US president)

9 January 1914 – Gypsy Rose Lee (entertainer)

9 January 1941 – Joan Baez (singer)

10 January 1945 – Rod Stewart (singer)

10 January 1953 – Pat Benetar (singer)

11 January 1971 – Mary J Blige (rap artist)

12 January 1729 – Edmund Burke (political theorist)

12 January 1951 – Kirstie Alley (actress)

12 January 1954 – Howard Stern (radio host)

13 January 1961 – Julia Louis-Dreyfus (actress)

14 January 1941 – Faye Dunaway (actress)

15 January 1906 – Aristotle Onassis (industrialist)

15 January 1929 – Martin Luther King Jr (civil rights leader)

16 January 1974 – Kate Moss (supermodel)

17 January 1927 – Tom Dooley (humanitarian)

17 January 1942 – Muhammad Ali (boxer)

17 January 1944 – Joe Frazier (boxer)

17 January 1949 – Andy Kaufman (comedian)

18 January 1882 – AA Milne (writer)

18 January 1904 – Cary Grant (actor)

18 January 1955 – Kevin Costner (actor)

19 January 1809 – Edgar Allen Poe (writer)

19 January 1839 – Paul Cezanne (artist)

19 January 1943 – Janis Joplin (singer)

19 January 1946 – Dolly Parton (singer)

20 January 1920 – Federico Fellini (film director)

20 January 1946 – David Lynch (film director)

The Tenth House

Capricorn is closely associated with the Tenth House, and the principles of the Tenth House are in keeping with the characteristics of Capricorn. The Tenth House indicates one's career tendencies, public image, and people who may have power or authority over you in day-to-day life, including the parent with greater authority. For more information on the Tenth House see the chapter, The Houses, in the Interpretation section.

Saturn

Capricorn is ruled by the planet Saturn, and principles of Saturn are in keeping with the characteristics of Capricorn. For details on Saturn and how to read it in a chart see the chapter, The Planets, in the Interpretation section.

Aquarius
(21 January to 18 February)

"Some people go to priests; others to poetry; I to my friends."
Virginia Woolf, Aquarius Sun sign, born 25 January 1882

Basic characteristics of the sign

Personal creed – *I know*

Positive/masculine sign

Element – Air

Energy – Fixed

Psychological type – Thinking

Glyph – ♒ represents watery waves, although has also been
linked to the serpent

Colour – Aqua

Body part – The calves and ankles

Metal – Uranium

Gemstones – Turquoise, aquamarine

Flower – Orchid

Trees – Fruit trees

Food – Fruits

People with an Aquarius Sun sign are generally:

✧ Playful

✧ Friendly

✧ Spontaneous

✧ Open-minded

✧ Caring

✧ Devoted

✧ Liberal

✧ Understanding

✧ Tolerant

✧ Benevolent

On the other hand, they can also be:

✧ Undependable

✧ Cold

✧ Aloof

✧ Mean

✧ Self-centred

✧ Unable to commit

✧ Judgmental

✧ Fickle

✧ Intractable

✧ Contrary

✧ Unpredictable

Aquarians love:

✧ Good conversation

✧ A boss who is more like a good mate

✧ Thinking outside the norm

✧ Fringe culture

✧ Independence

✧ Witty banter

✧ Committing to a cause

✧ Their friends, sometimes more than their family

But they can't stand:

✧ Soppiness

✧ Bores

✧ Predictability

✧ Chainstore clothing

✧ Conventional celebrations

✧ Tackiness

✧ Commitment

✧ Circular arguing

✧ Bosses being pernickety or authoritarian

✧ Television

✧ Suburbia

✧ People who try to be stereotypes

✧ Their privacy being invaded

✧ Popular culture in general

The Aquarian Character

Aquarians are radicals, they like to think outside the square. They are not anarchists; rather they like to take the shape of what is there and improve it in an original way. Any Aquarian will tell you that 'Who's Who' is littered with Aquarians, and it is true that they do seem to have more than their fair share of high achievers, especially in the sciences, filmmaking and writing. They also have more than their fair share of strong women and famous feminists, including Gertrude Stein, Alice Walker, Colette, Virginia Woolf, Betty Friedan, Susan B Anthony and Germaine Greer.

Aquarians are known for their open-minded approach to life and people. They make it their business to be accepting of all people and cultures. They are generally attracted to a more liberal, humanitarian brand of politics, and if they are interested in politics, they will throw themselves into it.

Their fixed quality helps them follow through ideas to their natural conclusion (as opposed to fellow air signs Gemini and Libra, who relish ideas but are flippant about their usefulness), but it can also make them quite aggressive in attacking their opponents. If they are not careful, they may find that their continuous support of a cause they hold dear may cause the narrowing of that broad-minded approach they prize so much. In its worst manifestation, this can develop into a hatred for their enemies that is capable of turning them into sceptics and pessimists.

"Vices are sometimes only virtues carried to excess!"
Charles Dickens (writer), Aquarius Sun sign, born 7 February 1812

Aquarians can't stand commitment and they will do anything to get out of confirming a time or place. If you invite your Aquarian friend out to dinner on Friday night, no matter how far in advance you ask, don't expect an answer until Friday morning. And even if they volunteer a time, it will bear no relation to the time they actually arrive.

Like Virgo, Aquarians can be a bit squeamish about bodies, and would prefer to live in the monastic cleanliness of their minds. This makes sharing personal space with others a little confronting for Aquarians. My Nana was an Aquarius Sun sign, and she married my grandfather because he was the first man she met who didn't 'maul' her. It wasn't so long ago that Aquarius was ruled by Saturn, and there are still facets of the Aquarian nature that like to do things in a well-mannered way.

"I only go out to get me a fresh appetite for being alone."
Lord Byron (poet), Aquarius Sun sign, born 22 January 1788

They love the idea of people, but as long as it is only in the abstract. They may love the idea of living in a commune, but the reality of all that shared space (especially the private spaces like the bathroom) can be too much.

They are also not the sort of person to take to a sentimental movie. Theirs will be the only dry eyes by the end. They are also skilled at giving such a devastating critique of a film, that even if you came out exalted by it, by the time you have sat through a post-film coffee with your Aquarian, you will be telling the people at work the next day, 'Oh yeah, it was OK . . .'

Aquarius at Work

You will find Aquarius doing whatever they can to differentiate themselves from the crowd, and if that means swallowing light bulbs for a living, then so be it. Actors, dancers, artists, transvestites, fashion designers, writers – anywhere out there on the fringes is where you'll find Aquarius.

Aquarians have a great eye for unique things so they can thrive at picking the next trends in clothing or furniture. Interior design and buying for retail stores are good careers for Aquarius, and vintage clothes and furniture stores often employ an Aquarian to scour the country op-shops for them.

Aquarians fall in love with things just because they are different – it can't be proven, but it's almost certain an Aquarian was behind the invention of twirling optic-fibre lamps, leg-warmers, fondue sets and snow-domes. Little wonder that it was the 1970s that embraced the Age of Aquarius.

Going Against the Grain

Germaine Greer probably best exemplifies the Aquarian brain at work. Her book *The Female Eunuch* (1971) revolutionised the way women thought about themselves and their roles, and it mobilised a whole generation of women to start making changes in their lives. Greer brought feminism to the common woman, and she did it in a radically different manner to those feminists who had come before her.

Firstly, she was a very attractive woman, with all the hallmarks of her Aquarian ascendant – open, attractive features, tall, slender legs and ankles, aquiline nose (*Life Magazine* dubbed her a 'saucy feminist that even men like'); and secondly her message was more about sexual liberation than the hardcore equal work/equal pay rhetoric that had previously dominated feminism.

Greer told women to start enjoying their bodies and their lives and not to consider themselves merely breeding machines.

"There are persons who, when they cease to shock us, cease to interest us."
FH Bradley (philosopher), Aquarius Sun sign, born 30 January 1846

She was notoriously promiscuous in her youth, but by the age of fifty had declared herself celibate. Her radical approach to writing has not changed over the years and her philosophy has evolved against the tides. Her most recent book shocked women for her stance on clitoral circumcision (for) and pap smears (against). She is a formidable opponent in a debate, and she still rises to the challenge of making the most eloquent man look inarticulate.

"Let's not quibble! I'm the foe of moderation, the champion of excess. If I may lift a line from a die-hard whose identity is lost in the shuffle, 'I'd rather be strongly wrong than weakly right.'"
Tallulah Bankhead (actress), Aquarius Sun sign, born 31 January 1903

In spite of her ability to shock, Greer is still thought of affectionately by many, even by those whom she deliberately went out to destroy. Aquarians can't help but be dangerously attractive, especially when they are doing what comes naturally to them – rubbing against the tide of conservatism and apathy and raising a few hackles and more than a few eyebrows along the way.

Aquarius Health
Foods that stimulate blood circulation, like chilli, as well as brain foods such as wheat grass, oats and barley, are good for the Aquarian. Red-coloured foods like beets, radishes, peppers, saffron and strawberries are of benefit. They should keep an eye on their iron and magnesium levels.

Yoga and tai chi or anything that slows the breath and means greater intake of air is good for the Aquarian brain, which will get gloomy without enough oxygen. Aquarians should avoid spring and carbonated waters for the same reason, as they need to retain the oxygen in the water, not burp it out with carbon dioxide. A change of scenery is required for relaxation.

Aquarius rules the calves and ankles, breath and eyesight. It is closely associated with the blood and circulation, with a tendency towards impure blood. The pathological action of Aquarius is towards nervousness, gloom and sensitiveness leading to habits and fixed ideas that make disease persist and linger. They are prone to varicose veins, hypertension and heart problems.

Typical Aquarian afflictions are: weak/impure blood, poor oxygenation, arteriosclerosis, heart disease, varicose veins; rheumatism, spasmodic disorders, spinal disorders; swelling of the feet/ankles; backache; hypersensitivity; lymphatic stasis; weak vision; conjunctivitis; and genital infections.

When seeking music for meditation, the Aquarian healing musical note is G. Oils for use in aromatherapy include costmary, hops, lavender, lemon verbena, parsley, patchouli, pine, star anise and sweet pea.

The Aquarius Partner

Approach from the side, never head on, as there is nothing that will scare an Aquarian off more than a full-frontal romance attack. They can't stand romantic nonsense like roses and candlelight, which they see as so predictable, tacky and unimaginative.

At this point, rose wilting pathetically, you may just want to put down your heart-shaped box of chocolates and run. No one would blame you. Not even Aquarius would blame you, and they will probably be quite remorseful next time they see you, once they've had a chance to calm down.

It is not that Aquarius really thinks you have no imagination (although she does love things to be a little bit unusual), she just got a bit of a shock. You were thinking of a nice night out, all she saw was a marriage proposal and a mortgage and a dozen snotty-nosed kids. The bars clanged down around her. She felt short of breath, claustrophobic, so she shot out the worst insult in her repertoire – that you are ordinary.

Now, what you have to do is very simple. Be her friend. But not just any old friend, make sure you are the wittiest and most intelligent friend on the planet, with a hint of mystery about you. Engage, intrigue, woo her all at the same time. Walk away. Let some time pass, hold out for several weeks if you can. 'Bump' into her; make an impression, make lots of eye contact, and then make an excuse. Get out of there. Then the next day, send her a little gift, something really unusual, with no subtext of romance.

You have to have her thinking that she is the one doing the wooing, and that you are the one playing hard to get. This goes double-plus if the Aquarian is male. Whatever you do, attack from left of field – they can fall in love, and they make wonderful, stable, faithful partners who are never short on conversation once in love; you just have to convince them it is their idea.

Aquarians are also not adverse to email. This is another way of casually engaging their attention and showing off your witty repartee.

Gifts for your Aquarius
"A new gadget that lasts only five minutes is worth more than an immortal work that bores everyone."
W Somerset Maugham (writer), Aquarius Sun sign, born 25 January 1874

Aquarians generally like unusual or quirky gifts. But quirky should not be read as 'whacky'. Aquarians hate anything that is crude or rude.

For something unusual, head to any antiques shop or second-hand bookshop and it will be full of stuff for your Aquarian. Ancient Tibetan mountain bells, a shoe snob, a collection of *Boy's Annuals* from the 1950s, a barber's clock that tells the time in mirror image – you get the idea. If it makes you stop and muse, 'isn't that unusual?', you are probably on the right track.

The Aquarian's colour is aqua. They may not wear it, but they seem to have it around, even more so than other signs and their colours, often in their bedroom colour schemes.

Some Aquarians like techno gadgets, the newer the better. A wrist-watch mobile telephone will cause a squeal of delight. Others are on a more humanitarian and environmental bent and will like anything you buy from Greenpeace, Oxfam or Community Aid Abroad. Don't forget your Aquarian when travelling. That is the perfect time to stock up on one-of-a-kinds.

Famous Aquarius Sun Signs

21 January 1905 – Christian Dior (fashion designer)

21 January 1940 – Jack Nicklaus (golfer)

21 January 1941 – Placido Domingo (opera singer)

21 January 1957 – Geena Davis (actress)

22 January 1788 – Lord Byron (poet)

AQUARIUS

22 January 1959 – Linda Blair (actress)

23 January 1832 – Edouard Manet (artist)

23 January 1899 – Humphrey Bogart (actor)

24 January 1941 – Neil Diamond (singer)

24 January 1949 – John Belushi (actor)

25 January 1759 – Robert Burns (poet)

25 January 1874 – W Somerset Maugham (writer)

25 January 1882 – Virginia Woolf (writer)

25 January 1924 – Corazon Aquino (political leader)

26 January 1925 – Paul Newman (actor)

26 January 1928 – Eartha Kitt (singer)

27 January 1766 – Wolfgang Amadeus Mozart (composer)

27 January 1832 – Lewis Carroll (writer)

28 January 1873 – Colette (writer)

28 January 1933 – Susan Sontag (writer)

28 January 1936 – Alan Alda (actor)

29 January 1860 – Anton Chekov (writer)

29 January 1939 – Germaine Greer (feminist/writer)

29 January 1945 – Tom Selleck (actor)

29 January 1954 – Oprah Winfrey (TV host)

30 January 1846 – FH Bradley (philosopher)

30 January 1882 – Franklin D Roosevelt (US president)

30 January 1937 – Vanessa Redgrave (actress)

31 January 1797 – Franz Schubert (composer)

31 January 1882 – Anna Pavlova (dancer)

31 January 1903 – Tallulah Bankhead (actress)

31 January 1919 – Jackie Robinson (baseballer)

31 January 1923 – Norman Mailer (writer)

1 February 1561 – Francis Bacon (writer)

1 February 1901 – Clark Gable (actor)

2 February 1882 – James Joyce (writer)

2 February 1902 – Charles Lindbergh (pilot)

2 February 1947 – Farrah Fawcett (actress)

3 February 1874 – Gertrude Stein (writer)

4 February 1921 – Betty Friedan (feminist)

4 February 1948 – Alice Cooper (musician)

AQUARIUS

4 February 1975 – Natalie Imbruglia (singer)

6 February 1895 – Babe Ruth (baseballer)

6 February 1911 – Ronald Reagan (US president)

6 February 1915 – Zsa Zsa Gabor (celebrity)

6 February 1931 – Rip Torn (actor)

7 February 1812 – Charles Dickens (writer)

7 February 1870 – Alfred Adler (psychiatrist)

7 February 1962 – Garth Brooks (singer)

8 February 1921 – Lana Turner (actress)

8 February 1925 – Jack Lemmon (actor)

8 February 1928 – Jules Verne (writer)

8 February 1931 – James Dean (actor)

9 February 1942 – Carole King (singer)

9 February 1943 – Joe Pesci (actor)

9 February 1945 – Mia Farrow (actress)

10 February 1494 – Rabelais (writer)

10 February 1890 – Boris Pasternak (writer)

10 February 1950 – Mark Spitz (swimmer)

11 February 1936 – Burt Reynolds (actor)

12 February 1809 – Abraham Lincoln (US president)

12 February 1908 – Charles Darwin (naturalist)

12 February 1968 – Chynna Phillips (singer)

13 February 1944 – Stockard Channing (actor)

14 February 1882 – John Barrymore (actor)

14 February 1894 – Jack Benny (comedian)

14 February 1944 – Carl Bernstein (journalist)

15 February 1951 – Jane Seymour (actress)

16 February 1935 – Sonny Bono (singer)

17 February 1963 – Michael Jordan (basketballer)

18 February 1933 – Yoko Ono (artist)

18 February 1954 – John Travolta (actor)

The Eleventh House

Aquarius is closely associated with the Eleventh House, and the principles of the Eleventh House are in keeping with the characteristics of Aquarius. The Eleventh House is the house of friends, hopes and wishes. It also shows how you deal with groups of people such as friends and workmates. For more information on the Eleventh House see the chapter, The Houses, in the Interpretation section.

Saturn and Uranus

Aquarius is ruled by Saturn and Uranus, and the principles of both planets are in keeping with the characteristics of Aquarius. For details on Saturn and Uranus and how to read them in a chart see the chapter, The Planets, in the Interpretation section.

Pisces
(19 February to 20 March)

"You can't teach the old Maestro a new tune."
Jack Kerouac (writer), Pisces Sun sign, born 12 March 1922

Basic characteristics of the sign

Personal creed – *I believe*

Negative/feminine sign

Element – Water

Energy – Mutable

Psychological type – Feeling

Glyph – ✵ represents two fish linked; refers also to the physical and spiritual sides of a person

Colour – Sea green

Body part – Feet

Gemstone – Moonstone

Flower – Waterlily

Tree – Willow

Food – Salad vegetables

People with a Pisces Sun sign are generally:

✦ Mystical

✦ Enchanting

✦ Emotional

✦ Loving

✦ Devoted

✦ Reverent

✦ Creative

✦ Easy-going

✦ Sensitive

✦ Instinctive

✦ Affectionate

✦ Submissive

✦ Unselfish

✦ Altruistic

On the other hand, they can also be:

✦ Escapist

✦ Idealistic

✦ Secretive

✧ Vague

✧ Weak-willed

✧ Easily led

✧ Always fishing for compliments

✧ Needy

✧ Lazy

✧ Manipulative

✧ Confused

✧ Depressed

✧ Irresponsible

✧ Inarticulate

✧ Duplicitous

✧ Goal-less

✧ Indecisive

Pisces love:

✧ Romance

✧ Feeling appreciated and needed

✧ Stability

✧ Mystical settings/enchantment

✧ Being encouraged to dream

✧ Sharing thoughts/dreams

✧ Having their input valued

✧ A role model

But they can't stand:
✧ Feeling vulnerable

✧ Feeling alone or unloved

✧ Being ignored

✧ Crude behaviour

✧ Noisy scenes

✧ Having no dreams

✧ Having no sense of structure

The Pisces Character
We have now come through the entire zodiac. We could say that: Libras will tell you the truth that you want to hear; Scorpios will tell you the truth because that is what you need to hear; Sagittarians will tell you the truth inadvertently; Capricorn is the master of tact and discretion; Aquarians know the truth, so why wouldn't you want to hear it? And then we come to Pisces, who are so tired of looking for the truth they suspect it doesn't exist. And so we return to Aries, where we rejuvenate our energy and look at things afresh. The cycle begins anew.

Understanding the Piscean character is as frustrating as trying to catch silverfish in your hands. Wishy-washy has been used more than once to describe their attitude to life, and in many respects, the description fits, but it doesn't quite work because it doesn't describe their motivation (or apparent lack of it).

The idea that Pisces is the final sign before we are reincarnated into an Aries again has often been used to describe the faraway look in Pisces' eyes and their tired disposition. They have simply had it with this physical reality, they are dying for a cup of tea and a lie down in the spirit world – or maybe a shot of adrenalin in Aries.

Pisceans are always quite pleased with this idea, as it boosts their flagging ego. However, their motivational problems could also be due to their ruling planets, Jupiter (the planet of religion and philosophy) and Neptune (the planet of mysticism and the fantasy world). With that combination you would hardly be spending any real quality time down on Earth if you could help it.

"In the sphere of thought, absurdity and perversity remain the masters of the world, and their dominion is suspended only for brief periods."
Arthur Schopenhauer (philosopher), Pisces Sun sign, born 22 February 1788

Pisces can be very indecisive and lack motivation if they need to do or get anything for themselves. They have been known to put up with terrible eyesight for an enormous period of time before they will get around to buying a pair of glasses.

This can appear as martyrdom, especially when they sometimes use excuses such as, 'There's no money left for that sort of thing' or 'I just don't have enough energy at the end of the day to get those sorts of things done' (there is more than a hint of truth in that). The truth is, Pisces would rather save their energy and resources to do things for other people.

If they are doing something for someone else, they find surprising reserves of strength. They will go to any lengths to give someone a hand, even taking food out of their own children's mouths to give to someone else's child. There is no sacrifice too large for them to make.

This is not so good if you are the child whose mother has just let you go hungry. Pisces find it difficult to distinguish between, friends, family and foes, and see everyone as worthy of their help. They see only a person in need, and their sensitive hearts have to fix the wrong so they can feel right in the world.

Pisces can allow themselves continually to be taken advantage of. They know it is happening, but believe the reward for being open-hearted and trusting is worth it. They can appear to be gullible, but this is not correct, as Pisces are never naïve (though they may like to pretend to be so as a defence). Pisces are rarely surprised by the depths to which humanity can sink, and can see most things coming from a mile off. But they just heave a big sigh and get on with it.

They have a great capacity to feel, and sometimes that can be quite overwhelming. Fellow water signs Cancer and Scorpio can protect their sensitivity with a hardened shell, even though they may be crying underneath. Pisces has no such defence. This is why some Pisces find relief from the world in drugs or escapist cults. Pisces find it a huge relief to have faith in something; they can be easy prey to the chap in the yellow dress proclaiming to be Jesus' former press secretary.

"If you were to ask me if I'd ever had the bad luck to miss my daily cocktail, I'd have to say that I doubt it; where certain things are concerned, I plan ahead."
Luis Buñuel (film director), Pisces Sun sign, born 22 February 1900

Pisces can have a strange relationship with possessions. They usually need many things around them, and can hoard like crazy, though they suffer a great deal of guilt collecting such symbols of materialism. Shopping soothes them, but they find it difficult to justify buying a few things for themselves. Like the dieter who denies herself, this can come out in a few ways.

Pisces could give in to temptation altogether and be quite a spendthrift, buying the best of everything but feeling incredibly guilty as well. Or they could buy a lot of things of lower quality but assure themselves that they were bargains. These people are thrifty in some ways (their shopping is full of generic brands), but not really efficient. These Pisces are indiscriminate op-shoppers who pick up all the things picked over in the bargain bucket.

But most Pisces quench their thirst by buying things for other people – every time you meet them they have a care package full of lovely things for you. They often start a conversation with 'I was in the shops the other day and I saw something that I thought you might need.' That way, they can buy quality but without the guilt attached.

Pisces at Work
"A daydream is a meal at which images are eaten. Some of us are gourmets, some gourmands, and a good many take their images precooked out of a can and swallow them down whole, absent-mindedly and with little relish."
WH Auden (poet), Pisces Sun sign, born 21 February 1907

Pisces are wonderfully imaginative and very visual. They dream with such clarity that they find it easy to translate their thoughts into visual metaphors, so they excel in film-making and painting.

But daydreaming has its problems. Never put a Pisces at a desk near a window, as their capacity for daydreaming knows no limits. They are also terrible procrastinators. But only if they are stuck in the wrong job – which fortunately for their little fishy soul, they usually don't stick at for long.

"We should take care not to make the intellect our god; it has, of course, powerful muscles, but no personality."
Albert Einstein (physicist), Pisces Sun sign, born 14 March 1879

Animation and website design are particularly Piscean careers. They are essentially lone pursuits with an enormous scope for creativity and fantasy. Pisces can usually visualise anything, and if their intellect is strong they can imagine themselves in the most complex problem. Einstein was said to imagine himself as part of an atom in order to think about a problem. He also considered his sleep very important and would sleep for ten or eleven hours each night before a big thinking day.

Musicians and artists and anyone who deals with bringing the realms of the subconscious to the surface normally have a lot of Pisces influence in their chart. Pisceans also make great actors. Though this seems incongruous with their sometimes painful shyness, the Piscean personality is fluid and changeable. They love to wear masks.

Pisces have an enormous capacity to care and empathise, so they make wonderful nurses, doctors, teachers and child-care workers. Counselling and social work are filled with Pisces, but they can have trouble keeping a professional distance from those they care for.

Movie Queen

"How boring moviemaking is . . . you work for one minute and then sit around for three hours."
Elizabeth Taylor (actress), Pisces Sun sign, born 27 February 1932

Eight-times married Elizabeth Taylor is known for her beautiful violet eyes, her glorious cleavage and her penchant for bourbon and failed love affairs. The film *Butterfield 8* won her an Oscar, but it was really *Who's Afraid of Virginia Woolf?* and the epic flop *Cleopatra* that catapulted her to the height of her career, and also to the height of her romance with Richard Burton. They had a tempestuous relationship, characterised by steamy exits and massive diamonds. One rock Burton bought her was 69 carats. 'A diamond,' she once said, 'is the only kind of ice that keeps a girl warm.'

In the early 1960s, Taylor was photographic royalty, the equivalent of her fellow water sign, Cancer Princess Diana in the 1980s and 90s. Her face sold newspaper and magazines like no other. Mattel made a Liz Taylor doll, complete with a little 69-carat diamond.

Oscar-winning screenwriter William Goldman once said about her: 'Elizabeth Taylor was famous, at least in legend, for never reading an entire script, just her own lines. No one's had a more fabulous career, maybe she knew something the rest of us didn't.'

Taylor's post-1960s films commanded attention but not a lot of respect, and she made a lot of television as her film roles dwindles. Later she released two perfumes, Passion and White Diamonds, which have probably made her more money than all her movies put together.

It was Taylor's love life that kept the public fascinated. She wore the studio's wedding gown when she married her first husband, bad-boy Nicky Hilton. On their *Queen Mary* honeymoon he abandoned her for drinking and gambling, and they separated after a few months.

Her next marriage was to English actor Michael Wilding, 19 years older; they had two sons, then a divorce in 1956. One day after the divorce, she married producer Mike Todd, with whom she had a daughter. Todd was killed when his plane, *The Lucky Liz*, crashed in New Mexico.

Six months later Taylor took up with Eddie Fisher, the best man at her wedding with Todd, in the scandal of the 1950s. The marriage ruined Fisher's career. They married on the same day as his divorce from his previous wife came through. And on their honeymoon, she received a telegram inviting her to star in *Cleopatra* with Welsh actor and tormented boozer, Richard Burton.

Burton said of their first meeting: 'She was the most sullen, uncommunicative and beautiful woman I had ever seen.' Even though Fisher was also working on the film, the Taylor-Burton affair gained momentum, so much so that the Vatican published a statement denouncing her 'erotic vagrancy'.

Taylor described this period as 'probably the most chaotic time of my life . . . it was fun and it was dark – oceans of tears, but there were some good times, too.' They married in 1964, but the signs were already ominous. When they travelled they rented the rooms above and below their own, so nobody could hear their fights. Drinking, brawling and affairs led to several separations and a divorce in 1974.

In 1975 Burton won her back, and they married in Botswana that year. Liz proclaimed: 'We are stuck together like chicken feathers to tar for love always.' They divorced four months later. Two other marriages followed.

Of her many relationships and husbands, Taylor said, 'What do you expect me to do? Sleep alone?'

Pisces Health

Milk and dairy products rarely agree with the Pisces con-stitution, and people with this sign who suffer from a lot of phlegm and tiredness due to overworked kidneys should consider a diet without dairy products. Lemon, lime, cranberry and apple juices can counter some of these problems as well. Fish is the best source of protein for Pisces. Their best grains are brown rice, bulgur wheat and quinoa; cabbage, celery and green juices are also good. Potato and sweet potato are good starch foods. Pisces should eat fresh salads daily to keep the bowels in order.

This is one of the addictive signs, so Pisceans should avoid intoxicants.

Pisces rules the feet and toes and the lymphatic system, and the functions of the glands in general.

Typical Pisces afflictions are: impure blood from overindul-gence, stagnant bowels and associated complications, obesity and cancer; alcoholism; lymphatic stasis, swollen ankles/feet, sores, ulcers; insomnia; tendency to catch pneumonia; corns, bunions. Pisces are neglectful of their own health in general.

When choosing music for meditation, the healing note for Pisces is B. Meditation oils include apple, camphor, cardamom, gardenia, hyacinth, jasmine, lily, mugwort, myrrh, palmarosa, sandalwood, vanilla and ylang-ylang.

The Pisces Partner

Pisces women are old-fashioned ladies at heart, and don't let them tell you any different. The odd one will attempt to put up the modern woman front, but she will turn to mush if you run around and open the car door for her. Treat her like she is the most precious and delicate flower you ever came across, and she will melt right there in front of you.

Keep the first date fairly formal. She loves to dress up and will be disappointed if she can't really wow you with her make-up and her clothes. The less relaxed the better, as Pisces will prefer the opportunity to wear her masks.

She will probably be nervous so you might have to take the reins of the conversation for the first half-hour or so (this is not always true, some Pisces women come into their own in romance and will be quite aggressive in their flirting – but the man must always initiate it). A night at the theatre or the ballet and she will be in her element. A nice idea for a daytime date is 'high tea' at a posh hotel. It's all marvellously civilised and a lot of fun. She'll love it.

Once things get a little more intimate, make any excuse to give her a foot massage. Pisceans completely bliss out as soon as you touch their feet.

With the Pisces male, let him play the macho man. He's not, of course (underneath he's as hard as marshmallow), but he loves to play the chivalrous male, at least until he can really relax with you. Let him open doors and buy you dinner and generally think he is the tough one. He needs to wear the mask society has taught him to wear as a little boy – because boys don't cry. But before long, he will be writing you poetry, and getting clucky over pictures of baby animals, and bawling his eyes out with you when you're sad.

Gifts for your Pisces

Because Pisces sometimes have to be forced into doing things for themselves, and are also notorious for ignoring their health, consider a voucher for a relaxation massage or a paid-up course in tai chi.

If your Pisces is the self-destructive type, stay away from presents of alcohol, but a great fantasy novel or a fantasy computer game will thrill them. Don't expect to see them for the next couple of days, though.

Pisces are soppy old sentimentalists for the most part, so frame a wedding photo of their grandparents or their parents or arrange a slide night for them – really rummage around in the box for some unusual old slides. Set the atmosphere with some well-chosen music. They will be misty-eyed and reaching for the tissues by the end of it.

If you have been away for some time and have received letters from them (Pisceans are fantastic letter writers, but terrible emailers), make them dinner and read through the letters over a bottle of red wine. This is a blue-ribbon winner with the nostalgic Pisces.

They like trinkets and old-fashioned things. Piscean women retain their girly quality throughout their lives. A music box or a china doll or teddy bear with the scent of eras past always goes down well.

Anything to encourage the considerable creative talents of Pisces is great, but getting them to sit down to do it in between all their commitments to other people is another thing. This is another example when booking them into a course like painting is for their own good, and they will have to go and enjoy it because they are doing it for you! They particularly like gifts associated with water.

Famous Pisces Sun Signs

19 February 1955 – Margaux Hemingway (actress)

19 February 1960 – Prince Andrew (British royalty)

19 February 1966 – Justine Bateman (actress)

20 February 1927 – Sidney Poitier (actor)

20 February 1949 – Ivana Trump (celebrity)

21 February 1903 – Anais Nin (writer)

21 February 1907 – WH Auden (poet)

22 February 1788 – Arthur Schopenhauer (philosopher)

22 February 1900 – Luis Buñuel (film director)

23 February 1908 – William McMahon (Australian prime minister)

23 February 1940 – Peter Fonda (actor)

24 February 1943 – George Harrison (musician)

25 February 1841 – Pierre Renoir (artist)

26 February 1916 – Jackie Gleason (comedian)

26 February 1928 – Fats Domino (singer)

26 February 1932 – Johnny Cash (singer)

27 February 1861 – Rudolph Steiner (philosopher/educator)

27 February 1930 – Joanne Woodward (actress)

27 February 1932 – Elizabeth Taylor (actress)

28 February 1473 – Nicolaus Copernicus (astronomer)

28 February 1890 – Vaslaw Nijinsky (dancer)

28 February 1940 – Mario Andretti (racing driver)

1 March 1927 – Harry Belafonte (singer)

1 March 1945 – Roger Daltrey (musician)

1 March 1954 – Ron Howard (film director)

2 March 1904 – Dr Seuss (children's writer)

2 March 1931 – Mikail Gorbachev (political leader)

2 March 1931 – Tom Wolfe (writer)

PISCES

2 March 1962 – Jon Bon Jovi (musician)

3 March 1911 – Jean Harlow (actress)

5 March 1908 – Rex Harrison (actor)

6 March 1806 – Elizabeth Barrett Browning (poet)

6 March 1926 – Alan Greenspan (economist)

6 March 1945 – Rob Reiner (film director)

7 March 1872 – Piet Mondrian (artist)

7 March 1875 – Maurice Ravel (composer)

8 March 1922 – Cyd Charisse (dancer)

8 March 1943 – Lynn Redgrave (actress)

9 March 1934 – Yuri Gargarin (astronaut)

9 March 1936 – Glenda Jackson (actress)

9 March 1943 – Bobby Fischer (chess champion)

10 March 1845 – Alexander III (Russian royalty)

10 March 1887 – Joseph Pulitzer (industrialist)

10 March 1964 – Prince Edward (British royalty)

11 March 1931 – Rupert Murdoch (publisher)

12 March 1922 – Jack Kerouac (writer)

12 March 1936 – Liza Minnelli (entertainer)

12 March 1948 – James Taylor (singer)

14 March 1879 – Albert Einstein (physicist)

14 March 1933 – Michael Caine (actor)

14 March 1947 – Billy Crystal (comedian)

15 March 1475 – Michelangelo (artist)

15 March 1935 – Jimmy Swaggart (religious figure)

16 March 1936 – Jerry Lewis (comedian)

17 March 1919 – Nat King Cole (musician)

17 March 1938 – Rudolf Nureyev (dancer)

17 March 1951 – Kurt Russell (actor)

17 March 1964 – Rob Lowe (actor)

18 March 1962 – Vanessa Williams (singer)

19 March 1947 – Glenn Close (actress)

19 March 1955 – Bruce Willis (actor)

20 March 1950 – William Hurt (actor)

20 March 1957 – Spike Lee (film director)

20 March 1958 – Holly Hunter (actor)

The Twelfth House

Pisces is closely associated with the Twelfth House, and the principles of the Twelfth House are in keeping with the characteristics of Pisces. The Twelfth House is the house of self-undoing, of the subconscious. For more information on the Twelfth House see the chapter, The Houses, in the Interpretation section.

Neptune and Jupiter

Pisces is ruled by Neptune and Jupiter, and the principles of both planets are in keeping with the characteristics of Pisces. For details on Neptune and Jupiter and how to read them in a chart see the chapter, The Planets, in the Interpretation section.

The Signs in Love

The following is a summary of compatibility between all the possible combinations of Sun signs. It has been included for fun as much as anything – a full comparison of star charts would be needed to really see the compatibility or otherwise of two people.

Aries/Aries

Temper tantrums are quite likely to erupt into major wars with this combination. Only one party can win and you know how little you like defeat – it is exactly the same for him. At heart, this relationship is hot and fiery. You should enjoy burning off some energy with some physical activities. Try to keep your battles out of your kitchen and on the tennis court. Passionate with problems.

Aries/Taurus

The Bull may have a little trouble with your free-spirited attitude but with some compromise it can work. This match can be a little bit dull for Aries at times, but stability may be what you need and your Bull could probably do with some revving up. Essentially, Aries needs to be first and best to be happy. Taurus needs to be assured that everything's safe and secure. If you can both assure each other of these things, you should be good for each other.

Aries/Gemini

A wonderful alliance. This is an exciting, sexual encounter that (dare I say it) can last! Both you and Gemini are so spontaneous and full of life there is no time for either of you to become bored. Intellectually, it will be a stimulating time as well.

Aries/Cancer

The Crab is far too sensitive and slow for your speedy and tempestuous nature. And you will have difficulty putting up with the Crab's nagging and negativity. Cancer has the energy to keep up with you, but will be directing it at different things. Tolerance through gritted teeth is the key phrase for both of you.

Aries/Leo

Exhilaration-plus. You both share the same likes and dislikes and you both lead a charmed life, always on the go searching out excitement, love and fun. The rest of the world will have to catch its breath as you pass by in a heady flash. However, you both love to be centre stage (Leo more than Aries), so are going to have to work out how you can both shine. Also, Aries is quite indifferent to other people's opinions whereas Leo sets a lot of store by what other people think. Leo should be careful not to upset Aries with the failings Leo perceives, and not to see Aries simply as a reflection of herself.

Aries/Virgo

Your impulsiveness is just too much for the Virgoan, and Virgo's practical, critical nature will drive you to drink. Barely patient sighs will abound. Avoid if possible.

Aries/Libra

Although opposites attract, an Aries can't tell his claret from his beaujolais, and may lack the sophistication required to keep a Libran happy, just as the Scales are a little too lazy to keep up with the amped-up Arian. Although the lovely Libran may be an inspired choice for a last-minute partner for the school reunion, this relationship probably doesn't have the legs to last.

Aries/Scorpio

This union is hot and heavy, but probably a little too hot to handle for the carefree Aries, as the possessive Scorpio will want to own you completely and give your free spirit a very short leash.

Aries/Sagittarius

Oh, what a lovely couple! (Wouldn't like to live with them though . . .) You are both fun-loving people and oblivious to the faults in each other that might drive other people crazy. You both love travel and adventure, and the Sagittarian ability to land on their feet will always see you on the sunny side of luck. Although don't expect to be dripping with money.

Aries/Capricorn

Finances are a big hurdle in this connection. You can spend it as fast as the Goat can make it, and that drives the bean-counting Capricorn to despair. You are both going to have to make some compromises.

Aries/Aquarius

Great conversation and a good game of chess; this must be the only union that keeps the Aries guessing about where the relationship is headed next. Who will call who, and when? Such conundrums will have the usually aloof Aries thinking about whether she wants to be with the even more indifferent Aquarius.

Aries/Pisces

Sexually this is not a bad alliance, but the emotional temperament of the Fish is just so different from Aries that it must put a strain on the relationship. Pisces will find your intellectualising superficial and you will find his emotional mind games exhausting.

Taurus/Taurus

Same-sign relationships are always a little trying. You appear to be perfect for one another, but can find yourself becoming irritated by each other's predicability and faults. However, with perseverance you will make a welcoming and serene home, and put on the most scrumptious dinner parties!

Taurus/Gemini

Taurus may find holding onto the flighty Gemini like trying to hold a handful of dry sand. Geminis don't like to sit down mentally for one minute, the Taurean loves to muse. The restless Gemini lives in a cerebral world of ideas and Taurus is very much based in the material. Also the great sex drive of the earth sign could find little comfort in Gemini's take-it-or-leave-it approach. Gemini loves change and Taurus resists it, so there's long odds on this one.

Taurus/Cancer

Pure bliss! Cancer likes to make a good home and gives a lot of physical affection, which is what every Taurus is looking for. But the Bull must be careful not to let fly on the odd occasion she feels the need to, as her Cancer is exceedingly sensitive and will crawl back into his shell if a nasty comment hits its mark. A lovely match.

Taurus/Leo

There is great sex appeal here for both partners. To the great joy of the Taurean, magnanimous Leo will shower her with the finer things in life. As long as Taurus swallows her jealousy and lets Leo show off a bit, all will go well. Leo must be careful not to dominate, as the equally obstinate Taurus, who is just a little slower off the mark, will brew to anger if she feels trodden upon. Longevity, stability, and loyalty characterise your relationship. Worth a red-hot go.

Taurus/Virgo

Usually love at first sight, Taurus and Virgo could be well advised to take things a little slower in the beginning of this earthy love tryst. Taurus could find Virgo's pedantic critiquing of his every move more than a little annoying. Also, where Taurus likes to wallow in deep emotion, Virgo is normally in control of her emotions. However, the common desire for material wealth and security may well see them through.

Taurus/Libra

Venus, the love goddess, rules both these signs and gives their pairing a sense of harmony. Both appreciate the finer things of life, so pots of money will be needed for these two to appease their desire for luxury. The success of this relationship will rest on Libra's sense of diplomacy and Taurus' patience. Taurus will have to allow the Libra her social wings, and Libra will have to be content to spend a few nights in, cuddled up with a decadent box of Belgian chocolates. Oh, what sacrifice!

Taurus/Scorpio

These signs sit exactly opposite to each other on the zodiac, and as with most opposite matchings they will be strongly physically attracted and intrigued by each other. Jealousy and possessiveness are big problems with this pair, with Scorpio being one of the few signs that can seemingly 'out-possess' Taurus. Taurus must appear to be wholly and solely committed at all times. In the long run, this can be wearing, even for the diligent Bull.

Taurus/Sagittarius

Sagittarius will be good-natured about the Taurean desire to nest, but no amount of berating will change the wanderlust Sag. The Sagittarian will happily philosophise with

Taurus about the pleasures of settling down with your one true soul mate to live the quiet life, and the next day find herself in a travel agent buying two tickets to Goa. Heartbroken, you will be underwhelmed by her tactless gift! Both must agree that no way is the better way, and to love each other for it.

Taurus/Capricorn

While Capricorn may seem aloof at first, the warm rays of Venus will soon melt this cautious exterior, and this match should be a good one. Be sure to have a few laughs every once in a while, and both be extra-generous in your flattery.

Taurus/Aquarius

Whoa, I don't even know how you guys found each other! Probably hunting for antiques, as that is the only place I can think of where you would both be likely to be at the same time. If you appear to be from opposite sides of the planet, then that is because you are, and it may be easier to leave it that way. If you insist on pursuing this difficult partnership, Taurus is going to have to let Aquarius have some space and Aquarius is going to have to divulge some of those secrets.

Taurus/Pisces

Romantic, imaginative and impressionable Pisces is just what Taurus is looking for. Taurus' earthy practicality can be a comfort for the highly emotional Pisces, and Pisces can allow the earthbound Taurus to dream a little. Usually a joy to behold.

Gemini/Gemini

Frenetic is one word to describe the pace of this pair. Life is so far in the fast lane they will have to build a bypass.

You won't find a more versatile, charming or vivacious couple. They will have fascinating conversations, have marvellous sex and throw a party twice a week for their many and varied friends. But the superficial nature of this coupling can become unstable. Complying to every restless whim could lead to a self-destructive lifestyle. One of you will have to try to keep this travelling circus on track, and are either of you willing to do so?

Gemini/Cancer

Warning, warning. Danger, danger. Gemini's scathing wit will cut the little Crab to the quick. Gemini has little patience for Cancer's moods and the first argument will be a doozey. You must be careful what you say to the Crab, because he has a magnifying glass to examine any remarks that might hurt his fragile ego. Passionate Cancer will fulfil Gemini's physical needs, and cheery Gemini will brighten Cancer's world, but all too soon Gemini's flirting will mortally wound the sensitive Cancer. Be wary.

Gemini/Leo

Finally, an ego large enough to laugh in the face of Gemini's flirtations! Leo will not see Gemini's coquetry as an insult to their relationship, but rather as an example of Leo's largesse in sharing his gorgeous and vivacious partner around. An affectionate pair who have a great time together, they will be constantly trying to upstage each other in social settings, but they both love a laugh and can see the funny side of their dramatic coupling. They will be in great demand at dinner parties.

Gemini/Virgo

Both are Mercury-ruled and have a mental approach to life, but where Virgo critiques, Gemini ridicules. They will have good conversations together because they both enjoy mental clarity, but Gemini can find Virgo's pernickety approach to learning exasperating.

Gemini/Libra

Love is in the air! Both are affectionate and fun-loving and love to entertain and travel. Sexually neither is jealous or demanding, and when Gemini wants to experiment Libra goes along for the ride. They will go through wads of money, but are otherwise a perfect match.

Gemini/Scorpio

Gemini will light Scorpio's embers but they will soon find out that sex isn't everything. Scorpio won't put up with Gemini's fickle nature, and Gemini will be under the constant scrutiny of Scorpio's suspicious nature. In turn, Scorpio is setting himself up for heartbreak by Gemini's light-hearted approach to love. Gemini loves people, Scorpio likes privacy. Be careful with one another.

Gemini/Sagittarius

It won't last long, but what a wild ride it will be! Gemini and Sagittarius sit exactly opposite in the zodiac and are fascinated by each other. They especially enjoy picking over each other's brains, for both have many and varied interests. They will talk for hours, plan excursions and get along like an oxygen-fed house on fire. Until it gets really serious and moves into the bedroom. Unfortunately neither is particularly demonstrative and neither will want to take too much responsibility for keeping the relationship afloat. Fortunately it will end amicably, and they will probably remain good mates.

Gemini/Capricorn

Philosophically, Capricorn needs the security of walls and floors, but Gemini likes to sleep in the open air; Capricorn needs routine and a regular pay cheque to feel at ease, but Gemini feels queasy whenever you mention either of these things. And where Capricorn worries about security, Gemini worries about keeping her freedom. All is not lost though – with understanding, Capricorn can show Gemini how to ground her constant curiosity, and Gemini can show Capricorn how to develop his sensual potential.

Gemini/Aquarius

Aquarius understands Gemini's inconsistency and will not take it to heart. In fact, Aquarius is likely to be just as inconsistent! They share a taste for the bizarre and meeting new people, and Aquarius can't get enough of Gemini's cheery attitude. Gemini is the seeker of knowledge, while Aquarius claims to have the knowledge. The sex runs hot and cold, but that is how these signs like it, and in marriage they are two affectionate companions rather than passionate lovers. A match like a comfy chair.

Gemini/Pisces

Gemini is likely to be very attracted to the Piscean dreamy nature, but his thoughtlessness will too easily hurt the emotional Pisces. Eventually, Gemini will be frustrated by the Fish's reluctance to deal with reality and overwhelmed by the Piscean need to be adored. Both possess qualities that the other could well do with, and persistence will pay off, but they must be prepared for a long road ahead. Compromise is the key word.

Cancer/Cancer

It's like looking in the mirror and that's the trouble. Cancers understand each other perfectly and know where the sensitive spots are, wounding without even trying. Both are too sensitive, too demanding, too dependent and need someone stronger. Each needs an enormous amount of

THE SIGNS IN LOVE

attention and reassurance, and resents the other for not giving enough. On the plus side, they're sensual bedmates whose erotic imaginations are sparked by each other. But that's rarely enough. This treadmill goes nowhere.

Cancer/Leo

Initially, Cancer might shy away from Leo's extroverted exuberance but give him a chance to shine and you will see that Leo's generous approach is just the medicine. Like the Moon reflects the Sun, you can both feed each others good qualities. Both take life very personally. Cancer's marvellous intuition tells them exactly how to handle the proud Leo ego. Leo's sunny disposition is a wonderful antidote for Cancer's blue days.

Cancer/Virgo

Cancer may have to warm up Virgo a little, but there is fire under the ice. This can turn into a secure, comfortable and affectionate relationship. Cancer's struggle for financial security works perfectly with goal-oriented Virgo. Cancer understands Virgo's fussy ways and steady Virgo helps balance variable Cancer. Cancer's dependency neatly complements both Virgo's need to protect and ability to make someone feel loved and needed.

Cancer/Libra

These two inhabit different worlds and probably should keep it that way. Cancer seeks an emotional partnering, and Libra seeks perfect intellectual communion. Libra has little time for Cancer's moods, and Libra's detached air makes Cancer feel insecure. They have a hard time establishing real sexual rapport, which exasperates Cancer. When Cancer turns critical, especially about Libra's extravagance, Libra starts looking elsewhere.

Cancer/Scorpio

Both signs value emotional commitment and Cancer's sensuality is ignited by Scorpio's dynamic passions. Cancer's possessiveness will actually make Scorpio feel reassured. Together they will build a little love cocoon and block out the rest of the world. This relationship has great intimacy, intensity, and depth. A recipe for great things getting better all the time.

Cancer/Sagittarius

Cancer will be awed by Sagittarius' worldly, philosophical knowledge and Sag will enjoy feeding Cancer's imagination. That said, they are probably better friends than lovers. Sagittarius will want to throw off the shackles every now and then and be less than pleased when Cancer panics and pulls them tighter. Cancer needs constant reassurance and will quickly exhaust Sagittarius' reserves of patience.

Cancer/Capricorn

There's an initial sexual attraction because they are on opposites sides of the zodiac. Compromise is the key. Career-oriented Capricorn can provide Cancer with security, but also many other interests that Cancer can see as competition. Cancer plays sensitive flower to Capricorn's domineering protector, but Cancer may take Capricorn's reserve as a personal rebuff and become moody and critical. This is worth the effort though, as once aligned it can make a lasting and fulfilling partnership.

Cancer/Aquarius

Cancer needs to feel close and secure; Aquarius is a lone wolf who will gobble up Cancer's warm, responsive nature if he feels trapped. And he is more than likely to feel trapped. Cancer can't understand Aquarius' cynical sense of humour, and Aquarius has little patience for Cancer's nagging. Not a great idea.

Cancer/Pisces

Pisces will love the protection Cancer offers from the outside world, and Cancer just loves having someone to love, especially someone as emotionally responsive as Pisces. Pisces is the dreamer, Cancer understands the dream and can make it a reality. They make a highly intuitive couple who know how to make the other smile. A match to be nurtured.

Leo/Leo

Cooperation. Ah, yes, not something that comes easily to either of you. As Leos, you are allowed, even expected to make all the decisions, and like two king lions in a pride you can expect to butt heads a little. Like a lot of same-sign relationships, you will be either extraordinarily happy and fulfilled or it will end in disaster – there is no middle ground. You must agree on who will be the leader and who the follower, and learn to swap roles once in a while.

Leo/Virgo

This is a difficult one to call. Any pairing relies on other parts of the chart being compatible, but with Leo and Virgo this is even more so the case. Leo will find Virgo's cool approach very sexy and Virgo will love the warmth of Leo. Magnanimous Leo will overlook Virgo's tendency to be critical, while Virgo will take pride in Leo's accomplishments. However, Virgo is more analytically astute than Leo, who may not appreciate being picked apart by Virgo. Leo may take for granted much of the work and assistance that Virgo provides.

Leo/Libra

The two will be attracted to each other immediately and enjoy fabulous sex romps, but when it gets down to the nitty-gritty of commitment, there may be some problems. Leo will not appreciate Libra's indecisiveness, which starts to irritate, and important matters will never be resolved as the Libran finds serious discussions too uncomfortable. When Leo inevitably decides it is time to take the lead, Libra may feel like they are being bossed about.

Leo/Scorpio

A clash of wills is imminent. There is strong attraction between these two because of their strength of character. There are definitely elements of conquest in your desire for each other and this makes the chase more passionate. Once you have each other, though, you might find that proud stubborn streak really annoying. Scorpio will fall hard and expect the same commitment from Leo, but Leo can't match the passion of Scorpio and has needs of his own. If you can find common ground it will be the affair of a lifetime, but it is more likely to end in tears.

Leo/Sagittarius

Sagittarians like to wander, and Leos are one of the few signs that won't see this as a slight to their enormous ego. You two will have a lot of fun and enjoy a wonderful life together, but Sagittarius will have to learn to mind her tongue, because her tactless comments can be a little too close to the truth for the proud Leo. Sag will keep introducing new ideas and experiences to keep Leo from getting into a rut. Sagittarius provides the humour, and Leo the panache. A good match.

Leo/Capricorn

Leo's cheerful temperament can take a bit of a battering from the somewhat cynical Capricorn. Leos are simple souls and they don't like too much intellectual detail. This bombastic approach can really irritate the Goat. Capricorn prefers classical simple elegance or a conservative, traditional style. Leo has a generous hand and loves rich color, warmth and a brilliance that borders on gaudiness. Sometimes, this translates into emotional terms also. Leos also thrive on the company of the opposite sex, but they prize fidelity. Notwithstanding, this usually isn't good enough for Capricorn.

Leo/Aquarius

Leo loves the world and Aquarius loves humanity. These two sit on opposite ends of the zodiac, which usually means a strong instantaneous sexual attraction. But it isn't always meant to be. Aquarius may be too aloof for Leo, who needs his ego stroked more than once or twice a day. Leo seems to dramatise inconsequential events and takes life too personally for Aquarius. But Leo loves a good surprise and Aquarius can certainly provide that.

Leo/Pisces

Leo will never have to compete for the spotlight, as Pisces will quite happily take the back seat. But Leo can easily dominate or trample Pisces' feelings, and this can be the source of considerable unhappiness. Leo can find Pisces dreaminess annoying. Pisceans are careful about expressing their feelings, whereas Leos are very open about how they feel. These emotional differences will add to the problems because although the Piscean needs a strong partner, Leo finds Pisces too clingy and stifling.

Virgo/Virgo

If you can target your drive for perfection, you will make an unbeatable team. Unfortunately, all Virgoans have areas of their life where they like to be absolutely precise and if these areas really clash, you could find yourself in a disastrous state. The constant self-criticism of the Virgo mind means areas of dissatisfaction will be many and varied. Try not to be too hard on yourself or each other and you will find many areas of happiness and joy.

Virgo/Libra

Libra loves to hear others' thoughts on any subject and they blithely accept different points of view. Virgo is the most critical of thinkers and is intolerant of illogical thinking. Virgo loves talking about politics and religion, but Libra lives by the old creed that you should never talk about either in polite company. At worst, Virgo views Libra as wishy-washy, and Libra sees Virgo as prim and intolerant. But, being a learning relationship (Virgo learning, Libra teaching) your different natures could complement each other, and you both can greatly benefit from the partnership.

Virgo/Scorpio

Scorpio will stride fearlessly into a challenging situation, where Virgo might tread more carefully, Scorpio may laugh at Virgo's timidity, but Virgo just considers his actions more prudent. Scorpio commits with driving passion, and although Virgo will make the same level of commitment it will be filtered through the intellect, filed away neatly, brought out again for closer scrutiny, a few typos fixed, and a clean copy printed. And still he will have a few more questions. Harmonising your different natures will take some effort, but there is much to be gained from having a go.

Virgo/Sagittarius

These two make great business partners. Sagittarius keeps the notion of the forest intact, while Virgo takes apart each tree, straightening every bough and sweeping away those pesky leaves. This pair will have great success if they realise their different approaches are complementary. As lovers, the compatibility is more difficult. As fellow mutable signs, they will find joy in communicating with each other, but Sagittarius, though passionate, is physically undemonstrative and Virgo's cool exterior needs more than a little push in that direction. But, with understanding, Sagittarius can get Virgo to laugh at herself a little more and Virgo can focus some of that Sag energy in productive ways.

Virgo/Capricorn

Wonderfully matched in many ways, you may find life a little too serene, even a little too predictable. Hard to believe as you both crave predicability, but you may have to make the effort every now and then to take a little walk on the wild side – provided you are both home for 'The Bill' and tucked into bed by 10 o'clock, of course! You are marvellously productive together, with Capricorn providing the strategy and Virgo the talent. You can rely on each other for an honest opinion and this makes life much easier and enjoyable.

Virgo/Aquarius

There is good mental rapport here. Virgo focuses on specific details and prefers to specialise in a certain area, while Aquarius takes a more global view and looks for inter-relationships in a large system. These are two fairly stand-offish signs and your aloofness may become a problem. Your physical relationship may be a bit cool or formal, and hopefully there are other astrological factors to provide warmth, affection and romantic attraction.

Virgo/Pisces

Ambiguity is the bane of Virgo's existence and he will go out of his way to quash it, or at least file it neatly in a folder marked: 'To be reconciled later'. Pisces wallows in ambiguity and is quite content to absorb lots of contradictory ideas. Virgo likes to carve out a niche, whereas Pisces drifts among a wider variety of interests. Virgo likes neat and tidy, Pisces loves a bit of clutter. Pisces is poetry to Virgo's facts. These differences do not necessarily conflict; neither of you is ambitious or egocentric and both are gentle, even shy people, so your sensitivity is a plus in this relationship.

Libra/Libra

For both of you, happiness shared is happiness quadrupled – your feelings only seem real when you share the experience. Both of you invest enormous energy and time into personal relationships, and you both feel incomplete without a partner for companionship. But you both want to be liked by everyone, all of the time, and you both avoid taking decisive stands or confronting personal disputes. Sometimes you will wish the other would take a stand for you, but generally your relationship will be harmonious and balanced.

Libra/Scorpio

Scorpio has an intense urge to merge with another and can become quite fixated on the object of their affections. Libra is no cold fish, but does like to keep some sense of proportion when it comes to a relationship. That is not to say that these differences are terminal. Libra learns from Scorpio and if other signs in the chart are compatible, all could be set for a very interesting coupling.

Libra/Sagittarius

A party duo, you are both outgoing, friendly people who enjoy each other's company immensely. Sagittarius provides the grandiose ideas, dreams, visions and wanderlust, and Libra puts them into perspective. Libra can be terribly sympathetic to these dreams and plans, but can be prone to going along with people even when there is plenty of doubt. Sagittarius can talk most people into anything, and compliant Libra is a sucker for this kind of enthusiasm – it can be a bit like the blind leading the blind! But what fun anyway – you will definitely have some laughs.

Libra/Capricorn

This can work, but you will have to accept your given roles and learn to love each others' foibles. Capricorn can keep Libra in the style to which she is accustomed, Libra can infuse some wine and laughter into Capricorn's orderly life. If Capricorn is the breadwinner and the keeper of the purse strings (just don't hold on too tight there Cap!) and Libra is happy to flit about, making sure Capricorn has a gorgeous home and clean children to come home to, you could share a very happy existence.

Libra/Aquarius

Both love a house full of friends, although sometimes Libra might wonder if Aquarius needs her friends as much as she needs her partner. You are great mates with a lust for conversation and you are mentally on a par. This relationship might appear casual from the outside, but don't let well-meaning friends and family make you have doubts (especially you, Libra). You both like things to be pretty breezy (Aquarius more so) and only you know if you are unhappy. To the happy couple!

Libra/Pisces

These affectionate, creative, artistic people take to each other immediately. But Pisces won't find the emotional support in Libra that he craves and Libra loves the romance and harmony, but flees from too much emotional commitment. Luxury and a lovely home are high on the wish lists of both signs, but Pisces is too lazy about making money and Libra is too extravagant about spending it. Libra feels stifled by Pisces, and Pisces eyes Libras many interests with suspicion. Physical rapport is never enough, but as long as it lasts, it will be fun.

Scorpio/Scorpio

This is intense. Those first heady weeks where young lovers spend days holed up in bed, living out the John and Yoko fantasy have probably turned into months and years for you two. Scorpios are all or nothing about a lot of things and relationships are especially intense. Neither of you have flings or even flirt without serious intent. Stormy fights and sizzling reunions may typify your relationship, which is likely to be either deeply satisfying or very destructive to you both. Just remember to come up for air every now and then, and don't forget your mother – she misses you.

Scorpio/Sagittarius

Sagittarius may feel like Scorpio is weighing her down, and Scorpio suspects that Sagittarius doesn't care as much as he does – he is probably right. Sag just doesn't have Scorpio's capacity for intense depth of feeling. Scorpio's possessiveness is flattering at first, but eventually she will find it frightening. Sagittarius needs a sense of freedom, Scorpio needs wholehearted commitment. You are so different from each other that it will take a lot of understanding for you to be together for any length of time.

Scorpio/Capricorn

Both are naturally suspicious and neither is flippant about giving away affection. Neither is likely to make a move without a guarantee that feelings are mutual. Scorpio's reserve is like a dyke holding back an ocean of emotion; Capricorn's reserve is like the gatekeeper to the oaken door, to the laser-alarmed hall, to the iron bars, to the Lockwood safe, to the little velvet box with the tricky lock that contains Capricorn's tender heart. Capricorn has a much greater capacity for detachment than Scorpio and can be strangely aloof at times, especially when feeling threatened. Scorpio is instinctive and passionate all of the time. There is no froth and bubble here, but neither of you want that anyway.

Scorpio/Aquarius

This combination is not as outrageous as you might think. True, Scorpio needs to possess the person and Aquarius wants to own the world, but these two desires are not mutually exclusive. The mental rapport between these signs is high and they will have great dinner conversation. Sex is good fun too, as both have a taste for the unusual. However, Scorpio will have to loosen the leash every once in a while and Aquarius will have to find ways to be more demonstrative if this is going to work. Definitely worth a try.

Scorpio/Pisces

Snap! Scorpio gives Pisces valuable emotional support, strength and leadership, as well as a deep, exciting sexual commitment. Scorpio's jealousy makes Pisces feel loved and Pisces' dependency is just what Scorpio is looking for. Communication is on a sensual, unspoken level. Both have intense feelings, and are interested in the mystical and the unusual. Heaven on Earth.

Sagittarius/Sagittarius

This pairing may eventually fizzle into just good friends, but you value friendship as much as love and you will have a lot of fun on the way. Your lust for life is unparalleled, and you will have a wild time thrilling each other with the next spontaneous adventure. The camaraderie between you is infectious and if you ever break up, it will be to the moans of your friends who loved going along for the ride. You most enjoy travel and talk together.

Sagittarius/Capricorn

Optimism and faith versus realism and doubt are likely to be hot topics in this coupling. Capricorn will find Sagittarius' grandiose plans amusing, Sagittarius will find Capricorn's reaction just a bit patronising. If your dissimilarities are not too extreme, you can complement rather than frustrate each other, with Sagittarius providing the energy and vision and Capricorn the steady hand.

Sagittarius/Aquarius

Progressive postmodernists, even in later life both of you will stay abreast of current trends in fashion, music, arts, literature, science and politics. Sagittarius tends towards the philosophical more than the sometimes cynical Aquarius, but neither of you is particularly sentimental. Your relationship may be very friendly but somewhat detached, but this is unlikely to be a problem. You both are independent and will give each other the space you crave. Your temperaments and interests are different but blend well and this should be an enjoyable, interesting relationship.

Sagittarius/Pisces

Lust abounds but the fire will soon fizzle. Pisces is a dreamer, not a doer, which will frustrate the get-up-and-go Sagittarius no end. Sagittarius, while loyal, will never know how to satisfy Pisces' need for attention and devotion, and her sharp tongue will hurt Pisces' romantic sensibilities. Pisces snuggles close but is constantly rebuffed by Sagittarius' struggle to free herself from heavy emotional demands. It won't be long before Sagittarius will fly the coop.

Capricorn/Capricorn

Together you can build a secure and stable life. You both have a high level of integrity, maturity and responsibility, and the ability to set reasonable goals and achieve high levels of success. You could be a very successful team in business activities as well. Light and laughter could be lacking so have a mob of kids to give you the light relief that you need. A long and fruitful life to you both!

Capricorn/Aquarius

You both admire each other greatly, but there is a certain aloofness that will be hard to thaw. Intellectually you are on a par and your talents are complementary to each other – you both love your work. Capricorn brings tenacity and reliability to the partnership while Aquarius brings ingenuity and sensitivity to current trends. With other parts of your chart bringing some warmth and sexual spark, this could be an interesting match.

Capricorn/Pisces

Like pieces of a puzzle, these two very different personalities fill in the weaknesses of the other. Capricorn dominates and will gladly take over the decision-making, Pisces will breathe a sigh of relief and drop the load. In turn, Pisces brings a breath of romance to Capricorn's fusty approach to life, and her lavish praise and doe-eyed affection delights Capricorn. Capricorn finds it difficult to verbally communicate his intense feelings – but he needn't worry with Pisces, she knows already.

Aquarius/Aquarius

Friends or lovers – can lovers still be friends? Of course, you both cry. But what happens when it seems lovers have become only friends? Neither of you likes to be at home much, so you will spend most of your intimate domestic life over cappuccinos in an inner-city café. Eventually the cracks might begin to show. You have an excellent mental rapport and your debates on politics, science and art are second to none, but your relationship may lack warmth and depth of feeling. You are both used to playing the aloof, hard-to-get one, but this will not do if you are going to make this work. You are going to have to make yourself a little vulnerable – are you up to the challenge?

Aquarius/Pisces

Pisces' romantic eroticism inspires Aquarius to experiment in new areas. Sexually this is fun, but sex is never enough to keep Aquarius interested. He is an intellectual and will find Pisces' dreamy philosophising a bit of fluff and eventually a bit of a bore. Pisces will never be able to get across the subtle emotional undertones in her understanding of life to the Aquarian. Eventually the outgoing Aquarius will start looking around, and Pisces can't endure that. Aquarius will become resentful and Pisces will be heartbroken. Not a happy story.

Pisces/Pisces

Oh, if only those weeks in the bedroom would never end. Sadly, eventually you're going to have to open the shutters and face the real world. One of you is going to have to be the responsible one. Both can be weak-willed and dependent, and you will drain the other emotionally. You both have a tendency to sink into a mire of self-pity and negativity, and accentuate each other's confusion and self-indulgence. You find it hard to cope with practical realities, and there's no one around to push you both in the right direction. Unless you are superstars with minders, maids, nannies and cooks to mind the daily grind, this sexy affair has no place to go.

Interpretation

Now you have the knowledge you need to start interpreting a natal chart. Hopefully it looks less strange to you now than it did at the start of the book. The glyphs should look familiar and you should be able to work out which sign a planet is in and which house a planet is in. You should also be able to tell your ascendant sign from looking at which sign has made its way up through your First House, and is rising over the ascendant.

Chart Shapes

The next thing to look at when interpreting your chart is the chart shape. There are seven main shapes, described below.

The Splay Shape

The most common of all chart shapes with the planets spread evenly throughout. This chart often indicates a healthy personality with an even distribution of talents and activities. However, if the planets do not connect strongly by aspect, the individual may have difficulty expressing their abilities fully.

The Bowl Shape

This is when all the planets fall into one half of the chart, with the other half being empty. If the planets are all at the top half, the focus is on the conscious activities of the individual. If they are all in the bottom half, the issues are of a subconscious and personal nature. If the planets fall in the left hemisphere, the issues are about taking control of one's destiny, while the right side is about the influence of others on your life.

The Bucket Shape

This is like the bowl, but with a rogue planet or planets facing from the other side. This creates a bridge to the other side and often means a powerful flow of highly concentrated energy. The aspects between the two sides will show how this energy will come out.

The Train Shape

This is four consecutive signs (or one third of the chart contains no planets). The empty section indicates a vulnerable part of the personality that may need attention.

The Bundle Shape

The opposite of the train shape, this can be the mark of a genius. All the planets are concentrated in one third of the chart. People with this chart often have very narrow and focused objectives – it is a rare chart shape, so be honoured if you have met someone with it!

The Sling Shape

This is the bundle shape but with a lone planet (or conjunction of planets) outside the third. This makes the attention on the separate planet or the conjunction very intense. People with this shape often have a vocational calling.

The Seesaw Shape
In this shape, the planets are divided in two, sitting opposite each other and staring each other down. As the name suggests, it means a personality whose actions can be contradictory, and who is pulled in opposite directions.

The Planets
We will now look at the planets in detail – after all, it is their energy that is driving your whole chart. Take careful note of how the planet was discovered and the mythology behind its naming, as these are important clues as to its role in your life. We will also look at the ascendant in detail. This chapter includes an interpretation of the ascendant in all twelve signs, and also looks at how the sign on the descendant can be read as a clue to your future marriage partner.

The 'planet' Chiron is discussed in-depth, plus the North and South Nodes and the Pas Fortuna. These objects are a little unusual and not all astrologers include all of them in a chart, but it is useful to know what they mean in case they do turn up in a chart you are interpreting.

The Sun
Our Sun is pretty similar to most stars in the universe. This big burning ball of gas makes up 99.86% of the solar system's mass and provides all the energy we need to sustain us.

The Sun can be divided into three main layers: a core, a radiative zone and a convective zone. Its energy is actually a thermonuclear reaction. It is constantly converting hydrogen to helium in the core, where the temperature is somewhere from 15 to 25 million degrees. The energy then scorches through the radiative layer and boils rapidly to the surface

Glyph – ☉

Sun's day – Sunday

Body parts – Heart, back

Metal – Gold

Spice – Cinnamon

Food – Corn

Colour – Gold

Rules – Leo

Represents in your chart – Your father

Occupation – Famous person or leader

in a process known as convection. Charged particles, called the solar wind, stream out at one million miles an hour.

If you stood on the Sun, its gravity would make you feel 38 times more heavy than you do on Earth. But if you did manage to stand on the Sun, you wouldn't have too much time to enjoy this weighty experience before you were burnt to a tiny wisp of carbon.

Magnetic fields within the Sun slow down the radiation of heat in some areas, causing sunspots, which are cool areas that appear to us as dark patches. Sunspot activity peaks every 11 years. The next peak is due in 2011.

As sunspots increase, so does flare activity. These are plumes of energy containing gamma-rays and x-rays and energised protons and neutrons, and each is the equivalent of one billion megatons of TNT spewing out in a matter of minutes. During this time the Sun bombards Earth's atmosphere with extra doses of solar radiation. This is called an active Sun and its energy can be quite ferocious. One such peak in 1989 caused power blackouts, knocked satellites out of orbit and disrupted radio communications.

The charged particles also excite oxygen and nitrogen in the atmosphere and create the aurora borealis, or northern lights. The prettier the aurora, the more solar radiation there is to come. An active Sun may also affect our climate. Scientists believe a small ice age from 1645 to 1715 corresponded to a time of reduced solar activity, and current rises in temperatures might be related in part to increased solar activity.

Coronal mass ejection is similar to a solar flare, in both form and effect. A bubble of gas and charged particles is ejected over several hours, which can threaten Earth's atmosphere. This can occur with or without solar flares.

Mythology of the Sun

The Roman god Apollo was the son of Jupiter and god of the Sun. Each day he drove his chariot of fiery horses across the sky to light the world, feed the plants and warm the backs of people working in the fields. He was also the god of healing, so sick people prayed to him.

Apollo had a human son called Phaethon. Phaethon nagged Apollo to let him borrow the Sun chariot and fly it across the sky. Being the caring parent that he was, Apollo agreed. Phaethon, proud as punch, took off like a bullet in the Sun chariot, up into the sky. But, like a forewarning to every teenager who was to come after him, he lost control of the horses. The chariot plunged towards Earth, a ball of fire threatening to burn up everything on the ground.

But grandfather Jupiter stepped in at the last moment, and stopped his fall with a thunder-bolt (and probably fixed up the excess on his insurance premium as well).

The Sun and Leo

The Sun rules Leo. You can see the Sun's influence in Leo's ability to be the catalyst. Their personalities tend to dominate a group, but in a life-giving way. Leo's fixed fire energy (much like the Sun is fixed fire) has the ability to bring people along with them, to feed people's egos and make them believe that anything is possible if you have the courage to take it on.

What the Sun means in your chart

The Sun is the largest body in the sky and it is where all life comes from. It is a very important planet in astrology and is given a great deal of weight. It is our motivation and our life force.

The Sun sign is the placement that people with the most rudimentary knowledge of astrology will know you by; but it is not necessarily how they will know you. It takes a long time for your Sun sign to become evident in your external appearance, and many people will assume you are more like your ascendant (which is your conscious self, that is, what you would like to be rather than what you are). Your Sun sign gives you clues as to how you can really let yourself shine

How to read the Sun in your chart

The sign in which the Sun falls describes the unravelling journey of your life. You may not even recognise your Sun sign in yourself until you are much older, because it shows us where we want to be and what our life preoccupations will be. It is our vitality and our life force and, ultimately, our sense of self. Like the Sun when it rises, overriding everything else in the sky, your Sun sign colours the influence of every planet in your chart. So the Sun is our ego and the catalyst for our behaviour.

The house in which the Sun falls shows where you want attention and admiration. It will also show where you really shine, where you feel most comfortable and at ease with your ability to take on the tasks at hand. For example, if your Sun is in the Third House, the house of communication, you are known as a good communicator and it is important for you to be recognised as such.

The Moon

> Glyph – ☽
>
> Moon's day – Monday
>
> Body part – Stomach
>
> Metal – Silver
>
> Herb – All mild herbs
>
> Food – Eggs
>
> Colour – Silver
>
> Rules – Cancer
>
> Represents in your chart – Your mother
>
> Occupation – Nurturer, cook or provider of food

The Moon's mass is only 1.2% of the Earth's mass, but it is nearly one-third the size of Earth in diameter. As small as it is, it is actually bigger than Pluto. Unlike Pluto, it is not a planet orbiting the Sun, but a satellite orbiting the Earth.

There are various theories about how it was created, but recent evidence indicates it formed when a huge collision tore a chunk of the Earth away. Therefore, like the four inner planets, the Moon is rocky. It's pockmarked with craters formed by asteroid impacts millions of years ago. Because there is no weather or atmosphere, the craters have not eroded and a footprint can sit undisturbed for centuries. Without atmosphere, temperatures vary wildly. Daytime temperatures on the sunny side reach 130°C; on the dark side it gets as cold as –150°C.

The Moon travels around the Earth at a little more than half a mile per second. It takes 27.3 days to orbit Earth and exactly the same amount of time to rotate on its axis, which means the Moon always shows us the same face. We see the Moon because of reflected sunlight. How much of it we see depends on its position in relation to the Earth and the Sun.

The Moon's orbit is called a sidereal month, and this is how long it takes the Moon to orbit the Earth in relation to a fixed star. Another measurement, called a synodic month, is measured in relation to the Sun and equals 29.5 days. Full and new moons are measured by the synodic month.

The Earth's gravity keeps the Moon in orbit, while the Moon's gravity creates tides on our oceans. The Moon's rotation speed is slowing and it is gradually drifting away from Earth.

We are still learning about the Moon. In 1998, the Lunar Prospector provided evidence that as much as six billion tonnes of ice sits near the Moon's poles. In June 1999, researchers discovered that a huge cloud of sodium gas trails behind the Moon.

Mythology of the Moon
The Moon is the subject of myths across all cultures. In Greek mythology, the goddess of the Moon is called Selene, and in Roman mythology Luna, but the two have been blended over the years. It seems that the Luna stories have gone by the wayside and the Selene stories have stayed with us.

Selene was an influential goddess, and many looked to her to help with their troubles. She fell in love with a mortal called Endymion, and together they had fifty daughters (heaven knows how many bathrooms they needed!).

But Endymion was only human and susceptible to disease, ageing and inevitably death. Selene could not bear the thought of losing her lover, so she cast a spell to make him sleep forever and therefore remain eternally youthful, living on in an unconscious state through the ages.

The Moon and Cancer

The changeability of the Moon and its phasal nature influences Cancer's moods, pushing them from one extreme to the other. Also, the Moon's ability to reflect the Sun is quite telling for a Cancer Sun sign, as Cancers can often let their own desires go wanting in order to see a loved one shine.

What the Moon means in your chart

The Moon represents your intuitive, emotional response to your environment. Just as the Moon reflects the Sun's light and the Sun is concerned with action, the Moon is concerned with reaction. In childhood, we are largely reactive. Without control over our environment or our emotions, we are raw in our emotional responses, crying out in pain when something hurts us and laughing until our bellies ache when something really tickles our fancy.

Looking at the Moon's sign, house and related aspects can be very instructive in showing us how we dealt with things when we were children – whether we were painfully shy, or cheeky and naughty, whether we had a natural compassion for others, or we struck out in hurt at those around us. These patterns of behaviour re-emerge throughout our lives, sometimes in the most painful ways. Looking at the placement of the Moon in your chart can help when trying to unlearn seemingly innate behaviour.

The Moon also corresponds to our protective instinct, to how we set up a home and how we pass on life's lessons to our children. Your Moon represents your mother, in the same way that your child's Moon will represent you as a mother, so you can see how mistakes can be repeated through generations or how to show your child the way to constructively build character and strength in the face of pain.

The Moon also represents all that is innate and subconscious, our natural habits, including eating habits, our views on the past, our moods and the imagination.

How to read the Moon in your chart

The sign in which the Moon falls describes the way you innately react to your environment and the intensity of your moods. For instance, the Moon in Aries indicates a short temper, but one that blows over quickly. It also means someone who is instinctively independent and rejects being 'mothered' too much.

The house in which the Moon falls describes your instinctive needs. For instance, the Moon in the Third House would mean you find emotional security in learning, whereas the Moon in the Second House would mean you find emotional security in material gains. This also represents where you want to make your home.

Mercury

Mercury looks a little like our Moon. This tiny world, which is only two-fifths the size of Earth, has been pummelled by asteroids over the millennia and is scarred by massive craters.

Glyph – ☿
Mercury's day – Wednesday
Body parts – Lungs, nervous system
Metal – Mercury
Herbs – Bitter-sweet herbs
Food – Wheat
Colour – Slate grey
Rules – Gemini, Virgo
Represents in your chart – All young people
Occupation – Writer, merchant

Mercury is halfway between Earth and the Sun, and the Sun's glare blocks our view of it most of the time. As the innermost planet, it has less than half Earth's gravity, and with barely a slip of atmosphere (which is thought to be helium). This lack of atmosphere means temperatures fluctuate wildly, from 400°C during the day to –195°C at night.

Mercury is one of the four terrestrial planets, made up mostly of rock and metal. It rotates very slowly (one day on Mercury takes 58.6 Earth days) but its orbit of the Sun takes only 88 days. Mercury has been known since ancient times.

Mythology of Mercury

Mercury was the god of merchants and of the thief. Mercury also invented the lyre. The son of Jupiter, his name comes from the Latin word 'mercari', meaning 'to make a deal'. Later, Mercury was associated with the Greek god Hermes, so messenger was added to his list of duties (as if he didn't have enough to do!). Both Mercury's and Hermes' symbol is the caduceus (two serpents twining around a rod) and a winged helmet called a petasus. On the coins of ancient Rome, Mercury is often represented as a clean-shaven young man, holding a money bag and sometimes his sacred animal, the cock.

Mercury was barely a day old before he had fulfilled his birthright as god of the thief and had stolen Apollo's cattle. The inventive little fellow had made the cows special shoes so no one could follow their tracks. Apollo was furious, but as he went to punish him, he heard Mercury playing his lyre. He fell in love with the instrument and decided to give Mercury his cattle and his shepherd staff in exchange for the gorgeous instrument.

When the first woman, Pandora, was made in heaven, every god contributed something to perfect her. Venus gave her beauty, Apollo music and so on. It was Mercury who gave her persuasion.

Mercury was also the god of science and business, which in this information age makes him an ultra-modern god. Being the god of communication, messages, business and thievery, he must be the god of the Internet as well.

Mercury and Gemini
The mercurial energy in Gemini gives the Twins their desire to communicate, and combined with the element of air, that communication is rapid. Ideas are picked up and put down, exchanges are quick-fire, and knowledge is speedily digested.

Mercury and Virgo
Mercury gives Virgo its intellectual, critical and analytical approach to life. Communication is important and Virgoans love books, magazines and writing. Whereas the Internet is the Gemini medium, Virgoans prefer a more tangible means of communicating, such as books.

What Mercury means in your chart

Communication, intellect and awareness are Mercury's calling cards, as are logic and reasoning, our manner of thinking, and how we create and express our thought processes. Mercury is the planet of conscious intelligence, and it will reveal how our memories work and how we choose to communicate conscious memories. It also tells us on what level we find communication satisfying, whether we speak only because we have to and would prefer to express ourselves by more tangible means, or whether we take real joy in having a good old chat.

Talking, thinking, sharing are the three words that best sum up the action of Mercury. Because this planet implores us to express ourselves, when Mercury goes retrograde (that is, when it appears to loop backwards across the sky), our communications will be challenged.

Body language is ruled by Mercury and its placement will tell you if you are a gesticulator whose heart is shown in an open sitting stance, or whether you stand in a closed stance and don't give too much away.

Mercury is never more than 28° from the Sun, so the sign Mercury is in is more than likely to be the sign your Sun is in. It is neither masculine nor feminine energy and assumes the gender of the sign it is in. It is the only planet that has this capability and is thought to bring reconciliation between the two sides of the personality. If you are at peace with Mercury, you are at peace with the communication within yourself. And this is a very powerful thing – if you have the ability to understand why you do things, you have the ability to control your destiny.

How to read Mercury in your chart

The sign in which Mercury falls describes the way you think and communicate, for instance, Mercury in Taurus would mean you think with purpose and with the view to coming up with considered and careful judgements.

The house in which Mercury falls describes where you choose to express your intelligence and communication. For instance, Mercury in the Tenth House would mean you express your intelligence in your career. In the Fourth House, it would mean you communicate best in a family situation.

Venus

Glyph – ♀

Venus's day – Friday

Body part – Kidneys, renal system

Metal – Copper

Herb – Mint

Food – Lollies, berries

Colour – Green

Rules – Taurus, Libra

Represents in your chart – Young women

Occupation – Artisan

The second planet is hot, hot, hot. Venus bakes under twice as much solar radiation as Earth and reaches temperatures of 480°C. It is also covered in a thick cloud of sulfuric acid gas about 95 times greater than the density of the atmosphere of Earth. This cloud actually rotates much faster than the planet itself (about once every four days compared to the planet's leisurely rotation of 241 days), and its weight would crush a human.

Venus is a little smaller than Earth with a mass of 80% and a diameter of 95%. Composed of rock and metal, the surface of Venus is mostly rocky desert.

It takes longer for Venus to rotate than it does to orbit the Sun, which it does in 225 Earth days. While all the planets orbit in an ellipse (an oval shape), Venus's orbit is close to a perfect circle. After the Sun and the Moon, it is the brightest object in the sky. The ancient Greeks believed it was actually two objects and even now it is referred to as the 'morning star' and the 'evening star'. Because it is so bright, Venus is the object of many UFO reports.

Mythology of Venus

Known as the goddess of love and pleasure, Venus was considered the mother of the Roman people. Her role was to bring joy to gods and humans. The daughter of Dione, her paternity is uncertain, but it is most likely that Jupiter was her father.

Venus married Vulcan, the god of metalwork, but was often unfaithful to him. Her many lovers included Mars, the god of war, and the handsome shepherd Adonis who made all the goddesses swoon. Mercury fathered her child Cupid, god of love. Ironically, Venus became known as the goddess of chastity in women. This was due to her ability to make herself into a virgin again at will.

Venus is also associated with the arrival of spring and is considered a nature goddess. She has very few myths of her own but because she so closely parallelled the Greek goddess Aphrodite, Aphrodite's myths are often told as hers.

Taurus and Venus

Venus gives Taureans their fondness for spending most of

their time, effort and money surrounding themselves with lovely, sensual things. Others may look on in amusement at their seeming excess, but to a Bull, beauty is inherent in the meaning of life. A happy home life and a stable relationship will complete the picture.

Libra and Venus
Venus combined with the element air, as it is in Libra, means beauty with the flirt, which gives some idea of the Libran social whirl. You could call it the party-double. A dinner party with a Taurean host will guarantee you excellent food, but a Libra host will make sure you never stand alone.

What Venus means in your chart
Like her goddess namesake, Venus is the planet of love, beauty, art and indulgence, and about what we want. Venus has many similar qualities to Jupiter, the planet of fortune, but with a more material bent, so it is sometimes called 'The Lesser Fortune'.

In childhood, the placement of Venus will reflect how we make friends and mix in school. Later in life it will become more about what we find beautiful and enjoyable and what we find beautiful in a partner. By looking at Venus in your chart, you can see where there may be problems in forming relationships, and strategies for avoiding those problems.

Venus also shapes the personal appearance, the personality, and the degree of success in the social world and in love. It dictates your ability to attract and hold admirers, your general popularity and your capacity for spending money. Someone with Venus in a difficult position in the horoscope (what astrologers call 'an afflicted Venus') might be indulgent to the point of vice, quarrelsome, or on the run from creditors for their frivolous extravagance.

The glyph of Venus has become a well-known symbol for women. Venus will show you what you aspire to be as a woman (strong, submissive, flirtatious, serious etc). In a man's chart, it reflects what he is looking for in an attractive partner.

How to read Venus in your chart

The sign in which Venus falls describes the way you seek enjoyment or pleasure and the way you seek romance. For instance, Venus in Leo would see you seeking pleasure in the drama of life, and you would enjoy having a relationship in a very dramatic way with torrid door-slamming arguments and passionate make-up embraces.

The house in which Venus falls describes where you find pleasure and romance. For instance, Venus in the Ninth House means you seek romance in exotic people and are attracted to people from other cultures. It means a love of learning, although it doesn't necessarily mean you will sit down and do the study (that is elsewhere in your chart). Venus in the Ninth House finds pleasure in trips to beautiful places and exotic things from foreign climes.

The Earth

Glyph – ⊕

The Earth is the third planet from the Sun and is remarkably similar to the other terrestrial planets, Mercury, Venus and Mars. All four consist of rock and metal as their primary ingredients. Each has a solid surface, unlike the gaseous surfaces of the planets of the outer solar system.

The Earth takes exactly 23 hours and 56 minutes to zip around on its axis, going at a breakneck speed of 1610 kilometres an hour. And you thought you were just quietly sitting there with your cup of tea! Not only is it spinning at such a dizzying rate, but it moves about 28 kilometres per second in its orbit of the Sun. A full orbit takes about 365.24 days.

Earth is a fabulous example of it all just coming together. Its distance from the Sun, the presence of water and the unique atmosphere of life-giving oxygen and nitrogen all conspired to form life as we know it some 3000 million years ago.

What the Earth means in your chart

Well, the Earth means nothing and everything, depending on how you look at it. In a chart, you do not see the Earth because that is the central point around which everything else revolves. It is where all the energy is concentrated, and it is also from this viewpoint that your chart is drawn.

Mars

Glyph – ♂
Mars' day – Tuesday
Body part – Head
Metal – Iron
Herbs – Ginger, cayenne pepper
Food – Onions
Colour – Red
Rules – Aries, Scorpio
Represents in your chart – Young men
Occupation – Warrior, competitor

For centuries, humans have been obsessed with this dusty, red planet. It seems if you were taking bets on which planet was most likely to support life, Mars would be the odds-on favourite. And there have been some exciting false alarms. Percival Lowell, an amateur astronomer who studied Mars in the early 1900s, thought he saw canals on its surface, which he believed must have been dug by Martians! Closer examination with modern telescopes and planetary probes showed they were optical illusions.

Mars is mostly rock and metal, with a mountainous terrain. Iron oxide dust gives the planet its reddish glow. The atmosphere is very thin and its orbit is elliptical. The odd comings and goings of Mars as seen from Earth confused scientists for centuries. It was Johannes Kepler, and later his colleague Nicolaus Copernicus who finally put the pieces of the puzzle together in the early 1600s, with the notion that planets orbited the Sun in an elliptical, rather than circular, pattern.

Mars' atmosphere and orbit cause wild temperature fluctuations, ranging from –137°C to a comfortable 26°C on summer days at the equator. Huge hurricane-like storms swirl around.

The two moons of Mars are called Phobos and Deimos, and they rise and fall on a day of a similar length to Earth's (that is, 24 hours and 37 minutes). No complaining about the year flying by though, as an orbit takes 687 days. Mars is about half the size of Earth.

There is evidence to suggest that Mars was warm and wet about 3.7 billion years ago. But the water froze as the planet cooled and there is nothing left but ice caps at the poles. There is evidence of water-bearing minerals in large amounts on its surface, and scientists hope the deposits will give some clues to the planet's history.

Mythology of Mars

The son of Jupiter and Juno, Mars is the god of war. He was regarded as the father of the Roman people because he was the father of Romulus, the founder of Rome. Mars was the husband of Nerio, a minor goddess who is often confused with Bellona, the goddess of war. This partnership probably would have made quite an impact on the tennis court in the mixed doubles.

Mars is often compared with the Greek god Ares, who was not as prominent in Greek mythology. Mars was quite important to the Roman army, whose soldiers worshipped him as the most prominent of the military gods, and considered him second in importance only to Jupiter. His festivals were held in March (named after him) and October.

Mars and Aries

Mars is the embodiment of masculine energy and so fits the sign Aries like a hand in a glove. Aries is full of positive, cardinal energy anyway, so probably doesn't need much more encouragement, but it is Mars that directs the drive for success.

Mars and Scorpio

Mars' influence over Scorpio is less pronounced than over Aries because Scorpio's prime ruler is Pluto. It is Mars' ruling of sexual energy combined with the watery Scorpion charm that can be deliciously dangerous, for the opposite sex at least. Rather than Scorpio's emotional ways and fixed energy being doused by Mars' fire, its power is enhanced by being harnessed in this way.

What Mars means in your chart

Mars is the 'red planet', fiery and energetic, with passion and determination to spare. Mars shows your general energy level – whether you are a can-do, will-do or a gonna-do sort of person. If you are feeling weary all the time and it's an effort to get out of bed in the morning, then you have issues with Mars. But you will also have complications in other areas in your life because of this lack of energy. By looking at Mars you can really tease out what is making you feel apathetic and begin to fix the problem.

Mars also represents the instinctive survival mechanism of fight or flight. Mars must be understood in conjunction with Venus. Venus is what we want, but Mars is how we get there. So Mars symbolises all those things that help us achieve our aims in life. It is the catalyst to all our behaviour, the energy that inspires us and keeps us motivated. Mars' energy can be constructive or destructive. As the god of war, Mars could be brutally violent. While this energy still emanates from the planet, it can be harnessed for stamina, ambition, courage and achievement.

Mars still rules the military, our sexual energy, weapons, accidents and, paradoxically, surgery. In medical astrology, it rules fevers, accidents and surgery – in short, all childhood disasters. And its exuberance and energy for life is similar to that of a child's.

How to read Mars in your chart

The sign in which Mars falls describes the way you assert yourself. For instance, if you have Mars in Capricorn, you have a deep reserve of energy that you use to best advantage. Mars is at its best in a sign like Capricorn, where the energy is focused and consistent but still undiluted and powerful. If you have Mars in Aries, you assert yourself impulsively. Mars is at home in Aries, so its effect is magnified. This means that although Mars in Aries means extra energy, it also means very little staying power.

The house in which Mars falls describes where you find your motivation. For instance, if Mars is in the Tenth House, you concentrate your energy on your career, which is where you feel most energised and powerful. If Mars is in the Second House, you are motivated by a desire for possessions.

Jupiter

Glyph – ♃

Jupiter's day – Thursday

Body part – Liver

Metal – Tin

Herb – Ginseng

Spice – Nutmeg

Food – Strawberries, honey

Colour – Purple

Rules – Sagittarius, Pisces

Represents in your chart – Your grandfather

Occupation – Lawyer, doctor, teacher

Jupiter is enormous, a ball of gas so massive it could hold all the other planets put together. You could stuff 1300 Earths into one Jupiter. And this giant thing rotates in nine hours and five minutes, though it takes 11.9 years to orbit the Sun.

The great red spot is Jupiter's most familiar feature. This is a swirling mass of clouds, like a great hurricane caused by the colossal winds that develop above the rapidly spinning planet – up to 400 kilometres per hour. The red spot is twice the size of Earth and has been raging for at least 300 years. It is one of several storms on Jupiter.

Jupiter's core is rock and it is many times the mass of Earth, but most of the planet is a thick gaseous murk. This appears smeared when viewing Jupiter through a telescope because the planet moves so rapidly beneath. Jupiter spins so fast that it bulges in the middle, making the diameter 7% greater at the equator than at the poles.

Its enormous pull of gravity makes Jupiter a beacon for asteroids and comets, and it has been saving Earth from certain destruction for many thousands of years by drawing asteroids into its mass. Maybe that's why they call it the lucky planet! In 1994, astronomers around the world watched as fragments of the Shoemaker-Levy 9 comet struck Jupiter. A bright cloud more than 13,600 kilometres in diameter erupted from the face of the planet.

Jupiter has at least 16 satellites. The four largest are the Galilean moons, Io, Europa, Ganymede and Callisto. They orbit on the same plane and are all visible by telescope.

Mythology of Jupiter
Jupiter is the supreme god of Roman religion and mythology. He is also called Jove and is closely associated with the Greek god Zeus. Jupiter was the son (along with Pluto and Neptune) of Saturn and the father of Mars.

Originally a sky deity associated with rain and agriculture, Jupiter developed into the great father god, prime protector of the state concerned with all aspects of life. His temple was worshipped with the spoils of war and magistrates paid homage to him with sacrifices. Jupiter was portrayed in two ways – as a powerful and benevolent leader of his people, dispensing wisdom and justice with generosity of spirit, and as a womaniser with a taste for gluttony.

Jupiter and Sagittarius
Jupiter gives Sagittarius its lucky aspect, its search for deeper meaning and the desire to travel.

Jupiter and Pisces
Jupiter's influence over Pisces is less pronounced than over Sagittarius because Pisces' prime ruler is Neptune. Jupiter gives Pisces its emphasis on wisdom and the deeper, universal concepts of life.

What Jupiter means in your chart
Jupiter is the lucky planet, a symbol of aspirations and hope. As the largest planet in the solar system, it represents expansion and expansive behaviour. Wherever it falls in the chart will be in an extravagant manner.

Like its namesake the king of the gods, Jupiter is a benevolent planet overseeing life and wisdom. Optimism, generosity, luck, humour and opportunity are all associated with this planet, as well as sports, games, pets and leisure time. Jupiter is also the guardian of the abstract mind, rules higher learning and is our catalyst for exploring ideas, both intellectually and spiritually. Jupiter forms our ideology and religious preferences, our ethics and morality. It will search far and wide for answers as Jupiter also rules long-distance travel. It also addresses our sense of optimism.

However, the largesse of this planet can deteriorate into laziness and sloth, and an afflicted Jupiter placement could mean weight gain and lack of motivation.

How to read Jupiter in your chart

The sign in which Jupiter falls describes the way you seek personal growth and wisdom, and the way the benefits flow to you. For instance, if you had Jupiter in Scorpio you would seek growth in all things hidden and mysterious. You would be attracted to professions such as the priesthood or private investigating. Jupiter in Scorpio also gives you luck in dealing with other people's money and resources, and in having these available when they are needed.

It takes Jupiter about twelve years to circle the zodiac (the planet visits an average of one sign a year), so people born in the same year as you are likely to have the same positioning as you do. Primary school teachers will tell you there is such a thing as a studious year (Jupiter in Virgo or Capricorn) and a year of the chatty ratbags (maybe Jupiter in sociable Libra). This has a lot to do with the planet Jupiter.

The house in which Jupiter falls describes where you choose to expand your world and where you have confidence. For instance, Jupiter in the Fifth House would mean confidence in romance, creative endeavours, socialising and gambling. It is the planet of largesse in the House of Magnanimity, so there is a danger of feeling so over-confident that you take one risk too many.

Saturn

Galileo Galilei was completely befuddled when he first laid eyes on Saturn. He did a little drawing in his notebook – a symbol with one large circle and two smaller ones – to attempt to describe his discovery. The rings appeared to him be like ears, and he considered the possibility that Saturn was not one object, but three.

Glyph – ♄

Saturn's day – Saturday

Body parts – Skeleton, teeth, hair, nails, skin, bones

Metal – Lead

Spice – Salt

Food – Dried fruit

Colour – Black

Rules – Capricorn, Aquarius

Represents in your chart – All old people

Occupation – Head of an organisation

For more than forty years debate raged about these 'ears', until Christiaan Huygens proposed that they might be rings. Giovanni Domenico Cassini discovered a gap between the rings, which he promptly named Cassini's division. He also proposed that the rings were not solid objects, but made of many small particles.

The sixth planet from the Sun has a rocky core and a gaseous surface. Saturn's claim to fame, however, is the intricate series of rings that encircle it. The rings are actually countless ice particles, ranging in size from one centimetre to one metre wide, splayed out in a disc-like orbit measuring one and a half kilometres across. You can spot three rings with a good telescope. The two outermost rings are separated by Cassini's division (which isn't actually a gap, but appears dark because it has less material in it). The middle ring is the brightest, and just inside it is a fuzzy one that can be difficult to spot.

Along with this whirligig of ice, Saturn has eighteen known satellites, made mostly of ice and rock. Titan is the largest and it orbits Saturn every sixteen days. Titan is larger than Mercury, and has a thick atmosphere that obscures its surface. It is not clear how many moons Saturn has, but there are likely to be at least twenty, possibly many more.

Saturn rotates at a fair pace, and a day is only ten hours and thirty-nine minutes. Its orbit of the Sun takes 29.5 years.

Mythology of Saturn

In Roman mythology, Saturn was a god of fertility and agriculture. He was married to Ops, the Roman goddess of the harvest, and was the father of Jupiter, Neptune and Pluto and the grandfather of Mars.

Saturn was king of Latium (modern-day Lazio in Italy), and was responsible for the remarkable achievements of the Golden Age of ancient Italy. Saturn introduced agriculture to his people by teaching them how to farm the land.

The Romans celebrated a festival for Saturn known as the Saturnalia, which began in mid-December and ended on 1 January. With cries of 'Jo Saturnalia!', the celebration included masquerades in the streets, big festive meals, visiting friends and the exchange of good-luck gifts called Strenae (lucky fruits). People decked their halls with garlands of laurel and green trees lit with candles. Masters and slaves would exchange places.

The early Christian church frowned upon this merriment and wanted to keep the birthday of Christ a solemn and religious event. They banned the Saturnalia and many other pagan customs, but to no avail. Eventually, the church decided to tame the Saturnalia and turn it into a celebration for Jesus. The joy of the Saturnalia was eventually transported to the joy of Christmas.

Saturn and Capricorn

Capricorns get their planning ability and their control fetish from Saturn. Capricorns often give the impression of being mature before their time, and this is old man Saturn's influence.

Saturn and Aquarius

Saturn's influence over Aquarius is less pronounced than over Capricorn because Aquarius' prime ruler is Uranus. Saturn gives Aquarians their innate wisdom. Its domain is knowledge and social structures, both major concerns of the Aquarian. Aquarians also like to keep a bit of distance from the world, which is how Saturn likes to rule, like a disciplinary professor.

What Saturn means in your chart

Saturn is where we feel hindered or blocked. It is where we find great challenges, and if they are overcome, there are great rewards to be had. Saturn is the planet that inspires the most fear and loathing of any of the ten, because the house in which it is placed will be where you have cause for frustration and concern. But the kind of disappointments that Saturn brings are also the source of the greatest motivation.

For instance, you might think having Saturn in the Tenth House would be the cause of great woe, as this is the house of career and ambition. But it doesn't mean you will spend the rest of yours days wrapped under a newspaper on the park bench, in a sorry state of destitution. Oprah Winfrey, Bill Clinton, Pablo Picasso and Albert Einstein all had Saturn in the Tenth House and all worked hard to make sure they were successful.

And that is the gift of Saturn. Look carefully at what is happening in your chart with Saturn and you will find that, although you have had difficulties in this area in the past, you have made quite a bit of progress and will continue to do so until you are really achieving what you want.

Saturn governs old age and the lessons it teaches us. It represents our attitude towards authority figures, tradition and wisdom. Structure and order in the way we conduct our affairs are all ruled by Saturn. Consolidation of assets are important here (yes, it is the dreaded planet of superannuation). Saturn concerns itself with karma and the lessons past experiences might bring.

How to read Saturn in your chart

The sign in which Saturn falls describes the way you feel safe and secure and, by process of elimination, where you feel inadequate. For instance, Saturn in Sagittarius means you need to know everything about a situation to feel secure. If the information is incomplete, you can't just roll with it, you have to wait until all the facts are in front of you.

The house in which Saturn falls describes where you feel blocked. For instance, Saturn in the Fifth House can mean you feel blocked in creativity. It also means you feel restricted when it comes to fun and games. You take romance far too seriously and are generally told to 'chill out' a lot.

Uranus

Glyph – ♅
Rules – Aquarius

Uranus is a ball of gas, with a cloudy surface, rapid winds

and a small rocky core, much like its gaseous neighbours Saturn, Neptune and Jupiter. But it is otherwise a very strange planet indeed. Uranus is the only planet to orbit the Sun east-west, and at a 98° tilt, so that it seems to be rolling around on its side. This means that one pole points at the Sun for months on end, giving the planet peculiar seasons.

Uranus has a lot of satellites and a very faint set of rings. It is believed to have sixteen regular and five irregular moons, making it the most populated planetary satellite system known, with Saturn coming a close second.

Uranus was the first planet to be discovered by telescope. It was discovered by William Herschel in 1781. Uranus is nineteen times further than Earth from the Sun, and was thought to be a star until Herschel pointed his telescope towards it and saw that it orbited the Sun. Uranus' orbit takes 84 years.

Mythology of Uranus
Uranus is named after the son of Gaia, mother Earth in Greek mythology. She produced Uranus to look after the sky. Uranus made rain fall to help the plants grow and provide water for the animals. Gaia and Uranus had many strangely shaped children, monsters and giants including the three Cyclopes, each with one huge eye protruding from their head.

Uranus couldn't stand the sight of his own children. He was a cruel father whose fear of his creations led him to banish them to the Underworld.

Gaia could not forgive Uranus for sending her first children to hell, so she encouraged their human-shaped children, the Titans, to rebel against their father. Led by the Titan Cronos (Saturn in Roman mythology), Uranus was overpowered by a sickle. Three drops of his blood fell on the Earth and formed the Furies, hideous bird-like creatures with a dog's head and bat's wings whose mission was to hound murderers, especially those who had killed their own. They were considered the spirits of revenge and justice.

Another drop of blood fell into the sea, creating the goddess Aphrodite (or Venus). Cronos married his sister Rhea and became King of the Titans. They had five children but Cronos feared that one of them would kill him, so he swallowed each one as it was born. At the birth of her sixth child, Rhea tricked Cronos into swallowing a stone wrapped in baby's clothing and gave the child to some nymphs who brought him up safely. This child was Zeus, known as Jupiter in the Roman myths.

Zeus choked his father and made him cough up the five lost babies – Hestia, Demeter, Hera and Hades (or Pluto) and Poseidon (or Neptune). And thus a dynasty was born.

Uranus and Aquarius
Aquarius embodies the Uranus ideals of independence and an unhindered intellect. Its emphasis on society as a whole is from the Uranus concern for humanitarian issues.

What Uranus means in your chart
Uranus is our ability to take a wider path, to break open the established neural pathways to think about things with fresh insight and a modern approach. It favours independence and originality and shows where we are different from the norm.

And it only requires difference, which does not necessarily mean radical. If career and ambition are the norm in your world, Uranus would show itself in conservative values such as marriage and motherhood. That is the nature of Uranus. Whatever you are expecting, you can be sure it will do exactly the opposite. Antisocial, uncooperative and contrary, this planet can just as easily be associated with humanitarian qualities, as with the dubious qualities of chaos and terror.

Uranus likes to mix it up a bit for some intellectual stimulation. Placement in a chart might emphasise desire for change for the sake of it and hence people who veer towards anarchy, rather than change with an emphasis on the good of the people, which is the place where most people have it.

It is considered the higher octave of the communicative Mercury energy, and rules all new technology. It doesn't raze to the ground in an effort to find new solutions (that's Pluto's territory). Rather it maintains the structure, but does a radical refurbishment.

How to read Uranus in your chart

Through the signs, Uranus moves so slowly that its effect is more on your generation than on you as an individual. It will show how your generation will shake up the establishment, and where it will be inventive in its thinking. If there is undue emphasis on this planet (for example, because the rest of your planets are on the other side, or it has many aspects to it), there is more influence on you as a person.

The house in which Uranus falls can give you insights into where you will rebel against the establishment or where you are different. A strong Uranus presence in your chart will mean a desire to disassociate yourself from the masses, who you will see as brainwashed by the flickering eye of television. A strong Uranus will lead you to think very clearly and carefully about why you do the things you do, and lead you to question their validity at times. These people can be very cynical of advertising, and almost impossible to hypnotise.

Through the houses, Uranus shows how you differentiate yourself, and in what area your genius lies. For instance, if you have Uranus in your Seventh House, you would choose to have a less conventional marriage (if you got married at all).

Neptune

> Glyph – Ψ
> Rules – Pisces

Neptune spends most of the time being the eighth planet from the Sun, but every now and then it exchanges this title with Pluto and becomes the ninth planet. This is because Pluto's orbit is highly elliptical or stretched. The last time Neptune was the outermost planet was from 1979 till 11 February 1999, when it crossed back again. It won't be the ninth planet for another 228 years.

Neptune is the usual cornucopia of ice, hydrogen, helium and methane, with a quick rotation that fuels rapidly swirling winds and a myriad of storm systems surrounding a rocky core. The planet has a faint set of rings and eight known moons. It is also thought to contain a deep ocean of water. It takes nineteen hours and twelve minutes to rotate on its axis, but 165 years to orbit the Sun.

Neptune wasn't spotted in the usual way, by sight, but was discovered in 1846 after mathematical calculations of Uranus's movements predicted the existence of another large body.

Mythology of Neptune

Neptune was the Roman god of the sea. He carried a trident, which looks like a large three-pronged garden fork, and he rode a dolphin or a horse. When the sea is rough enough to show white tops on the waves, these are sometimes called sea horses after Neptune's horse. Neptune was also called the earth-shaker because he was the god of earthquakes.

Neptune's Greek equivalent was Poseidon, who was a much more important god in Greek mythology. The planet Neptune is also heavily associated with the Greek myths of Orpheus, a celebrated musician. The music of his lyre was so beautiful that when he played, wild beasts were soothed, trees danced and rivers stood still.

Orpheus (Neptune) married the nymph Eurydice. When Aristaeus tried to rape her, she fled, was bitten by a snake, and died. Orpheus descended to Hades searching for her. He was granted the chance to regain Eurydice if he could refrain from looking at her until he had led her back to sunlight. Orpheus could not resist, and Eurydice vanished forever. Grieving inconsolably, he became a recluse and wandered for many years.

Neptune and Pisces

Neptune can be seen in Pisces in their dreamy qualities and their weakness for drugs or religion (sometimes both). Pisces is the only sign to be ruled by Neptune, and it is this planet that carries us over from this life to the next.

What Neptune means in your chart

Neptune is the higher octave of Venus, meaning it takes Venus's concerns to a more spiritual level. It is the desire for spirituality, to search longer and harder for evidence of another realm.

Neptune is the planet of illusion and dissolves worldliness; it is concerned with fantasy, escapism, drugs and spirituality. It is the desire for greater perfection in the world, and its placement will show where you seek that perfection. In essence, Neptune is creating an illusion, of what is enchanting on the outside and captivating within. This includes drugs, alcohol, trances and hypnosis, delusion, hypochondria, abnormality, sleep and dreams.

Neptune rules the oceans. Poetry, music and dance are among the trance-like activities this planet favours. It also rules movies, television, theatre, fashion and all forms of glamour. Animation is a very Neptunian art form.

How to read Neptune in your chart

The sign in which Neptune falls describes the way we attain our dreams and whether we are successful. Neptune spends roughly fourteen years at each sign, so its effect is generational and it usually signifies the grand illusion of each generation.

For example, the baby-boomers (born 1942–57) have Neptune in Libra. This signified an intense desire for peace and love, but also a lack of motivation. Libra is the sign of romance, and so the baby-boomers have very idealistic and sometimes unrealistic expectations of love, and this has manifested itself in a huge upsurge in the divorce rate. The next generation (born 1956–71) with Neptune in Scorpio sought rebirth through drugs, and thus the hedonistic seventies were born.

The house in which Neptune falls describes where you are required to have faith and trust, as well as where you may encounter confusion and loss. It is through these events that you gain greater spirituality and insight.

It is also where we turn a blind eye and dream. For example, if you have Neptune in your Second House, the house of material goods, you are haphazard about your possessions. You probably don't think you really deserve your possessions and would be much better off pretending they belonged to someone else – you would then take better care of them.

Paradoxically, you are also very skilled at dreaming up get-rich-quick schemes (Neptune is the planet of imagination), but holding on to your hard-won gains is a different story.

If there is undue emphasis on this planet, there is more influence on you as a person.

Pluto

Glyph – ♀
Rules – Scorpio

Relatively little is known about this tiny planet with the strange orbit. Its composition is presumed to be rock and ice, with a thin atmosphere of nitrogen, carbon monoxide and methane. We have only ever gathered very fuzzy images of this cold planet.

Pluto is only about two-thirds the size of Earth's Moon, and its 248-year orbit is off-centre in relation to the Sun, which causes the planet to cross the orbital path of Neptune. From

1979 until early 1999, Pluto was the eighth planet from the Sun. It is now the solar system's most distant planet and will remain the ninth planet for 228 years. Fortunately, the orbits of Pluto and Neptune are too different for them to ever collide. And though they are neighbours, they are also always more than one billion miles apart.

Pluto was discovered in 1930, by amateur American astronomer Clyde Tombaugh. Its one Moon, Charon, was discovered in 1978. It is larger in proportion to its planet than any other satellite in the solar system, and scientists think it may be a chunk that broke off Pluto in a collision with another large object.

Some astronomers think Pluto may have wandered into our system from a more distant region known as the Kuiper belt. If that's the case, Pluto is not a planet at all, but probably similar to a large asteroid or comet. Others have also suggested that Pluto may have once been a Moon of Neptune.

There have been some recent moves to strip Pluto of its planet status, because: all the other planets in the outer solar system are gaseous, giant planets whereas Pluto is a small solid object; Pluto is only a little more than half the size of any other planet; Pluto's orbit is by far the most eccentric of all the planets; and Pluto's orbit is the only planetary orbit which crosses that of another planet (Neptune).

However, Pluto will retain its planet status. As a compromise, it will probably also become the first in a new class of celestial objects known as a Trans-Neptunian Object (TNO). So Pluto may soon be sporting a dual passport of sorts.

Mythology of Pluto

According to the Roman myth, the three sons of Cronos and Rhea – Jupiter, Neptune and Pluto (known in Greek mythology as Zeus, Poseidon and Hades) – each drew lots to determine which part of the world they would rule. Jupiter and Neptune received the sky and the seas respectively, and Pluto was left with the Underworld, known as Hades.

Pluto ruled the realm of the dead alone, until he became enamoured of the beautiful goddess Persephone. Although their relationship began shakily – Pluto abducted his future bride and whisked her away in a chariot – their union was peaceful, and Persephone became Queen of the Underworld.

Pluto and Scorpio

Pluto's influence can be seen in Scorpio's obsession with sex, death, birth and rebirth. Pluto embodies the issues that the Scorpio mind loves to tackle. Water gives Scorpio its emotional capabilities and its fixed quadruplicity its stable nature, but Pluto gives Scorpio its simmering rage and obsession with answering the big questions in life.

What Pluto means in your chart

Pluto takes the energy of fiery Mars to a more intense and spiritual level, although some astrologers think Pluto has more in common with the emotional Moon.

This planet is about transformation, regeneration and rebirth, death, sex and obsession. When you consider the time that it was discovered, in the first year of the Great Depression and at the beginning of the events that led to World War II, you get an idea of where Pluto is coming from.

These events were tragic, but (you would hope) society has learned some big lessons from them. Whatever Pluto does, it provides us with massive change and asks us to transcend what we know, redeem ourselves in the process and come out stronger as a result. Pluto relies on the fact that we will find a will and a way to survive.

There are two sides to Pluto. One side is interested in universal welfare and in cooperating with others for the greatest good of all. Psychic abilities and the ability to extend one's consciousness throughout the universe fall into this realm. Pluto beseeches the masses to look inward (and to their subconscious) to see what's there. It revolutionises the thinking of a whole generation and ensures that each generation leaves its mark and tries to make the world a little bit better.

On the other side, Pluto rules destruction, death, obsession, kidnapping, coercion, viruses and waste, atomic energy, crime and the underworld, along with many forms of subversive activity like terrorism and dictatorships.

How to read Pluto in your chart

The sign in which Pluto falls describes the way you regenerate, and because Pluto takes such a long time to pass through a sign (because of its eccentric orbit, this can take anywhere from twelve to twenty-one years), it is a generational sign. In fact, along with Neptune, it could be considered the sign of the generation gap. Often when a generation has the most productivity in its youth, the regeneration is not apparent, but as the generation grows older and takes over the positions of power, its impact becomes imbued in the fabric of society.

For instance, the last generation that had Pluto in Gemini undermined the established wisdom and replaced it with new ideas about communication and energy (Freud and Jung in psychology, Einstein and Planck in physics, Picasso in art). But it wasn't until this generation grew up that its ideas became part of the norm.

The house in which Pluto falls describes where your greatest influence or obsession is. For instance, with Pluto in the Third House (the house of communication) your words can heal or kill. This placement gives your communications great power. Therapists or salespersons often have this position.

If there is undue emphasis on this planet there is more influence on you as a person.

Lunar Nodes

North Node Glyph – ☊
South Node Glyph – ☋

The two lunar nodes are where the Moon's orbit meets the (imaginary) intersection of the Earth's orbit around the Sun. This path is called the ecliptic. When the Sun and Moon meet at this intersection, or node, an eclipse occurs. The node signifies the exact point where the Sun and Moon 'collide' in the sky.

So the nodes are not planets, but crossings. The North Node is when the Moon is passing south to north, and the South Node is when Moon is passing north to south. The nodes stand exactly opposite each other on the astrological chart. Many computer-generated charts will not even bother putting the South Node in, as it is obvious where it should go.

Sometimes the North Node is called the ascending node, as it is made when the Moon is ascending from south to north. Hindu astrology calls it the Dragon's Head. The South Node is also known as the descending node, or the Dragon's Tail.

The lunar nodes travel backwards at the rate of about three minutes a day, so it takes eighteen and a half years for a lunar node return to occur.

What the nodes mean in your chart

The North Node is where you will find growth and development and the South Node represents what you should be trying to shrug off. While the South Node indicates subconscious behaviours that might be sabotaging your efforts, the North Node represents the positive strategies you should use to counter them.

It takes one and a half years for the nodes to change signs, so they should be given weight only after you have assessed the rest of the chart.

Ascendant

Glyph – ASC

Your ascendant, or rising sign, is one of the first things an astrologer will look at when assessing your chart. The ascendant is the sign whose cusp was rising in the First House when you were born. It is probably what you will most recognise in yourself, how you relate to the world and the mask you wear to greet the day. The ascendant is more about how we think we should be, rather than what we are, and more about what we think our motivations should be, rather than what they are.

It is the filter through which all the other influences of the planets and houses and signs come. The ascendant will distinguish the different hues in disposition, temperament and physical appearance in people born on the same day, but at different times.

By looking at the sign in the First House, you can also tell which cusp was rising in your Seventh House, which is said to tell you what sort of person you will be attracted to in love. Below is an outline of what the ascendant means in each Sun sign.

Aries ascendant comes across as headstrong and full of energy, with a can-do attitude. You like to be seen to be first. Aries ascendant generally gives a slim, sporty body with a fast metabolism and a square face. You are attracted to attractive people, with a fair-minded nature and lovely manners.

Taurus ascendant means graceful living, and harmony in motion is what you would like to project. You don't like to appear ruffled and you like to throw a good dinner party. Taurus ascendant usually gives a solid body with a slower metabolism, but graceful movements and an attractive face. You are attracted to dark, handsome, intense types.

Gemini ascendant means witty and clever. You like to be seen as a communicator, so busy that sometimes life seems like a contest. Gemini ascendant usually gives a lithe body with a fast metabolism and pretty hands. You usually look younger than your years. You are attracted to jolly, happy-go-lucky types.

Cancer ascendant likes to be seen as caring for everyone and as quite sensitive, and you always like your family to come first. You use your intuition to solve problems. Cancer ascendant gives large soulful eyes and paler skin, with a heart-shaped face. You are attracted to ambitious, successful types.

Leo ascendant likes to be seen as a very generous person with a great deal of integrity, in charge and the centre of attention. You like to be glamorous, especially when you go out. Leo ascendant usually gives a solid body, attractive features, with great hair. You are attracted to unusual types.

Virgo ascendant likes to be seen as doing a great job in the background, to be thought of as practical, logical and objective. You like to communicate well and clearly. Virgo ascendant usually gives a solid body with piercing eyes, usually blue or grey in Caucasians. You are attracted to dreamy types.

Libra ascendant likes to be seen as the social butterfly, keeping the peace and solving injustice – you are always political in your dealings with people. You like harmony and take pride in your appearance, enjoying good-quality clothes. Libra ascendant usually gives an overall very attractive appearance, with an oval face and pretty features. You are attracted to energetic types.

Scorpio ascendant likes to be seen as determined with a reserve of power; intense and magnetic and very sexy. You strive to give off an air of charisma by being just a little bit mysterious. Scorpio ascendant usually gives darker features and an intense gaze. You are attracted to sensual types.

Sagittarius ascendant likes to be seen as optimistic, happy, worldly and interesting in their views on philosophy. You like to look always ready to take off. Sagittarius ascendant gives a sporty physique with large hands and bone structure. You are attracted to flirty, chatty types.

Capricorn ascendant likes to be seen as ambitious and goal-driven, always with a practical agenda to fix a problem. You like to be seen as prudent and trustworthy, never frivolous. Capricorn ascendant usually gives a solid build with square hands and lovely skin. You are attracted to sensitive, moody types.

Aquarius ascendant likes to be seen as doing things differently and as a lateral thinker. You like to dress a little eccentrically as an expression of your individuality. Friends are very important to you. Aquarius ascendant usually gives a bony appearance, with lovely legs and an aquiline nose. Your eyes appear sharp and intelligent. You are attracted to stylish types.

Pisces ascendant likes to be seen as very easy-going, with a dreamy nature that has better things to do than sit around all day in reality. You like to be idealistic and don't like to be bogged down in the practicalities of life. Pisces ascendant usually gives winsome, liquid eyes. You are attracted to organised, intellectual types.

Pars Fortuna

Glyph – ⊗

The Pars Fortuna (or the part of fortune) is a point in the chart derived from the positions of the Sun, the Moon and the ascendant. The Pars Fortuna is the most popular of over forty such parts used – these points are called arabic parts and they express relationships of distance and direction between three sensitive points in the chart.

The house in which the Pars Fortuna is positioned represents the area where the person's endeavours are most likely to come to fruition. The sign it is in indicates the best approach to those endeavours.

The 'fortune' is not necessarily materialistic or even tangible, although it can be. It depends very much on the sign and house location. Whether it is physical, intellectual, emotional or spiritual, cultivating this part of your personality will allow you to experience harmony and well-being.

Chiron

Glyph – ⚷

Chiron was discovered on 1 November 1977 by Charles T Kowal, who spotted an object inside the orbit of Uranus. On closer inspection, it appeared to be a significantly sized planet. But Chiron did not lend itself to such easy classification, and while the media went into a frenzy announcing the discovery of a tenth planet, cooler heads said that it was more likely to be a minor planet like Ceres, Eros and Hidalgo. Chiron was quietly given minor planet status.

Still, many astronomers had the niggling feeling that Chiron did not quite fit this classification either. For one thing, it appeared to be very bright for a minor planet such a long distance away. And its orbit was more than a little eccentric. When Chiron is closest to the Sun (the perihelion) it is actually closer than Saturn; at its furthermost point (the aphelion) it almost reaches Uranus's orbit.

When a tail was discovered behind Chiron, it was thought this unusual object must be a comet, though a comet so huge (more than 50,000 times the volume of an average comet) that perhaps it was an asteroid. Another unusual feature of Chiron compared with other comets is that, because of its enormity, it is actually collecting more ice and matter into its matrix as it goes. Usually comets burn off gas as they approach the Sun, only to pick up some of their body weight again out in the colder climes past Uranus. Chiron actually keeps most of its heft under a layer of dust as it approaches the Sun, so some of the gases never burn. Hence its amazing size, though how it became so big in the first place is unknown.

While the debate was raging about Chiron, something altogether different came into view. Its name is Damocles, and it posed similar problems to Chiron. Damocles' orbit of the Sun is even more eccentric; it heads out into the cold of the outer solar system, past Uranus, then does a quick U-turn and zooms back in, crossing the orbit of Mars. Because it is cutting such fine corners, its entire orbit takes only forty-one years, compared to Uranus' eighty-four years.

Now at least thirty-two objects of this type have been found. They have been called centaurs by astronomers—not quite asteroid, not quite comet, not quite minor planet.

Though no longer alone, Chiron is still unique in that it has minor planet status as well as short-period comet status. The other centaurs have not shown cometary behaviour, so they remain in the minor-planet category only, but the coma and tail of Chiron have deemed it a little bit different.

Mythology of Chiron

Chiron is often confused with the Sagittarian centaur. Centaurs were a mortal race, with the legs of a horse and the body of a man. Rowdy louts who were barely tolerated in Olympian society, they could drink all night and get up fresh as a daisy for a session of archery in the morning.

Chiron didn't have anything to do with this race; his centaur-like form was actually a defect from birth. He was Saturn's bastard son. Saturn fell in love with a sea-nymph, Philyra, but Saturn was married to Rhea and they had their own children including Pluto, Neptune and Jupiter.

To hide their illicit affair, Saturn and Philyra turned themselves into horses when they were together. This had unforseen consequences for their unborn child and when Philyra delivered Chiron, she was so ashamed of his centaur-like form that she abandoned the child on Mount Pelion and begged the gods to turn her into a tree.

The little baby Chiron didn't die, but he did grow up alone. He used all the hurt from his abandonment to throw himself into study and mastering the arts. He became a master musician and even the stones stopped to listen to his sorrowful tunes. He later became known to the Olympian community as a wise being and parents sent their sons to Chiron to be tutored.

Chiron mentored heroes such as Jason, Achilles and Hercules. His teachings synthesised the disciplines of the physical, spiritual and intellectual, because only by integrating all three does a person's true nature reveal itself. This teaching is still the basis of most vocational spiritual training.

Chiron was wounded by an arrow from the bow of Hercules. Hercules had been visiting the good centaur Pholus when a posse of nasty centaurs attacked them. Hercules chased the marauders, when Chiron himself was accidentally struck by one of Hercules' poisoned arrows. The wound was deep and would have been fatal, but since poor old Chiron was an immortal, he couldn't die, and its pain led him to a search for healing.

In his search for a cure, Chiron was the discoverer of medicine, which he then taught to others. After many years, Chiron gave up his immortality to Prometheus. Jupiter was so taken by the way that Chiron used his talents and abilities that he made a new constellation to honour the life of Chiron – Sagittarius.

What Chiron means in your chart

Chiron is still not used as a matter of course in astrological charts, but there is a growing feeling in the astrological community that it fills in some obvious gaps, and that its influence is quite unique. It has been included here so you can look at it in your chart and add to the growing ledger of knowledge in this exciting new area.

A newly discovered body like Chiron gives astrologers a whole realm of possibilities to consider. Often they first look at the myth surrounding the name to gain clues as to the meaning of the planet. Astronomers do not name planets flippantly. They carefully consider the myths that have gone before them, and their own instincts as to the nature of the planet.

Chiron was a bastard child, born with a birth defect and abandoned at birth, but he used his differences to help others find their place in the world. In this way, Chiron is seen as the planet of alienation, of where we find ourselves painfully at odds with what is perceived as 'normal'. Unlike Uranus, where we find a great deal of joy in our eccentricity, Chiron is associated with an affliction – both born (his birth defect) and made (his wound from Hercules) – that we must make peace with and find a way to use for our own benefit.

It is also where we find an integration of our spiritual, mental and emotional sides. The house where Chiron is placed can give us clues as to where we can achieve this union.

One way to tell the nature of a newly discovered body is to look at major events in the world around the same time. Chiron was sighted in 1977, when the building blocks were being laid for the biological revolution in cloning. At this time we discovered how to synthesise insulin and we mapped out the genome for a virus (an important precursor to the mapping of the human genome that is now giving us such massive advancements in medicine), the first human gene was cloned and we discovered how to synthesise a bacterial gene.

Our attitudes to birth and death were also changing rapidly, for example, precedents were set to allow parents to decide to disconnect comatose or brain-dead children from a respirator, thus releasing them from the pain of the material into the spiritual (think of Chiron's merciful release from the pain of his wound). As well, the first-reported commercial surrogate motherhood arrangement went ahead in the US, and the first 'test-tube baby', Louise Brown, was born as a result of IVF treatment.

What holds these discoveries together is not only their obvious links to life, death and healing, but that they also often came from a synthesis of two or more sciences.

Some key Chiron words have been identified as:

✦ Healing

✦ Integration and synthesis

✦ Maverick

✦ Questing

✦ Guiding

✦ Doorway or loophole

✦ Mentor

✦ Turning point

✦ Catalyst

✦ Stepping stone

✦ Passageway through a matrix

✦ Common ground

✦ Holistic

✦ Balance

✦ Mediator

✧ Koan (in Zen Buddhism)

✧ Synergy

How to read Chiron in your chart

The sign in which Chiron falls shows the way in which your affliction is dealt with and how you might deal with its effects.

The house in which Chiron falls shows where your affliction manifests itself.

Introduction to Planets in Signs

The planet's influence in a sign is how the energy (planet) shows itself through the filter of behaviour (sign). The planets in the signs should be read carefully and with particular care to weighting each influence properly.

Planets move slowly through the signs. Even the fastest-moving planet, the Moon, takes several days to pass through a sign. The three furthermost planets, Uranus, Neptune and Pluto, take so long to move out of signs that their influence is said to be generational rather than personal. Saturn and Jupiter also take a long time to move, so be careful when assigning their influence on a chart. The exception to this is when they are particularly well-aspected or if they are standing alone in the chart – then the sign plays a big part, as well as the house. Any planet that stands alone on the opposite side of the chart to a lot of activity, and is also well-aspected, will exert a lot of influence over the chart.

The Generational Planets

These planets move too slowly to say specific things about you as a person; rather they will tell more of the mood of your generation. Uranus takes seven years to go through a sign, Neptune almost fourteen years and Pluto takes an average of twenty-one years (Pluto's wobbly orbit makes its path less stable.)

Everyone born within a few days of your own birthday was probably born with the same planets in the same signs, so their charts should always be read with an eye for their aspects and with deference to the houses they reside in.

You will notice also that some planets in signs have the word 'exalted', 'fall', 'dignity' or 'detriment' following them. This means that, for example, some signs match the energy of certain planets so well that they are said to be in exaltation, or exalted. The opposite of this is fall, meaning that when a planet is in the sign opposite to the sign in which it finds exaltation, that planet's energy is stifled. Dignities are favourable positions, phases or aspects assumed by a planet. A planet is said to be in detriment when it is in the sign opposite of the sign that it rules. See the Glossary at the back of the book for a full description.

Aries

The sign of Aries is the sign of action, impetus and motivation. A planet in Aries will be in overdrive, its energy always apparent.

The Sun in Aries (exalted) is what we know as an Aries Sun sign, which means the entire character wants to be first with ideas, and is likely to be the motivating force behind any big plan. For a more in-depth look at the Sun in Aries, see the chapter on Aries earlier in the book.

The Moon in Aries are emotionally assertive and powerful people, who like to be in the driver's seat in their domestic environments. Women with this position like to be first, men with this position are attracted to powerful women.

Mercury in Aries is a mind in action, fast-thinking and talking; this placement attacks study and information with a voracious energy. Self-willed and confident with their thoughts, these people can appear arrogant.

Venus in Aries (detriment) is action in the expression of affection, and these people have a deep-seated desire for romantic attention. Passionate in love, they are also very wanting (Elizabeth Taylor and Marilyn Monroe have this placement) and they demand constant excitement. Once the first spark of passion dies, these people tend to move on or start an argument to liven things up.

Mars in Aries (dignity) expresses the driving energy of Mars through the personal style of action (Aries), and these people have loads of energy that they express in constant activity. They are assertive with great leadership ability, but they can also be careless, impatient and impulsive.

Jupiter in Aries people find luck when they charge right in with the intention to get it done. Jupiter is also our religious and philosophical beliefs. Jupiter in this sign means we get bored with the pernickety details and are attracted to easily consumed religion and ideals.

Saturn in Aries (fall) means that to feel safe and secure people with this placement must take the initiative. Never tell a Saturn in Aries to 'just wait here' in a crisis – if they do obey (not likely anyway) they will have torn all their hair out and be about to extract their fingernails by the time you get back.

Uranus in Aries is the energy of independence and innovation in the sign of action and impetus – Uranus likes it here. Excessive haste can be a problem, and a few accidents are likely, but this is a great placement for new inventions and shocking new ideas.

Neptune in Aries boosts the imagination. The imagination is excitable and vibrant.

Pluto in Aries is a can-do generation, and Pluto makes motivation very strong. It means people will come up with extreme and energetic solutions to problems.

Taurus

Planets placed here will take a longer time to get moving, but their forward motion is much more difficult to stop once begun.

The Sun in Taurus are deliberate, materially oriented and not a little bit stubborn. For more information on the Sun in Taurus, see the chapter on Taurus earlier in the book.

The Moon in Taurus (exaltation) is emotional energy expressed in this fertile, earthy sign. The Moon is where we can be moody, but the inertia effect of Taurus can minimise this, though it can ensure that when sadness does set in, it can be very hard to throw off.

Mercury in Taurus likes to think about practical problems thoroughly and considers abstract thought or musing a complete waste of time. Attitudes are generally conservative and hard to budge.

Venus in Taurus (dignity) is decadence plus, and people with this sign crave sensual experience. They love to be massaged and touched and they always have dessert.

Mars in Taurus is practical and consistent, and people with this placement will always get the job done, if in the least imaginative but most sensible way. This Mars may take longer to start, but won't stop until the job is done.

Jupiter in Taurus thinks that the bigger the problem, the more money you should throw at it. Their philosophy of life will tend towards the materialistic rather than the spiritual.

Saturn in Taurus people need to know where their next meal is coming from to feel secure. Once this is taken care of, they can take on the world.

Uranus in Taurus (fall) sees the erratic nature of Uranus curbed by the Taurean desire to consider all things slowly before action.

Neptune in Taurus sees the dreams and ideals of a generation tending towards material things.

Pluto in Taurus (detriment) is a generation obsessed with material and sensual pleasures. The last time Pluto was in Taurus was from about 1853 to 1883, the generation whose push for material progress led into the Industrial Age.

Gemini

Gemini is the sign of communication and any planet here will tend to express itself through communicating. This sign is also adept at doing two things at once.

The Sun in Gemini makes a person restless and skilled at gathering information for the purpose of communication. For more information on the Sun in Gemini see the chapter on Gemini earlier in the book.

The Moon in Gemini means an emotional need to communicate, and people here feel better once they have aired how they feel. They are probably quite good at getting their feelings across – their faces will express a thousand words before the mouth even begins to form them. This person's mother was probably quite chatty.

Mercury in Gemini (dignity) makes the ability to communicate easy and the collection and dissemination of information a priority. Clarity of thought is a feature, but this placement could also mean a gossiper.

Venus in Gemini likes variety in romance. They tend to distance themselves from emotional entanglements by dissecting the situation intellectually.

Mars in Gemini can spread themselves a little thin, but they are good at putting their energy into several projects at once. Women will attract men who talk a lot and like to be on the move.

Jupiter in Gemini (detriment) can aid people in learning different languages and communicating on the world stage.

Saturn in Gemini people feel secure when they have freedom to move around, and when the lines of communication are open. They feel very insecure working under management that keeps them in the dark.

Uranus in Gemini will shock people by expressing weird, socially unacceptable ideas. The last generation born with this placement (1943–49) fuelled the social upheavals of the 1960s.

Neptune in Gemini people like to verbalise their fantasy world and to dash from one fantasy to the next.

Pluto in Gemini means regeneration in the area of ideas. The last generation born with this placement began the modern art movement, suffrage for women and made huge break-throughs in the sciences. In this placement, Pluto burns the old ideas and starts afresh.

Cancer

This is the sign of moods and mood swings. Any planet placed here will express itself through the emotions.

The Sun in Cancer is nurturing and sustaining when positive, whining and grasping when negative. For more information on the Sun in Cancer see the chapter on Cancer earlier in the book.

The Moon in Cancer (dignity) is emotion expressed through the home and family. This is a very sensitive, percep-tive placement, and sensual impressions last longer as memories in the mind than words or pictures. Action is a good antidote to the moodiness inherent in this placement.

Mercury in Cancer people have long memories, especially for sentimental events. They are swayed by arguments with emotional appeal and their thinking is naturally compas-sionate. They are often accused of being illogical, but their logic is from the heart rather than the head, so attempts at critical thinking will seem superficial.

Venus in Cancer people need a comfortable home to make them happy, as this is where they express their creativity. They are reserved socially but are prone to make their partner the object of considerable attention. They place a lot of emphasis on the success of their relationships and can become quite maudlin when things don't seem to be going well.

Mars in Cancer (fall) is action dominated by the emotions and moods – these guys can be just a little highly strung, and prone to the occasional outburst. Women in this sign are very strong. This placement can lead to more than a few arguments.

Jupiter in Cancer (exalted) is good luck in exaltation, and that has to be fun! Jupiter here emphasises the virtues of compassion, and conventional religion and morals. It protects during childhood and retirement. Just remember, good luck can be squandered, so use it wisely.

Saturn in Cancer (detriment) looks for a stable home in order to feel secure. They may have trouble expressing emotions.

Uranus in Cancer can lend extra difficulty in committing to an emotional relationship. The expression of the emotions can tend towards the hysterical if this is not balanced well by other placements in the chart.

Neptune in Cancer means the fantasies of this generation are more to do with emotional issues, and with the home and the homeland.

Pluto in Cancer is obsessive about the home. The last generation to have this (1914–39) ensured that the suburban sprawl became a reality.

Leo

Leo is the sign of creativity and self-expression. Any planet placed here will tend to express itself dramatically.

The Sun in Leo (dignity) is seen here in its full glory. Leos are dramatic and always centre-stage. For more information on the Sun in Leo see the chapter on Leo earlier in the book.

The Moon in Leo expresses their emotions with more than a touch of dramatic flair. The home is their stage, so life is never dull. Women with this placement are particularly breathtaking.

Mercury in Leo makes up their mind very quickly, and often without all the facts. They are usually very quick to grasp the big picture. They have a high opinion of their mental agility, which may not be justified. They argue with an appeal to your better nature, rather than bothering with logic or details.

Venus in Leo people have love as their stage, and you are playing Romeo to their Juliet. Be prepared for slamming doors and passionate make-up embraces, but you may find yourself looking for the hidden camera, wondering whether this performance is for you alone.

Mars in Leo like to argue with arm-waving gesticulations and dramatic exits. Their grand schemes are awe-inspiring, but they won't put up with anyone finding fault. Depending on the rest of the chart, the schemes may sometimes be impractical or lacking in substance.

Jupiter in Leo can make for a big spender – of someone else's money if they can find it.

Saturn in Leo (detriment) needs others' respect and admiration to feel secure. They are often very conservative in their creative endeavours.

Uranus in Leo (detriment) in the generation born 1955–62 is eccentricity in the sign of leadership. It means questioning of the status quo, and this generation will solve problems by changing the leadership.

Neptune in Leo (exalted) in the generation born 1914–29 made jazz popular, and later rock 'n' roll. Leo likes to turn fantasies into an aggressive, creative form. This placement of Neptune produces a generation that can fight for their dreams and ideals, and was the generation that instigated World War II.

Pluto in Leo in the generation born 1939–57 is the generation commonly referred to as the baby-boomers, a very powerful group if only for their sheer weight of numbers. An obsession with youth marks this generation, and a need for absolute power saw the emergence of the Cold War, many dictatorships, but also many democracies. Pluto in Leo likes to be extravagant in one area to the detriment of others, and treats material goods as status symbols.

Virgo
Virgo is the sign for details and the sign of work, so any planet placed here will express itself in the details, and in work and service of some sort.

The Sun in Virgo is communication with particular attention to details. This sign is concerned with information dissemination in a more practical, earthy manner than its airy counterpart Gemini. The Sun in Virgo is examined in more detail (that should make you happy!) in the chapter on Virgo earlier in the book.

The Moon in Virgo is emotionally critical of themselves, and they tend to underestimate their abilities. The Moon in this sign is an image of purity, and you like to keep yourself emotionally unsullied. This can make you a little shy and introverted.

Mercury in Virgo (dignity and exalted) is a powerful brain with the capacity for clear thought in the face of the most tangled issues. People with this placement pick everything apart, then put it back together into its most logical form. They are pedants in thought, and can be impatient when other people's thinking seems a little patchy. They make great bureaucrats because they have no fear of red tape, but they also make excellent lawyers and investigative journalists.

Venus in Virgo (fall) tend to categorise people as a matter of course and can appear to have a very high standard when it comes to friends. This critical approach often comes from a lack of self-confidence.

Mars in Virgo means a flair and energy for details and work. This makes them valuable in many areas of life, but especially in craft and work.

Jupiter in Virgo (detriment) is idealism in an orderly structure, but it is also detail and the big picture, which can cancel each other out. They like their philosophies to have a practical purpose.

Saturn in Virgo may lack self-confidence, but could eventually turn this around to be quite sure of their abilities and talents. They feel secure when working, especially if serving someone's purpose. This is a diligent placement, but they must find their own reserves of confidence, and turn what they learn from self-criticism into armour.

Uranus in Virgo will make people look for improvements in their lives in the small significant details. This generation did not invent the car, but they put in suspension, air-con and a rear spoiler (well, it might have been a Moon in Leo who came up that little flourish, but you get the idea). This also means a revolution in health, and the last generation to have this (1962–68) was responsible for the health-shop revolution.

Neptune in Virgo (detriment) will mean compassion and confusion, where fantasies are reduced to just getting and keeping a job. The most recent generation with this placement was born in 1928–43.

Pluto in Virgo (exalted) saw the potency of this placement increased by the subsequent transit of Uranus through Virgo. This generation (1956–71) has made many breakthroughs in medicine by rediscovering the mind-body connection through the discovery of hormones and brain chemistry. It was also a time of greater power for the working class.

Libra

Libra is the sign of balance in judgment, beauty, art, charm and the immediate social set. It is a reactive sign and any planet found in Libra will show this as well.

The Sun in Libra (fall) Balance is all important to Libra, and Librans tend to counterbalance their surroundings. For more information on the Sun in Libra see the chapter on Libra earlier in the book.

The Moon in Libra needs harmony in the home, both in beauty and in vibe. They need emotional calm to feel good, and they tend to avoid confrontation to this end.

Mercury in Libra is an active mind that sees both sides of everything, and is very good at strategy and at reconciling opposing forces. They can diffuse an argument by seeming to agree and disagree all at once. This can be an indecisive placement and they tend to think better with someone around to bounce ideas off.

Venus in Libra (dignity) people value appearances and try to make a good impression through clothing, grooming and nice manners. They value relationships as a creative form of expression and can place too much importance on this aspect of their life.

Mars in Libra (detriment) will generally create indecision. Mars likes just the one thing to go straight ahead with, but Libra can see many sides and options. They are good strategists though (they can see the multiple results of any decision) and are excellent at moderating and reconciling other people's conflicts. They are also quite talented at chess.

Jupiter in Libra likes to have a partner around when philosophising or making big decisions. Jupiter is your intuitive sense of the big picture, and Libra tends to slow that down by processing through the mind and weighing up each pro and con, but the philosophy will be the better for it.

Saturn in Libra (exalted) must have ideas neatly balanced to feel comfortable. They rely on having a partner in order to feel secure in any sphere (marriage, a best friend or a business partner), and they have a great fear of going it alone.

Uranus in Libra is a generation that hates to be crowded in relationships and demands personal space for their own interests. They like to do marriage a little unconventionally.

Neptune in Libra was born 1943–56 and is a generation that fantasised and idealised relationships, love, peace, harmony and justice – they were the kids of the 'California Dreaming' and when the world asked them to go to war in

Vietnam, in true Libra form, they pulled the scales back to love-ins and flower power. Most of this generation were also born with Pluto in Leo, so they tried to marry their love of peace and harmony with an obsession with individuality – a difficult mix.

Pluto in Libra was born 1972–84 and will be obsessed with art and beauty (expect this generation to pretty up the cities) and justice for everyone. Once this generation moves into positions of power, energy will be put into bridging the gap between rich and poor. Marriage is taken very seriously by this group, but not in its traditional form, as Pluto tends to destroy to build anew. There will probably also be reform in the law.

Scorpio

Scorpio is the sign of extremes, and planets in this sign are intensified.

The Sun in Scorpio are the soothsayers of the zodiac, intense characters who have great insight into the underpinnings of the personality and the universe. For more information on the Sun in Scorpio see the chapter on Scorpio earlier in the book.

The Moon in Scorpio (fall) has emotions in the sign of extremes. If your partner has this, make sure you always get home from work on time, because their suspicious heart will have you locked in a passionate embrace with Cheryl from accounts before you can explain you stopped to pick up some milk. Expect to have a great sex life though, with a few dramatic mood swings on the way.

Mercury in Scorpio is the original 'suspicious mind'. This brain takes great joy in looking through the cracks in the door. They can spot a weakness in an opponent ten feet away, and pay no heed to compassion when seeking a remark that can take your breath away with its nastiness. These people are intuitive.

Venus in Scorpio is passionate in relationships, and this is the sign of the dark temptress. This placement can be possessive and jealous when it comes to their partner, and if it doesn't work out, there will be great bitterness. Venus in Scorpio finds beauty in the underworld, so can find themselves entangled in illicit pleasures.

Mars in Scorpio brings emotional commitment into action. These people never take a course of action lightly, and will adhere to the plan until the end. Other parts of the chart deal with whether the plan is well-thought out or even worth doing, but once activated there is very little that can stop this sign.

Jupiter in Scorpio is feeling happy and at home in the sign of birth, death and regeneration. Sound like the *Addams Family*? It simply means they are attracted to all things hidden and mysterious (they probably love a good murder mystery) and have luck in healing others and uncovering secrets.

Saturn in Scorpio needs a sexual relationship to feel secure, and has a deep-seated, almost irrational fear of the unknown and the underworld. Still, the fact that you are reading this about yourself means you are well on the way to conquering this fear – keep up the good work!

Uranus in Scorpio (exalted) is the planet of the unexpected exalted in the sign of sex, death and religion. This placement is responsible for this generation's (born 1975–81) renewed interest in the occult (and consequently, television shows like *Buffy* and *Charmed* being marketed directly at them). They like to experiment with sex and taboos, and made the accoutrements of body piercing and PVC very fashionable when they were in their teens.

Neptune in Scorpio is the generation (born 1956–1970) that dreamed about rebirth and regeneration, but Neptune is actually wishy-washy about getting things done. Manifestations of these Scorpio-like dreams included dramatic violence and explicit sex in films. The illusion of this age was that people could be reborn through drugs.

Pluto in Scorpio (dignity) This planet destroys to build anew, so we will see this generation (born 1984–95) rewrite the book on sex and bring the biological revolution to its full fruition, including experimenting with human cloning.

Sagittarius
This is the most open sign in the zodiac.

The Sun in Sagittarius is clumsy, but with a lot of luck, these people make it through life by the skin of their teeth with a smile on their face. Travel and higher learning are important to these people, they never lie and have no tact. For more information on the Sun in Sagittarius see the chapter on Sagittarius earlier in the book.

The Moon in Sagittarius needs emotional freedom and hates boundaries in matters of the heart. They have an optimistic heart that believes everything will turn out all right. Travel and study feed their souls.

Mercury in Sagittarius (detriment) likes to think big, and becomes frustrated if asked to think about details. To them, the philosophy of an idea is the important thing, they don't really care if it is practical or not. This mind tends to pick an intuitive path through information, rather than stopping to look at the details.

Venus in Sagittarius are idealistic in love, and need a friend as much as a partner. They like to wander in a relationship both philosophically and physically (but they probably won't cheat, as they are fairly conservative about that), and they find beauty in study and travel. Love-making style is pretty straightforward in this placement, and they are best off falling in love with a friend.

Mars in Sagittarius set their sights so far, they may lose their goal. Action is focused on the big picture and they like to use their legs to get where they want to be. Travelling is a manner in which this placement uses its energy.

Jupiter in Sagittarius (dignity) can be so lucky with this placement that they come to rely on it to get them out of self-made predicaments. Whichever house this planet and sign is in, is likely to be where they lead an especially charmed existence.

Saturn in Sagittarius is a conservative attitude to philosophy, beliefs and foreign cultures. This placement feels most secure when there is freedom of speech and they know what is going on.

Uranus in Sagittarius Uranus here (the generation born 1981–88) loves to have eccentric principles, tell shocking stories and shock with their philosophies. Karl Marx had this placement.

Neptune in Sagittarius The fantasies of this generation (born 1970–84) concentrated on philosophy and foreign cultures.

Neptune can fog the philosophical visions of its contemporaries, and it can turn principles into illusions. Karl Marx had this placement also.

Pluto in Sagittarius in the generation born 1995–2008 is obsessed with long journeys. The space race will be back on the agenda when this generation takes power.

Capricorn
This sign will put any planet to work in its signature organised and disciplined manner.

The Sun in Capricorn shows control, organisation and planning. These people need an ambition to build their character on. For more information on the Sun in Capricorn see the chapter on Capricorn earlier in the book.

The Moon in Capricorn (detriment) is controlled emotion, at least to the outside world. These people feel as deeply as anyone else, but they would never cry in public. There is an emotional need to be organised and get things done.

Mercury in Capricorn is highly perceptive in all things tangible. These people make great engineers and mathematicians, or in any profession where the goal posts are not likely to move. The senses are heightened in this position. As children, their mothers could never sneak medicine into their orange juice.

Venus in Capricorn seeks status and security in relationships. These people are not above marrying for money. This placement approaches love pragmatically, and would never get involved in a long-distance love affair.

Mars in Capricorn (exalted) has deep reserves of energy that they put to considerable use. This placement has the great ability to pace themselves, and they are best suited to working in a practical area with obvious results at the end of each day.

Jupiter in Capricorn (fall) may mean material wealth is important, and this sign can give luck in this area.

Saturn in Capricorn (dignity) emphasises materialism and these people fear not having possessions.

Uranus in Capricorn in the generation born 1988–95 is extreme attitudes in the sign of conservative values (the previous generation to have this placement was responsible for the upright and uptight Victorian era). It was also a time when materialism was taken to new heights.

Neptune in Capricorn is practical imagination based on the world around us, one that is useful in science. This generation (born 1984–98) will dream of wealth and fame. This is a rather productive placement for this not particularly productive planet.

Pluto in Capricorn Revolt in the establishment, Pluto is death and rebirth in the sign of authority. People born with this placement (1760–70) inspired the French and American Revolutions.

Aquarius
This sign makes every planet act with an eccentric flair and a social conscience.

The Sun in Aquarius (detriment) means visionaries and eccentrics, genius or craziness – people with the Sun in Aquarius seem to skip to a different beat. For more information on the Sun in Aquarius see the chapter on Aquarius earlier in the book.

The Moon in Aquarius is very assertive feminine energy, and is often connected to the women's liberation movement. People with this placement nurture from a distance and will gravitate towards relationships with people with a similar tendency, like the Moon in Sagittarius.

Mercury in Aquarius need to learn by themselves, and can seem to learn in a vacuum. Information is processed rapidly and dispassionately, with an eye for the unusual.

Venus in Aquarius rebels against anything or anyone who might want to domesticate them – they like to have intellectual partnerships and they need to be friends first and foremost with love interests. They can seem a little calculating in love.

Mars in Aquarius seeks to act with their intellect, and these people will come across as aggressive in their thinking. They like to think about new ways to sort out old problems, which can be a bit hit and miss. Some old ways are ripe for change, other ways are done in the traditional manner because it is tried and true. Mars in Aquarius tends not to make that definition.

Jupiter in Aquarius is attracted to unorthodox belief systems, maybe even cults. The beliefs and ethical systems these people adhere to are very original, and may even be systems they have come up with themselves. There is an emphasis on the creation and promotion of new ideas.

Saturn in Aquarius (dignity) needs authoritative opinions to feel secure. They also need a lot of friends and acquaintances, and fear being lonely.

Uranus in Aquarius (dignity) The union movement (a very Aquarian idea) took off with the last generation (born

1912–20) to have this placement. That group fought for the eight-hour day. This generation (born 1995–2002) is likely to take the very Uranus concept of technology and reinvent and extend it. Humanitarian and democratic ideals, progressive social change and scientific advances are likely when this planet is at work here in its home sign.

Neptune in Aquarius (fall) This group (born 1998–2012) will dream of freedom and independence. Many of the generation that fought the American Civil War had this placement. This group is more likely to dream of freedom in a more abstract sense, and come up with more technological solutions. Quirkiness and individuality will be highly prized.

Pluto in Aquarius Liberty, Fraternity and Equality, the calling card of the French Revolution, has a distinctly Aquarian ring to it, and no wonder. Pluto, the planet of death and rebirth, was in the sign of radical change and equality for all people, Aquarius, at that time.

Pisces

It has been said that planets in Pisces act like they are on drugs. On what sort of drugs depends on the aspects.

The Sun in Pisces can be alone in a crowded room, and that is just fine with them. Characterised by a faraway look, they are sympathetic to the point of empathy and emotional to the point of drowning. They are full of the wisdom of the universe but usually lack the energy to convey it. For more information on the Sun in Pisces see the chapter on Pisces earlier in the book.

The Moon in Pisces is a highly sympathetic, sensitive and shy placement. These people treat their home like a refuge, and they would do well to develop thicker skins for their own peace of mind.

Mercury in Pisces (detriment and fall) have artistic minds that remember in astonishing detail if an emotional impression is made on them – police love them as witnesses to the crime scene, yet though they can tell you the colour of the burglar's left nostril, they can't remember the name of the street their grandparents lived on.

Venus in Pisces (exalted) increases the artistic sensibility, but can bring difficulties in relationships. People with this placement often have trouble marrying their romantic notions of the dashing prince with the reality slouching on the couch eating baked beans from the can and watching the wrestling. Pisces wants to be self-sacrificing, but in this position people may be so caught up in their own conflicting feelings that they can forget about the other person's feelings altogether.

Mars in Pisces has most of the energy going into the imagination, and people with this placement are left with little energy to carry out their imaginings. It can be useful in the arts.

Jupiter in Pisces (dignity) sees the imagination enlarged in this position, and these people have the ability to grasp, even if only for a moment, the Very Big Picture. Awe-inspiring though that might be, this is not a terribly practical position, although it is excellent for musical talent and dancing – it adds an ancient bacchanal quality to the energy.

Saturn in Pisces makes people very vulnerable and sensitive, and particularly worried about matters of faith. They feel better when their intuitive powers are on track, and they can fear losing their grip on reality.

Uranus in Pisces Though so radical in other signs, Uranus finds it difficult to manifest itself in a physical manner here. Genius in the imaginings tends to stay in the imaginings. This generation (born 1919–27) did bring us Walt Disney and animation, though.

Neptune in Pisces (dignity) increases the imagination, but it is also very subtle. Daydreaming is intensified. When this planet is afflicted there is danger of self-undoing in drink or drugs.

Pluto in Pisces (fall) The generations born with this placement (early 1800s, next here in 2043) are obsessive in their fantasising and drug-taking. Opium was popular in the 1800s – I wonder what will be the drug of undoing in 2043?

The Houses

A house is a term used by astrologers to define the twelve sectors of the sky that clearly delineate the twelve main areas in our life. Each planet will fall into one of these houses. You may have many planets in one house, and many houses without planets, or they may be beautifully spread across the whole chart. The empty houses have a meaning as well. So, when you are reading a chart, you will be looking carefully at the position of the planets and noting which house and which sign they are in.

Houses One to Six are concerned with a person's self-development and expression, in other words, their internal issues. Houses Seven to Twelve are concerned with how a person relates to others and learns to cooperate with people and forces outside themself, in other words, their external issues.

The difference in meaning between a house and a sign is quite subtle. For instance, what is the difference between a planet in the First House and a planet in Aries? The answer is that the house indicates *where* a planet will have influence, and the sign is *how* a planet will have influence. The house is usually a place or a thing. The sign is usually a method.

The three main components to a chart can be broken down in this way:

✧ A planet is WHAT energy needs to be expressed or understood.

✧ A sign is HOW that planet's energy shows itself as a psychological drive or a personal style.

✧ A house is WHERE that planet's energy comes up as a situation, or in what areas of life it occurs.

There are various interpretations that can be made in a chart as to what a house represents:

1. A house represents where to express a planet's energy. This is the most common and most important interpretation. For instance, if you have Mars in the Seventh House (in other words, the planet of action and anger in the house of love and beauty), you will be restless in relationships, anxious to start them, but quick to move on.

2. A house represents where a planet's energy is used as a strategy. For instance, if you have Mars in the Seventh House this means you will use aggression as a strategy in starting, continuing and ending relationships.

3. A house represents an area of life where the planet's energy will manifest itself as an event or a person. For instance if you have Mars in the Seventh House, Mars will manifest itself as a hot-headed partner with whom you have a lot of passionate arguments.

4. A house represents a place where the planet's lessons are learned. For instance, with Mars in the Seventh House, the lesson Mars has to give us is to use aggression as a positive force in relationships rather than letting it build into frustration. This person could be calm and considered in all other aspects of her life, but lets her temper get in the way of her relationships. Once she learns to use this energy in a constructive way, she will succeed like nothing else in her relationship.

A house can also represent a physical manifestation of a process of the mind (such as an illness or a body feature), or where to direct that energy (such as a career path). As you can see, placements can be interpreted in two or more ways. The first example is the most common way to interpret a house and its planet, but the others are equally valid.

And these interpretations are not mutually exclusive. When reading a chart, one interpretation will have more of a ring of truth to it than others, but all should be evident in some way.

As a novice in chart reading, it is probably best to commit interpretation number 1 to memory, and slowly add the others as you become more accustomed to reading charts.

Planets in the Houses

Following is a description of the twelve houses, with a summary of interpretations of the planets in the different houses. These interpretations are by no mean exhaustive, and if you have been reading attentively you should be able to draw your own conclusions – so be brave, have a good guess and see how you go. By all means look each of your planets up, but learn to trust your own reading as well.

The First House
The First House is the house of the personal appearance, it is how you want to be, rather than how you are. It is associated with the sign Aries and the planet Mars. It is how you want to look in physical appearance and personal style; the image you maintain; your look, moves, gestures, body language, habitual movements; how you appear to others on a superficial or first-impression level; the image you project to others who know you personally (but it is the Tenth House that will show how you are known by your public image or reputation); how you may have presented yourself as a child; and the mask your inner soul wears to show itself in the outer world.

When people find out you are interested in astrology, they will invariably ask, 'Well, what am I then?' If you don't know them well, you will invariably pick their First House influences, rather than their Sun sign. No amount of explaining about the influence of the First House will convince someone that you actually can't judge a person's Sun sign on face value, but you can have a pretty good go at their ascendant and their First House.

The First House is usually referred to as the house of the self. It sits in the east and was where the Sun rose on the day of your birth, so it is the house of sunrise and new beginnings. This is focused on the individual: the self and the voyage of discovery that defines every personality, looking at such questions as who are you? what will you become? how do you realise your potential?

The First House is about our approach to life and the individual qualities we refer to as our personality. The packaging is also governed by the First House – the physical body, the way in which we present ourselves, the head and face.

The First House shows your outward character traits. Any planet in the First House will give you the outward traits of the sign that this planet rules. A planet in the First House will be instrumental in how that person sees himself and how others see him. A planet in the First House will be very evident in the childhood years, and what we believe our personality to be until we find the motivation of our Sun sign. For example, if your little Sagittarian child seems as shy as a mouse, is very secretive and would prefer to play alone, she probably has Pluto in the First House, which gives her the appearance of a Scorpio child. She will not bloom into her rough-and-tumble Sagittarian ways until the teen years, and sometimes even later.

The ruler of the First House is also said to be the ruler of the whole chart. Later in this chapter we talk about how to correctly weight a chart. The chart ruler **may** have more influence than the other planets.

A sign in the First House is known as the ascendant and is instrumental in the first impression we have of someone physically, their type of body, the shape of their face, and so forth. For instance, you could be a Gemini with a Taurus ascendant, so instead of being born with the classic Gemini streamlined sporty body, you will be born in the Taurean model, with a sluggish metabolism.

The Sun in the First House gives you the traits of Leo. You like to be seen as dramatic and attention-loving and the centre of the action at all times. People are attracted by your flair.

The Moon in the First House gives you the traits of Cancer. You like to be seen as emotional, moody and perceptive. People are attracted by your caring nature.

Mercury in the First House gives you the traits of Gemini and Virgo. You like to be seen as curious and communicative. People are attracted by your conversation.

Venus in the First House gives you the traits of Libra and Taurus. You like to be seen as artistic, fair and just a little self-indulgent. People are attracted by your charm and sensuality.

Mars in the First House gives you the traits of Aries. You like to be seen as the action person; 'attack' and 'take charge' are your key words. People are attracted by your zesty energy.

Jupiter in the First House gives you the traits of Sagittarius. You like to be seen as optimistic, lucky and with a tendency to say the first thing that pops into your head. People are attracted by your happy smile.

Saturn in the First House gives you the traits of Capricorn. You like to be seen as ambitious, well-organised and cautious. People are attracted by your level-headedness.

Uranus in the First House gives you the traits of Aquarius. You like to be seen as independent, an intellectual and just a little bit weird. People are attracted by your unusual clothes.

Neptune in the First House gives you the traits of Pisces. You like to be seen as trusting, imaginative and dreamy. People are attracted by your liquid eyes.

Pluto in the First House gives you the traits of Scorpio. You like to be seen as intense, mysterious and intuitive. People are attracted by your emotional strength.

The Second House

The Second House reflects your attitudes about the material world, your philosophy towards money, possessions, finances and your earning and spending capacity. It is associated with the sign Taurus and the planet Venus.

Planets that fall in the Second House indicate your attitudes towards wealth and material goods, whether you are a scrooge or spendthrift, a miser or a two-bob millionaire. They will also indicate how and where you are likely to spend your money – on yourself, on your children or on setting up soup kitchens for the needy.

On a deeper level, this house also reveals your sense of self-worth (or self-wealth). This house deals with what a person values, both within themselves and outside themselves. It signifies where your emotional and financial security lie, and its sign and planet will show you whether you value financial security over emotional security or vice versa.

The Sun in the Second House will focus the conscious awareness on money and possessions. Possessions are very important to someone with this placement, and they may be used to compensate for a lack of self-worth.

The Moon in the Second House will make money and the sense of self-worth fluctuate as if pulled by the tides – make sure you put some aside when the tide is high.

Mercury in the Second House will mean communication is important to your sense of self-worth and increases the chance that your income will depend on your communication skills.

Venus in the Second House is the planet of love in the house of possessions. Beautiful and artistic things are what you value, romance is where you find self-worth.

Mars in the Second House is easy come, easy go. Mars thinks money is for making and spending, not for hoarding.

Jupiter in the Second House gives you a happy-go-lucky attitude to money. That doesn't mean you will be rich, just that you know the money will turn up when you most need it, so there is no need to stress about it.

Saturn in the Second House is what we regard as important, so important that we are fearful we are going to blow it. With this placement you fear poverty, and will do anything to avoid it.

Uranus in the Second House will ensure you never get paid in a usual way. Freelancers, actors and people paid on commission often have this one, receiving lump sums and then nothing for months.

Neptune in the Second House dreams about being rich, but that is where the money stays – in their dreams. Guilt is commonly associated with money in this placement.

Pluto in the Second House means, with this planet of extremes, that money is either an obsession or absolutely of no importance. You are either a millionaire or a hobo.

The Third House
The Third House describes your relationship to your siblings and your early schooling. It is associated with the sign Gemini and the planet Mercury.

It will describe how you relate to your siblings, such as whether you fight like cats and dogs, or unite together against the enemy. It describes your neighbours in a similar manner. It also describes how we learned to relate to our peers at school and at home, and thus it describes how we get along with our workmates and colleagues now.

It describes how we were educated in our early life. If you experienced a difficult time at school, have a good look in your Third House for complications. As it describes our early schooling, so it describes how we now process language and how our brain retains information. It shows in what style you communicate, whether you are calm and lucid or frantic and confused.

The Third House also relates to short trips, although this is not so important in a natal chart, but is more useful when working out 'transitions' and using astrology for forecasting.

The Sun in the Third House is where you want admiration, and this placement means you want it through communication. This will make you appear like a Gemini in this regard. At least one sibling will be a show-off.

The Moon in the Third House means emotions are communicated easily. At least one sibling will be an emotional type.

Mercury in the Third House is at home here. This makes people very good at school and they excel in verbal and writing skills. At least one sibling is a chatterbox.

Venus in the Third House knows how to charm with words. At least one sibling will be a charmer as well.

Mars in the Third House wastes no time telling it like it is so that they can move on to the next battle. At least one sibling will be aggressive.

Jupiter in the Third House means communications are cheerful and free-flowing, but there's a tendency to talk big and tell too much. Relations with siblings are happy.

Saturn in the Third House is cautious in communication to the point of being constipated, and this placement can be the cause of a speech impediment in your youth. Older siblings picked on you, while younger siblings relied on you too much.

Uranus in the Third House tends to say and write shocking things. At least one sibling will be a little eccentric.

Neptune in the Third House is imaginative in communication, especially good for artistic pursuits, but no good for accounting. At least one sibling will be a dreamy type.

Pluto in the Third House gives your communications great and influential power – use them wisely. Relations with your siblings are extreme, either love or hate with nothing in between.

The Fourth House

The key concerns of the Fourth House are the home, the home circumstances, the family and caring for somebody.

The Fourth House is closely associated with Cancer and the Moon.

The relationship with the stronger parent figure is a major feature of this house. This could be either the mother or father, but usually it is the parent who had the most influence over your growing up.

The Fourth House is about our sense of belonging, how we conduct ourselves in private, and about our childhood conditioning. An analogy is made between the home, the womb and the grave, thus the Fourth House is about the manner in which we enter and leave life. It reflects the first few years of your life and, paradoxically, the last years, and will point to what you will become as you get older.

It is not only about our family home, but it is about the home we set up for our own family, and the values we intend to pass on to our children. Are we sentimental about the home, are meal times strict or is the home used as a place to sleep and nothing more? It shows the 'feel' of your home and how you tend to act there.

A planet in the Fourth House will reflect, among other things, our background and our views on family values. For instance, Mercury in the Fourth House indicates a background where learning was important. It may also mean a rational approach to family affairs and an unsentimental approach to the home.

The Sun in the Fourth House rules the roost. The home is ostentatious and just a little gaudy and a tribute to your family life, with lots of framed pictures of family hanging about. Your influential parent is outgoing and vivacious.

The Moon in the Fourth House has a more potent power, because the Moon's home is here. Home is your refuge, and your family life is paramount. Your influential parent is moody and emotional.

Mercury in the Fourth House means home is a hubbub of communications with talkback on the radio competing with the TV, the computer, the chatter of children and the phone ringing. Retirees like to talk and write, a good placement for finally getting around to writing those memoirs. Your influential parent is a talker and a traveller.

Venus in the Fourth House means home life is harmonious and beautiful, filled with tasteful furnishings. Retirement is comfortable. Your influential parent is charming and self-indulgent.

Mars in the Fourth House means you will take up jogging when all your friends have retired to the front porch. Home is where you are most active, energetic and argumentative. Conflict rules here. Your influential parent is aggressive and argumentative.

Jupiter in the Fourth House means a large house with a great view, with a tendency to travel and study in your retirement. You were always just a little bit spoiled at home. This is an extremely good placement for a comfortable life. Your influential parent is a jolly type who seems to know everything.

Saturn in the Fourth House leads to a fear of domestic instability which makes you work hard to establish a stable, permanent home. This placement can mean that your childhood home was unstable, and you determine this will not be the case for your family. Your influential parent is very distant.

Uranus in the Fourth House means your home and family life are probably a little unusual. You will develop eccentric opinions as you get older. Your influential parent is very independent, brilliant or just plain crazy.

Neptune in the Fourth House means you would love to live by the sea. You were a little bit different from your family and sometimes felt you didn't really belong. Your influential parent is more than a little confusing, sensitive and sympathetic, but not to be relied upon in times of crisis.

Pluto in the Fourth House means you can go home to recharge. You are strong at home, though home may also be a place of power struggles. Your influential parent is powerful to the point of being overwhelming.

The Fifth House
The Fifth House is all about your creativity and how you express it. It is closely allied with Leo and the Sun. It is about how you spend your leisure time and has a great deal of influence on your attitude towards children.

Love and romance, children and creativity, sports and games, gambling and speculation, and how you have fun in general all belong in this house. All the other houses up to this point dealt with staying alive. This is the first house that says 'Let's enjoy ourselves'. This house shows romantic interests, but not marriage. That's the job of the Seventh House.

The Sun in the Fifth House will always put love first. The creative urge is strengthened here. Lovers and the first child will be fiery and dramatic.

The Moon in the Fifth House means your romantic interests will tend to be on the moody side. This placement tends to attract 'poor-me' types in romance. The first-born will be moody.

Mercury in the Fifth House means you express yourself creatively through writing and speaking. You will fall in love with a talker. The first child will be a chatterbox.

Venus in the Fifth House means your lovers are always charmers, and you are creative, artistic and self-indulgent. The first child will be a charmer.

Mars in the Fifth House means your outlet for energy is in the house of fun, so you love sports and games. The first child will be active and energetic.

Jupiter in the Fifth House means more fun, confidence in romance, confidence in creative pursuits and confidence in gambling. The first child will tend to be a jovial, happy-go-lucky type.

Saturn in the Fifth House denotes caution in fun and games. Undue importance is placed on romance. Saturn can be very good for creative projects that take forever to do and require endless patience. The first child will be difficult.

Uranus in the Fifth House means an attraction to unusual types in romance and an innovative sense of the creative. Uranus will have your parents tearing their hair out as you bring home one bizarre date after another. The first child will be either a genius or an eccentric, but more than a little accident-prone, so keep watch.

Neptune in the Fifth House can make us fall in love with our rose-coloured glasses turned on to the full spectrum. There is a tendency here to find a 'soul mate' on every street corner. Neptune here is very creative in the arts. The first child will be dreamy and imaginative.

Pluto in the Fifth House means intense relationships followed by periods of celibacy and a tendency to become obsessed with your lover to boot. Games are never just games to you, you take them very seriously. Games are also where you recharge. The first child will be stubborn and intense.

The Sixth House

The Sixth House shows how you work, as opposed to your career (which is governed by the Tenth House). If the job you have is shown by your Sixth House then it's just a job, not a career. The planets that fall in the Sixth House show how you like to work, what your work environment should be like for you to feel comfortable. Virgo and Mercury have strong ties to the Sixth House.

The Sixth House also rules co-workers and subordinates. It indicates the quality of service you give to others as well as the quality of service they give to you, so this house rules, by extension, servants of all sorts. The other things to look for here are conditions of health, the type of ailments to which you are prone and what diet serves you best.

The Sun in the Sixth House means you have to shine in the workplace and you need recognition for what you do to feel good about your world. The people who work for you tend towards the showy.

The Moon in the Sixth House means you have an emotional need to work and your office will be a home away from home. The people who work for you are moody and need mothering.

Mercury in the Sixth House means work will involve speaking, writing or travelling, no matter what your career. The people who work for you are talkative and communicative.

Venus in the Sixth House means you need a pleasant work environment, and even if you work in an office, you will insist on a cubicle with a window. The people who work for you are charming.

Mars in the Sixth House is action and aggression in the workplace. You like to be up and about, talking and getting things done. The people who work for you will also be aggressive and energetic.

Jupiter in the Sixth House is lucky in finding jobs and in health, but also means you are likely to become bored before you get the real benefits in a job. Jupiter rules the legs, so walk around to keep your brain on the job. The people who work for you are happy types or foreigners with interesting backgrounds.

Saturn in the Sixth House means frustration in the workplace, such as being overlooked for promotions. It can also mean great success once these obstacles have been overcome. Work is very important to this placement and this position frequently gives fabulous organisational skills. The people who work under you can be obstinate and seem like they are frustrating your efforts.

Uranus in the Sixth House needs independence in the workplace. They can't stand having someone looking over their shoulder. This is a good thing too, because often the way you work is quite eccentric and would confuse any boss, but works just fine for you. Hi-tech jobs are best for you.

The people who work under you are of a similarly eccentric bent.

Neptune in the Sixth House means you will be best working with the poor or in a job where you need to use your imagination. You can feel imprisoned in an office job and find yourself daydreaming a lot. The people who work under you tend to drain you both materially and emotionally.

Pluto in the Sixth House means you need to be obsessed about your work. Office jobs will result in office politics and power struggles. The people who work under you tend to be absolutely for you, or can't stand you at all. Watch the latter.

The Seventh House

The Seventh House is concerned with your relationships with others. This is the house that shows you what your partners and partnerships are like, as well as you known enemies (hidden enemies are revealed in the Twelfth House). It will tell you what you are looking for in a partner personality-wise. It also deals with conflict and personality clashes.

The Seventh House is closely allied with Libra and Venus. It looks at deep love relationships and marriage. The sign on the cusp of the Seventh House shows what sort of people are attracted to you for long-term relationships.

It is also helpful to look at the Seventh House when planning a long-term business partnership to see what conflicts may arise.

The Sun in the Seventh House will give you a sunny partner, with traits similar to Leo. There is a strong focus on partners and marriage with this placement, and you feel more outgoing in general when in a good relationship.

The Moon in the Seventh House will give a moody partner. Your attitude towards your partner will be quite cyclical. You will find it easier to express your emotions while in a supportive relationship, but that is able to include your moods. You will tend towards the mothering or the be-mothered types.

Mercury in the Seventh House will give an intellectual, talkative partner, who may be quite flirtatious. Talk will be a big part of your relationship.

Venus in the Seventh House will give a charming partner. You may find yourself becoming more self-indulgent after marriage.

Mars in the Seventh House will give an active, aggressive partner. Married life will never be dull, with lots of activity interspersed with the occasional argument. You will find yourself becoming more aggressive after marriage.

Jupiter in the Seventh House will give you luck and confidence in love. Just don't overreach yourself with this placement, and you will end up with a dream partner – maybe someone exotic, or wealthy. Overconfidence could see you going through a long line of wonderful prospects and finding yourself lonely and (to use a terribly old-fashioned expression) on the shelf. You will find yourself luckier after marriage.

Saturn in the Seventh House people are often better off waiting to get married until they have established their own personality and have a very good idea of what they need from a partner. Saturn usually gives an older partner.

Uranus in the Seventh House may never marry, as she loves her independence too much. This placement favours an unusual or eccentric partner or partnership, or a genius partner.

Neptune in the Seventh House is a little like Neptune in the Fifth House. You tend to approach marriage with the rose-coloured tint on your glasses set high. This placement gives a highly artistic, sensitive and romantic partner – or a drug-addicted bigamist. The unfortunate thing about this placement is that you will be the last to know which one you married.

Pluto in the Seventh House is all or nothing. Love or hate your partner, your feelings will never be wishy-washy. Pluto will give a very intense partner.

The Eighth House

The Eighth House is the house of sex. Sounds fun? While the Fifth House is about romance and, the Seventh House about marriage, the Eighth House is about biological energy and procreation, of which sex is a big part (but only one part). This house shows one's sexual tastes and desires. It is closely allied with Scorpio and Pluto.

The Eighth House also shows the effect society's rules have on you (are you a rebel or a conformist?) as well as the effect you have on the values of those around you (are you a paragon of virtue inspiring others to greater moral heights, or are you like the rest of the rabble?).

It also indicates the access you may have to other people's money and resources, including your partner's money. It tells you about your partner's finances and the things that they value, and how you approach that with them.

It also has a lot to do with birth and death and matters of the occult and the afterlife.

The Sun in the Eighth House means a dramatic approach to sex. You fulfil yourself in the house where your Sun lives, and a career in health, rehabilitation or finance would be fulfilling.

The Moon in the Eighth House means emotionally you need to heal and nurture. This placement wants to accumulate its own money and possessions – living off Daddy's gold Amex card is not for you.

Mercury in the Eighth House is a dirty talker. This placement also likes to talk and think about money, sex and health.

Venus in the Eighth House is a sucker for a four-poster bed in the flickering light of a full candelabra. Venus enjoys possessions, especially if they have been provided by someone else.

Mars in the Eighth House is a credit-card blow-out waiting to happen. The Eighth House is other people's money and Mars just loves to spend. This placement won't wait around to see if you are interested. They will make the moves and move on very quickly if their passions are not reciprocated. Sex can seem like an Olympic event – how many positions can one person know?

Jupiter in the Eighth House craves people of exotic backgrounds. People throw money at you with this placement – the difficulties come when it is time to pay it back.

Saturn in the Eighth House likes a planned sex life and not too many surprises. Credit can be hard to come across with this placement, but these people are excellent at managing other people's money. They are very rigid on social rules.

Uranus in the Eighth House loves to break the taboos and be a little kinky. This placement revels in breaking the social rules.

Neptune in the Eighth House sees sex as a dreamy affair. Neptune puts the blinkers on when it comes to business partners in this house – make sure you are the one managing the books.

Pluto in the Eighth House means sex is an obsession. You are either celibate or promiscuous. Try not to indulge in power-tripping when handling your partner's money or business affairs.

The Ninth House

The Ninth House describes our philosophy on life. Are we deeply spiritual or do we find God in a bottle of bourbon? Our religious and ethical beliefs are described here in the same vein. The Ninth House is closely associated with Sagittarius and Jupiter. Activities which serve to expand our horizons sit here – these include travel, publishing, publicity, advertising, politics, and cultural pursuits, and even sport.

The Ninth House rules higher education and it shows us how we choose to expand our world, whether through work or travel, or in more sedate pastimes like reading or watching the television. The sign that rules the Ninth House cusp shows us this.

Less usual circumstances that it relates to include court decisions, a second marriage and in-laws. The Ninth House can also describe the job or health of your mother.

The Ninth House can be thought of as dealing with the concerns of the Third House (early schooling, short trips and magazine articles) on a larger scale (tertiary education, long journeys, and books and the foreign media).

The Sun in the Ninth House loves to shine in study and higher learning and gains a great deal from overseas travel. You have a greater than normal interest in religion, philosophy and the big picture issues, and prefer to deal with general principles rather than specific facts.

The Moon in the Ninth House means you tend to have philosophies based on principles of the heart rather than those of logic. There is a strong emotional need to travel and study.

Mercury in the Ninth House likes to scrutinise life philosophies, take them apart and put them back together, but they have no emotional ties to them. To people in this placement, one idea is as good as the next.

Venus in the Ninth House finds pleasure in study and travel but may lack motivation. You may find love overseas, or be attracted to a foreigner at home. You admire philosophy for its grace of expression, but generally feel that 'live and let live' is the best policy. You are not likely to travel to anywhere dirty or ugly – Tuscany or Paris is your speed.

Mars in the Ninth House is a placement that can spawn a crusader.

Jupiter in the Ninth House gives luck in long-distance travel and higher education. Just take off and see the world at your whim – the energies have conspired to protect you.

Saturn in the Ninth House struggles with university as they are much better at learning in a hands-on environment. This placement will prefer a more dogmatic philosophy.

Uranus in the Ninth House is anarchy in the house of beliefs – perhaps you were raised by conservative Christians? You will love shocking them with your latest devotion to the doctrines of a way-out cult and you will love venturing far off the beaten track, ignoring all the advice in your guidebook.

Neptune in the Ninth House is where philosophy and travel occupy your dreamscape. You are drawn to the sea for long trips.

Pluto in the Ninth House means long journeys revitalise you and study is balm to your soul. You will enjoy studying anything that might be instrumental in solving hidden mysteries.

The Tenth House

The Tenth House indicates one's career tendencies, public image, and the people who may have power or authority over you in day-to-day life. It is about the parent with the most authority. It is the house where we discover our ambition and it shows us where we can put that ambition to good use. It is closely associated with Capricorn and Saturn.

When choosing a career direction it is important to look at what is going on in your Tenth House, as it will show where your ambition lies, a most important aspect to a fulfilling career. Aspects (see the chapter in Aspects in this section) are critical to working out where your career path lies.

This house is power balanced with responsibility, and it will show how we manage both.

The Sun in the Tenth House shines in public, and will do well in whatever profession they choose. They will gain an authoritative position as a matter of course.

The Moon in the Tenth House means attitudes to your career go through phases, but you generally feel happier when in a caring 'feminine' career like nursing or social work. Other Moon careers include working in hotels and restaurants, as well as the dairy industry.

Mercury in the Tenth House means mental stimulation is important in your career choice, as is the circulation of information. Short trips could also form a part of your career path, like truck or taxi driving. Writing, public speaking, sales or journalism will all be satisfying careers.

Venus in the Tenth House means networking and public relations are skills you put to good use in your career. Art and design, curating, beauty, jewellery, floristry and fashion design are all Venus careers. Whatever you do, you will always look good doing it.

Mars in the Tenth House means that whatever you do, you know you can do it better than the boss, and you are not above shouting him down about it as well. Mars means rapid advancement in a career, as long as that boss you yelled at has no say in who gets the promotions. Mars makes you ambitious, but may be your undoing as well. Mars occupations are in the military, police, fire officers, anything requiring energy, initiative and action.

Jupiter in the Tenth House means work in the pursuit of your ideals will be the most satisfying career for you. Luck is strong in your career, and the boss will tend to like you and give you a leg-up every now and then – don't squander your good luck.

Saturn in the Tenth House take a while to get going in their careers, but with their diligence, eventually succeed. They are organised and disciplined. Saturn is usually a planet to fear, but it is at home in the Tenth House and will fair you well, after a time.

Uranus in the Tenth House has been perfectly suited by the technological revolution – turning up to work on a skateboard at 3 p.m. to work into the night on cutting-edge projects on the Internet suits this placement down to its shoeless feet. Forget the corporate ladder, you need a place to express your eccentricities.

Neptune in the Tenth House means you will flounder unless you can focus your dreamy side into a career path – try filmmaking, art or fashion design, a Neptunian career like marine biology, or areas like charities, medicine, prisons, halfway houses and nursing homes, which Neptune also rules. Without this focus, you may become one of the poor, sick, imprisoned or substance-abusing people who also have Neptune here – motivation enough to find your niche?

Pluto in the Tenth House means you must attempt to match your career with your twin desires for power and to serve society. Politics, religion, the police, psychology and medicine (Pluto is the planet of healing) are all careers where you can synthesise these disparate desires.

The Eleventh House

The Eleventh House is the house of friends, hopes and wishes. It also shows how you deal with groups of people like friends, acquaintances, classmates, workmates and church groups, but not very close friends. This house is especially concerned with how you integrate yourself into the greater community. It is strongly aligned with Aquarius and Uranus.

The Eleventh House is your house of social conscience and will show your attitude to charities. This house also indicates money directly earned from career matters. It will not, however, tell you how to keep a hold on that money – that is the domain of the Second House, so it is possible to have a strong Eleventh House, meaning that the income from your career is excellent, but also to have a weak Second House, which means the money is spent as soon as it is made.

The Eleventh House can be thought of as an extension of the Fifth House, which shows where we are creative in a personal manner. It shows us where we are creative in the wider, social sense. It reveals your broader ambitions after your career, your hopes and wishes and your political activity.

The Sun in the Eleventh House means you will have loads of friends and acquaintances and enjoy being in clubs and societies. You enjoy being part of political action, generally on a large scale, but this can indicate a smaller scale as well. You may have trouble forming close personal relationships.

The Moon in the Eleventh House means involvement in community politics is likely. You like taking a role in the large social groups that you tend to move in. Your friends can be described as moody. Your hopes and wishes tend to be more whim-like than fixed goals.

Mercury in the Eleventh House will not tolerate friends who can't hold their own in a social situation, and will not suffer anyone who is too shy to speak for themselves.

Acquaintances tend to flit in and out of your life. Your friends are talkers, writers, travellers and the flow of conversation is important to you. Writing down your goals is a good way to keep yourself on track.

Venus in the Eleventh House means you find social satisfaction in a large group of friends and many acquaintances. You value taste and artistic ability in your friends, and you like them to be well-dressed when you meet them for coffee. Your wishes are fixed upon material things.

Mars in the Eleventh House people are well-connected networkers who are superficially close to a vast amount of people – everyone seems to know and love them. Mainly because they are scared. Mars in this placement can make you very aggressive in social situations, and the force of your personality will impose itself on the group. You will have equally assertive friends. You set your goals and then go for them, without a second thought. The phrase 'be careful what you wish for because you might even get it' is pertinent here.

Jupiter in the Eleventh House makes you so charming in friendship, people seem to clamour to be seen with you. With such variety, it is easy to make mistakes and choose your friends from the wealthy or those with social status over people of true worth. You will seem to receive all that you wish for – don't get complacent, or your luck will run out. Your ambitions are very broad-based and you are comfortable enlisting help from your acquaintances where others would err on the side of politeness.

Saturn in the Eleventh House means you were painfully shy in your youth, so you have either overcome this obstacle to be very adept in social situations (and considerate of those who are still shy) or you have resolved to stick to your few very close friends. You have older or more mature friends. Luck does not come easily when it comes to achieving your ambitions, but that's OK, you have learnt not to rely on it anyway. Not such a bad spot for this difficult planet.

Uranus in the Eleventh House means friends who are somewhat bizarre, and they usually have a common ideological interest to you. Your long-term ambitions are very original and you probably have an unusual plan to achieve them by circumventing the normal channels.

Neptune in the Eleventh House is long-term ambition deeply rooted in fantasy land, and goals tend to change with the fashions. Friends will be artistic and gentle types. 'Friends' will also drain you emotionally and take you for a ride; unfortunately you have great difficulty in distinguishing real friends from the others. You tend to be shy in large groups.

Pluto in the Eleventh House means you find personal power in group situations and have a natural ability for politics. You have only a few very close friends whom you treat with extreme deference. Your hopes and wishes can become your obsessions – you will no doubt achieve what you set out to do. Make sure it is what you really want.

The Twelfth House
The Twelfth House is the house of self-undoing, where we subconsciously sabotage ourselves. In this house you find restrictions, hidden enemies (as opposed to open enemies, shown by the Seventh House) and psychological problems. Any planet in this house represents something we are hiding from the world and frequently from ourselves as well. It is associated with Pisces and Neptune.

This is a continuation of the issues brought up in the Sixth and Ninth Houses, but with a more mystical bent. It represents a desire for a union with a greater reality. It is the last house before the cycle begins again, and is where the lessons from the previous eleven houses are evident, including accumulated mistakes.

It involves hospitals and prisons and serious illness. It used to be called the house of sorrows, but the guys in public relations thought the Twelfth House had enough problems without a depressing name as well.

The Sun in the Twelfth House means privacy is treasured. They are sensitive souls who need to retreat from the real world every now and then to recharge. They can often be night owls and they generally have esoteric interests and are keen observers of human nature. They need to be encouraged to bring their insights into the wider realm.

The Moon in the Twelfth House means you are shy and sensitive, and often hide your emotions and mood swings. You prefer to do good works behind the scenes, with compassion and imagination. Your home is your refuge. You need to be encouraged to let your emotions show.

Mercury in the Twelfth House have little confidence in their ability to express themselves, which is a great pity, because their ideas are often carefully considered and mindful of the wants of all involved. They need to be encouraged to speak out on issues close to their heart.

Venus in the Twelfth House can mean only a few close friends and shyness in social settings. They need to be encouraged to be more open about their feelings to friends and let them into their confidence. They should also try to push themselves at parties to speak up a little more, maybe even talk to someone outside their friendship group.

Mars in the Twelfth House bottles their anger – beware of the inevitable explosion. They like to work behind the scenes, so watch that they aren't plotting or conspiring. People with this placement need to be encouraged to speak up when they are offended.

Jupiter in the Twelfth House can hide their joy. This placement brings luck in protecting you from physical harm. Often the religious or spiritual world is preferable to the real world for these people. They need to be encouraged to laugh because the whole world laughs with you, and you know whose company you cry with.

Saturn in the Twelfth House suppresses sadness, which only builds to the inevitable. They suffer from an immobilising fear of the future and authority. People with this placement have to find ways to express their inner purpose and put their talents as behind-the-scenes organisers to good use, which will help them build self-confidence.

Uranus in the Twelfth House hides their eccentricity and genius. These people possess a strange and wonderful imagination, and they can relieve this pressure valve by taking on an interest that extends their consciousness, like yoga or meditation. Probably reluctant at first, they will surprise themselves at their talent for such things, and the benefits they get from them.

Neptune in the Twelfth House hides their dreamy, imaginative side. They will have vivid dreams but the meaning will remain hidden from them. They should be encouraged to keep a dream diary. This placement is quite harmonious, as Neptune is at home here, liking his reveries hidden.

Pluto in the Twelfth House can mean hidden rage bubbling beneath the surface. Watch for this one, an escape valve must be found. Abilities in the healing professions are heightened. An interest in psychology or the occult could help uncover your hidden nature.

Aspects
Relationships Between Planets
After looking at the position of the planets in the signs and the houses, the third major area of chart study concerns the angles formed between pairs of planets. These angles are called aspects.

Understanding how aspects are formed is quite simple. If you take any two planets on a chart, and from the centre of the chart draw a line to each planet, the angle formed by these two lines is an aspect. Remember that a full circle is made up of 360 degrees, so an aspect angle can be as small as 0° (planets in the same position) or as large as 180° (planets exactly opposite each other).

You don't need to just look at aspects formed by planets. Technically, you can use any calculated position, such as the midheaven, or the orbit intersection of the Sun and the Moon (Moon nodes). However, you should be careful how much emphasis you place on these aspects.

How do we know which aspects are significant? Tables 6 and 7 of in the Reference section describe the most commonly used aspects in popular astrology. At first glance, the important aspects might seem to be simply whole numbers, but the first trick to working out aspects lies in a simple mathematical rule:

◇ Degrees in a circle divided by a low number = whole number of degrees

For example, let's start with the number 2. We have 360° in a circle divided by 2, which equals 180°, a whole number. This aspect leaves the planets directly opposite each other in the sky and is logically called an opposition. Such a relationship is a constant tug-of-war between the two planets involved.

Let's also try the number 4. 360° divided by 4 equals 90°. This aspect is a square and the angle is a right angle, like the corner of a square.

The next formula you can use to calculate aspects is based on the number of signs between the two planets. Each sign, as you will recall, is 30°. The distance between the planets in an opposition is exactly six signs. For a square aspect, the distance between planets is three signs.

Many aspects are not multiples of 30°, such as the one you get by dividing 360 by 5. This gives you an aspect called a quintile, which is 72°, a perfectly good whole number. However, two planets in a quintile are 2.4 signs apart! So, although this is a whole number aspect, it is not a convenient one for the purposes of astrology. As a consequence, most astrologers completely ignore this aspect.

The Preferred Aspect

Indeed, most astrologers only use aspects that are an even number of signs apart. It is clear why this is so when you examine the aspects in a chart. Let's say you have the Sun 5° into Aries and the Moon 5° into Libra. It will be immediately obvious that they have a relationship – they will be the same distance from the start of their respective signs. The only thing that remains is to count the number of signs between them (six) and you instantly have your aspect (an opposition).

With a little practice, you can work out the major aspects without even drawing up the chart. So it is probably for this reason, as well as it being quite aesthetically pleasing, that the major aspects are all multiples of 30°. Using this logic, the quincunx of 150° (five-twelfths of 360°) is quite acceptable, being exactly five star signs apart.

At this point, I can hear murmurs of disapproval from the numerologists, as the number 5, among others, is over-looked in popular astrology. After all, 5 is the number of man, arcanely represented by the pentacle, and it is the mind that sits over the four elements. And what of the magical number 7 – the favourite number of half the Western world? Should it be relegated to the aspect bin because 360° divided by 7 is 51.428571 recurring?

Fear not! For those with a penchant for numbers there is the Harmonic Aspects Method (not to be confused with harmonic astrology, which is a different kettle of fish cooking on the same stove).

Harmonic aspects are quite unlimited and allow any two planets to be aspected. For example, if two planets are 137°30'08" apart, then you divide 360 by 1597 and move the result 610 times around the chart. All you have to do now is determine the significance of an aspect 610/1597th of a circle . . .

As you can see, harmonic aspects could get out of control. In practice, most astrologers using this method limit them-selves to division by numbers between 1 and 12, but many extend this to 36.

Below is a basic categorisation of the harmonic aspects.

Type of Aspect	360 divided by...	Description
Conscious (Overt)	1, 2, 3, 4, 6, 8 & 12	These are recognisable major Aspects. These will be obvious in a person's character.
Pre-conscious (Potential)	5, 7, 9, 10 & 11	These Aspects represent potential characteristics that might be easily developed into conscious ones.
Subconscious (Latent)	13 to 36	You may never discover these mysteries of character unless you know a good hypnotist.

Good and Bad Aspects

You will have realised by now that there are hundreds of aspects lying dormant in your chart. If you are not careful, you can lose sight of the big picture. It's a bit like looking at a painting – if you look too closely at the brush-strokes you miss the overall effect. The method advised here is to identify the strongest major aspects. You'll find that this is more than sufficient information to round out your astrological portrait.

If you've already used the Reference section to create your own chart, be aware that the techniques you have used are not accurate enough for aspects. You will probably need to have your chart drawn up by an astrologer or a web service – in which case many aspects will be calculated for you.

Below are the five aspects generally recognised to be the most significant.

✧ 0° = Conjunction. This is a blending of planetary energy. This is the most powerful aspect and will generally combine the energy of the planets involved. Intensity is often the result.

✧ 180° = Opposition (major aspect). This is a powerful aspect that will put the planets at odds with each other and produce difficulties. Often the expression of one planet results in the obstruction of the other and vice versa.

✧ 120° = Trine. This is a strong harmonious relationship between two planets.

✧ 90° = Square. This is a tense relationship that brings planetary energy into conflict.

✧ 60° = Sextile. This is a moderate harmonious aspect that brings both planets into harmony, like the trine but not as strong.

✧ 150° = Quincunx. A blending of energy which causes dilemma and forces revision.

Aspects are generally seen to be tense or harmonious, because of the attributes of the individual signs.

Earlier we saw that each sign is either positive or negative and is associated with one of four elements. Let's take a trine aspect of 120°. Planets in this aspect will be four signs apart and therefore they will be the same element and have the same polarity. You can see this illustrated in the diagram below.

If you had the Moon in Aries and the Sun in Sagittarius, these planets are expressed dynamically and intuitively (in line with the element fire). For this reason they have a harmonious relationship and there is no conflict between them.

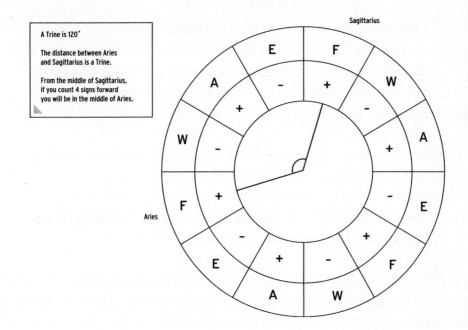

A Trine is 120°

The distance between Aries and Sagittarius is a Trine.

From the middle of Sagittarius, if you count 4 signs forward you will be in the middle of Aries.

Signs don't necessarily have to be of the same element. Fire and air combinations are also harmonious, as are water and earth. This generally applies to sextiles, which are 60° apart.

The following table summarises the effect of different energies brought together by the major aspects.

Aspect	Signs Apart	Same +/-	Elemental Harmony	Effect
Conjunction	0	Yes	Excellent	Intensity
Opposition*	6	Yes	Good	Usually Conflict
Square	3	No	Poor	Tense Conflict
Trine	4	Yes	Excellent	Strong Harmony
Sextile	2	Yes	Good	Weak Harmony
Quincunx	5	No	Poor	Weak Conflict

* Oppositions should be seen as potentially harmonious but requiring a degree of effort to find the balance

The result is that planets will combine to either moderate or stimulate each other's influence. When in tension, there will be conflict, and the influence of one or the other will be obstructed. On the other hand, a harmonious relationship will see the energy of each planet complement the other.

In all cases there is a conflict of interest between the two planets. In harmonious aspects they will probably work it out themselves. In tense aspects, a little conscious effort will be required to straighten the path.

Degree of Error

Of course, most of the aspects in your chart will be far from exact. So how exact does an aspect have to be? And how do you compare a weak aspect between the Sun and the Moon to a strong aspect between Pluto and the asteroid Chiron? There are no easy answers to these questions. Instead, a careful analysis of the various aspects in your chart will lead you to your own conclusions. With that in mind, here are a few tips which may come in handy.

The degree of error allowed for an aspect is called an orb. For a conjunction, astrologers typically allow a large orb of up to 8° (which means that two planets can be 8° apart and remain in conjunction). As a guide, apply an Orb of 3° to 4° degrees to an opposition, trine or square. For a sextile or quincunx, apply an orb of 1° to 2°. Use your own judgement as to what constitutes a reasonable orb in each situation. There are also a few other factors involved.

If an aspect is within 1°, feel free to label it 'exact' and give it extra weight in the overall chart. Conjunctions can be exact within 2°, but you need to be a bit stricter regarding a sextile or quincunx.

As a general rule, the further/smaller the planets, the smaller the orb. The Sun occupies 0.5° of the sky, which is significant by comparison to every planet other than the Moon. So you can be a little more lenient with the orbs of the Moon and the Sun. In contrast, be a little stricter with the orbs of aspects involving the outer planets (Uranus, Neptune and particularly Pluto).

Your astrologer may be able to tell whether the two planets in an aspect are applying (becoming more exact) or separating (becoming less exact).This would have an effect on weak aspects with the Moon, especially if you lack an exact time of birth. Although the effect of birth time on aspects is minimal compared to the way it effects the placement of the houses, it can easily influence Moon aspects.

Finally, certain aspects will have different significance depending on the planets involved. Uranus, Neptune and Pluto are viewed as the 'social' planets. Because they spend so long in each sign, many people born across a length of time (sometimes years) will have these planets in the same sign. So aspects formed by these planets (particularly with each other) are less significant in a natal chart.

Remember to use your instincts. It is not necessary to understand every detail of a natal chart at first viewing. As you come to understand how your chart represents you, the obscure details will become clearer.

One more thing . . .

A chart drawn on paper assumes that the planets obediently follow a straight path across the sky. If we find a Sun/Moon conjunction in a chart, should we expect to see an eclipse in the sky? In truth, the Sun could be 20° north and the Moon 10° south – that's a total of 30°! So keep in mind that a conjunction means that two planets are in the same degree of the same sign – not eclipsing each other in the sky. The same consideration applies to all aspects.

Interpreting Aspects

The rest of this chapter is devoted to interpreting various aspects that may appear in your chart. Remember that aspects are applied after considering the planets' positions in their signs and houses, so the interpretation given to a particular aspect will vary greatly from one chart to the next. So, use the following as a guide and attempt to make an interpretation of your own chart based on your understanding of your chart and the other aspects involved.

Sun/Moon

Conjunction Your ego is expressed emotionally and the two are barely discernible. The lines between your conscious and subconscious thoughts are blurred. Your frankness gives people confidence in their relationships with you. You act passionately.

Opposition Your sensitive side is exposed in fits and starts as the flip-side of a badly managed will. Try to develop a routine of focused development followed by self-imposed down-time.

Trine Your emotional needs are easily satisfied while you focus on your goals. You are generally balanced and associate well with the opposite sex.

Square Your direction and motivation lack emotional colour and your pursuit of happiness is hampered.

Sun/Mercury

The conjunction is the only major aspect made by Mercury to the Sun.

Conjunction Your ideas are dynamic and you are quite convincing when you want to be. But the subjectivity of your ego can flaw the ideas it helps form. You can think for days but a too-perfect conjunction could cause a bit of a meltdown.

Sun/Venus

The conjunction is the only major aspect made by Venus to the Sun, other than the sextile.

Conjunction You know what you want and how to enjoy it. You come on strong in your relationships and sometimes forget to invite your emotions. You relish sitting in the front row of a 50-seat theatre.

Sun/Mars

Conjunction You are an activist by nature, perhaps aggressively if the mood so takes you. People give you the jobs they're not sure how to do. This is a very 'masculine' aspect.

Opposition You achieve results through conflict and when this doesn't work you tend to overreact. You are prone to aggression and animosity.

Trine You act with focus and get what you want just by taking it. You can achieve much and need only choose wisely.

Square You often find yourself 'back to square one' after a rash display of misguided action. This can lead to a defeatist attitude, which you stubbornly cling to.

Sun/Jupiter

Conjunction Luck and optimism move in your circles. Whether it be initiating party games or forming political parties, people are attracted to social movements that materialise around you. Watch your vanity.

Opposition You have abundant energy to grow, but find it difficult to plot your course. You over accommodate with a certain pomposity and try to talk up your failures as success.

Trine Travel comes easily and early, and you are constantly growing in maturity. Don't waste time planning your next move.

Square Your life takes you extravagantly in directions you feel at odds with. Realigning your goals will cause conflict with others.

Sun/Saturn

Conjunction You are focused on the outcome of what you are striving to achieve. Life's lessons have a great significance for you – and if you're lucky, one of those lessons will teach you how to relax. Remember that discipline is the fastest route to where you are going.

Opposition Something often gets in the way of your goals and hurts your confidence. This leaves you feeling somewhat maligned.

Trine You make excellent life choices because you learn from past mistakes. You may even find yourself manufacturing life lessons for their own sake.

Square By your own reckoning, nothing you do is right. Any attempt to resolve your dissatisfaction with discipline is held to ransom by misguided energy. Gain is achieved through hard work.

Sun/Uranus
Conjunction You lead an unorthodox life and your intentions seem strange. But for those not disturbed by your behaviour, you have a great deal of flair. Too many external restrictions will affect you on all levels.

Opposition Your way of life and unusual experiences have attributed to a weird perception of people and events. Such views are full of contradictions and hamper growth.

Trine Your theories are sound and much of your success comes from that. You are the life of the party.

Square Your nonconformity results in conflict rather than the desired mental stimulation. You claim authority on many matters but the result is a matter for the authorities.

Sun/Neptune
Conjunction You tend to idealise your involvement with the world, which works marvellously while the world is cooperating. Your natural desire for escape is consuming and so you should choose your 'exit' signs wisely. Art and music will suit you well.

Opposition You imagine failure, rather than ways to succeed. Your disillusionment tempts unhealthy escapism.

Trine You are psychically attuned to success. Good ideas arise from daydreams provided you don't overindulge your imagination.

Square Your daydreaming is antiproductive. You have high aspirations, but distract yourself and curtail your pursuit of success with imaginative excuses.

Sun/Pluto
Conjunction Your actions have impact and you can initiate dramatic change. Be careful what you put your mind to, because situations could back-fire with misguided intentions.

Opposition The conscious and unconscious parts of your mind struggle for dominance and neither acts in support of the other when the situation calls for it.

Trine You are insightful and influential. You are a catalyst for many types of change.

Square Your unconscious takes over at inopportune moments and otherwise rarely produces the goods when needed. You undermine yourself unconsciously.

Moon/Mercury
Conjunction You have no trouble verbalising your feelings or telling everyone about your love life. Your logic has a subjective edge to it.

Opposition You have trouble expressing your feelings and overuse your words. Your decision-making lacks subjective balance.

Trine You communicate your feelings and connect with people very well. You are able to acknowledge and validate your feelings while problem-solving.

Square You are distracted by your internal emotional state when you try to be objective.

Moon/Venus
Conjunction For you, art is a state of mind. You make decisions based on instinct and often in favour of your senses.

Opposition You have trouble satisfying your emotional needs through daily pleasures and pursuits. You are somewhat masochistic.

Trine You have a happy home life and people feel very comfortable with you. Few things give you a sense of urgency about your actions.

Square You feel that the pursuit of the physical aspects of your life short-change your need for emotional balance.

Moon/Mars
Conjunction You step on toes as you tackle sensitive moments head-on. You summon passion with ease and achieve success with your unthinking brashness.

Opposition You attack problems dispassionately and your aggression is erratically directed. You have difficulty acting on your feelings.

Trine You are courageous and are usually the one to initiate the resolution of conflict. Your self-confidence is inspirational to others.

Square You are somewhat self-destructive and undermine your emotional progress with rash actions.

Moon/Jupiter
Conjunction You are more emotionally mature than those around you. You are big on the welfare of others and certainly the welfare of yourself.

Opposition Your benevolence is not properly directed. And aspects of your life that are emotionally significant tend to suffer.

Trine You are good-spirited and like to share it around. You are expansive and have many good friends.

Square Your emotional needs are overridden by your sense of wider social generosity.

Moon/Saturn
Conjunction You don't express your emotions spontaneously, as past lessons are fresh in your mind. You benefit from disciplined risk-taking when it comes to your feelings.

Opposition You have a conscience that takes no heed of your emotions. Likewise, your feelings are often made redundant by a lack of insight into their cause.

Trine You learn successfully from emotional lessons even though you are not emotionally expressive.

Square Your poor handling of your emotions undermines your actions. You are critical of your feelings and suppress them accordingly.

Moon/Uranus
Conjunction You tend to be moody and your reactions to sensitive issues can be erratic. You are drawn to novelty and change in your emotional life.

Opposition Your independent nature leaves you lacking emotional support when you need it most.

Trine Although it is a little antisocial, you get a great deal out of acknowledging your feelings in an unconventional way.

Square Seeking emotional security in strange ways leaves you more unstable.

Moon/Neptune
Conjunction You are emotionally intuitive and even over-sensitive to the emotions of others. Your imagination is fuel for artistic expression.

Opposition You find it hard to take stock of your own feelings relative to the feelings of others.

Trine You are healthily sensitive to the emotions of those around you, and importantly to your own emotions as well.

Square Other people's needs are overbearing and conflict with your own. This affects your emotional confidence.

Moon/Pluto
Conjunction People have difficulty avoiding your influence. You are fascinated by death and transformation and inclined towards the spiritual.

Opposition You are an emotional loose cannon and any beneficial effect you could easily achieve is left unfulfilled.

Trine There is power and significance attached to many of your feelings, giving you positive impetus for change.

Square You find it hard to let go of the old and accept the new. Any change is negatively coloured by your emotional overreactions.

Mercury/Venus
Of the aspects dealt with here, the only major aspect concerning Mercury and Venus is the conjunction.

Conjunction You are good at presenting the needs and wants of yourself and others. You also love to talk.

Mercury/Mars

Conjunction You are direct in thought and action. Your lines of argument tend to be aggressive and quite compelling.

Opposition You can organise your thoughts well enough, but the heat of the moment leaves you lost for words.

Trine You fight your wars with a keen mind. You prefer to stay clear of sentimentality.

Square You are unable to say what you think without coming down hard on your audience. Your action lacks rationality.

Mercury/Jupiter

Conjunction Your keen mental faculties offer you a broader forum in which to develop a greater knowledge and belief system.

Opposition You want to organise your experiences into general systems of knowledge, but this is better suited to simple situations.

Trine Your way of thinking benefits your drive for development and broader sense of knowledge.

Square Your general development is hindered by the distraction of immediate considerations.

Mercury/Saturn

Conjunction You are a logical and clear thinker. You have exacting methodologies and measured, premeditated action.

Opposition You are somewhat reserved and suspicious. Your thinking short-changes you before you act, which is due more to an active imagination than to past experience.

Trine While growing up you developed a good way of thinking through problems. You have the capacity for clear judgement.

Square There is a conflict between your natural way of thinking and the way you were brought up to think. With resulting deficiencies in your methods, you often feel subject to criticism.

Mercury/Uranus
Conjunction Mentally you are super-quick on your feet.

Opposition You have eccentric opinions and tend to change your mind a lot.

Trine You are attracted to humanitarian, scientific or occult pursuits.

Square You have crazy ideas and often jump to conclusions.

Mercury/Neptune
Conjunction You have a vivid imagination, which you communicate excellently.

Opposition You are mentally sensitive to the thoughts and intents of others.

Trine Your visualisation is excellent and you are attracted to the visual arts.

Square You are absent-minded and subject to tricks of the mind.

Mercury/Pluto
Conjunction Your penetrating mind drives you to the depths of mystery.

Opposition You are prone to danger as you easily stumble on nasty secrets.

Trine You are sensitive to the subtle interplay of energy and meaning in social situations.

Square You tell it like it is and people tend to strongly disagree.

Venus/Mars
Conjunction Your actions and opinions are highly influenced by your feelings about things. You possess vitality and creativity.

Opposition Your relationships are many but the way you express yourself depends on the person you are with. You make poor decisions when you must choose a soft or hard approach.

Trine You relate to people objectively and successfully. You have a refined will, yet remain dynamic.

Square You have difficult relationships that blow hot and cold. Your social conduct lacks refinement and you lack control of your desires.

Venus/Jupiter
Conjunction You are comfortable in the pursuit of greater

life knowledge although this is fairly self-serving. It pleases you to be benevolent.

Opposition You tend to indulge in meaningless activity and you can come across as boring. You are easy-going and tend towards relationships that have little to offer you.

Trine You like to share ideas and you are optimistic. You benefit from setting high standards for yourself and tend towards philosophical or religious pursuits.

Square You fail to reconcile your philosophy with your basic wants. While overindulgent, you are not often satisfied.

Venus/Saturn
Conjunction Your understanding of other people is driven by a calculated analysis of their motivations. You are patient and open to the basic laws of nature and harmony.

Opposition You rarely open up to others due to a fear of criticism. You like to control relationships and often feel lonely.

Trine You have an artistic sense of order and balance which may result in an interest in mathematics or other pure sciences. You opt for relationships with obvious practical benefits.

Square You lack confidence in your relationships. You are emotionally blocked and somewhat antisocial.

Venus/Uranus
Conjunction You have ever-changing attractions to people and know little difference between friendship and love.

Opposition You are emotionally unstable, with a penchant for unhealthy exotic experiences.

Trine You are fun-loving, spontaneous and see the bright side of situations.

Square Your infatuations come in bursts and cannot be depended on to last.

Venus/Neptune
Conjunction You are aesthetically sensitive, with much healing potential.

Opposition You are prone to physical dependencies and addictions.

Trine You are romantic and inclined towards non-goal oriented pursuits.

Square Your unconscious mind is the source of conflict in relationships.

Venus/Pluto
Conjunction Emotional death and rebirth occur frequently with you.

Opposition Hard-to-control compassion leads to relation-ship problems.

Trine You regenerate your spiritual side through expres-sions of love.

Square You are inclined towards unhealthy emotional involvements.

Mars/Jupiter

Conjunction You are energetic and enthusiastic in your beliefs and philosophies. You are competitive and confident.

Opposition Much of your energy goes to waste on misguided projects. Lack of success breeds indulgence and laziness.

Trine You are actively benevolent without concern for your own needs, knowing they will be met. There is little restriction in your life.

Square You dangerously overstep your boundaries and lack judicious self-control. You have fanatical inclinations and poor timing.

Mars/Saturn

Conjunction You approach your life with ambition and military discipline. You have excellent concentration and self-restraint.

Opposition You are ambitious but restrained by your conscience. You lack assertiveness when action is required.

Trine You possess good constructive energy which you seldom waste. Your willpower and patience make you well suited to positions of authority.

Square You find your efforts constantly frustrated. You may be cynical or bitter from a few too many failures.

Mars/Uranus

Conjunction You are a natural leader of the revolution as you rebel with great success against restrictions and conservative ideas.

Opposition You are prone to outbursts of irritability.

Trine You have abundant energy which you use efficiently and resourcefully.

Square You jump to act without any consideration of the consequences.

Mars/Neptune
Conjunction You have lofty spiritual ambitions with sublime intentions.

Opposition You have desires that are aggressive or which you find hard to control.

Trine You are spiritual and keenly sensitive to falseness in others.

Square You are unaware of your bad habits.

Mars/Pluto
Conjunction You have great endurance and an unflinching constitution.

Opposition You act with deception without really understanding the reasons.

Trine You have well-developed insight combined with a strong sense of fact.

Square You make sacrifices to suit your ego.

Jupiter/Uranus
Conjunction You enjoy the advantage of opportunity – an unexpected help. Your life philosophy is always original.

Opposition Your optimism is often inappropriate and difficulties are unexpected.

Trine Your creativity is inspirational and you have what is known as 'good karma'.

Square While claiming interest in the greater good, you act only for your own good.

Jupiter/Saturn

Conjunction You are kind and generous in a way that seeks to empower others to act for themselves. You prefer philosophies that are practical and workable.

Opposition You are burdened with responsibility which you feel is not yours to carry. You lack the imagination to achieve resolution.

Trine You possess sound common sense of ethical and philosophical issues. These gifts are ideal for business or political pursuits.

Square You experience conflict between desires for expansion and the need for consolidation of experience. You miss opportunities or act too early.

Jupiter/Neptune

Conjunction You have a reserve of imaginative energy, best used in the pursuit of knowledge and philosophy.

Opposition You find it hard to fulfil your promises and have distorted spiritual ideals.

Trine You are spiritually receptive and intuitive.

Square You are impractical and your achievements can lack substance.

Jupiter/Pluto

Conjunction You are inspired to heal and engage in spirituality.

Opposition You create conflict by forcing your fanaticism on others.

Trine Your faith is powerful and can result in meaningful changes.

Square You rebel against the norm for selfish reasons.

Saturn/Uranus

Conjunction You develop practical habits as a basis for a creative use of energy.

Opposition Your criticisms are dogmatic and your erratic behaviour causes conflict.

Trine Universal laws are accessible to your intuition.

Square You have radical ideas at odds with conservative actions.

Saturn/Neptune

Conjunction You have good concentration, and discipline makes dreams a reality.

Opposition Your fears are irrational, although they are a clear result of past experiences.

Trine You favour secrecy and subversion in your endeavours.

Square You are prone to being under psychological attack.

Saturn/Pluto
Conjunction You are patient and focused on secret plans.

Opposition Your vindictiveness arises from an unfortunate past.

Trine You are conversant with the laws of the sublime.

Square Your efforts are often blocked by events on a social level.

The Angles
We have talked at length about the ascendant and how it reveals itself in the personality. The **ascendant** is one of the four angles and its placement is very important for our understanding of how we reveal ourselves to the world – the social mask that we wear. This is the most important angle, but the other three should be included in any reading of a chart.

The second-most important angle is the **midheaven** (also known as the MC), which shows how we wish to impress ourselves on the world at large. It expresses our bigger concerns, and how we would like to be thought of by society as a whole. The ascendant is what people see when they first meet you. The midheaven is what others hear about you.

The **descendant** is what we are looking for in other people, what sort of person we gravitate towards and what sort of life partner we will choose. If you have Pisces on your descendant, your partner will be described as dreamy and imaginative and not a little bit mystical.

The **IC** is the part of ourselves that we are prone to hiding from the world, and also that part that is the least acknowledged and hidden from ourselves. In adults, it defines our deepest motivations and indicates our sense of 'home'.

There is a beautiful logic to these angles. The sign in one angle will always be the opposite sign to the angle on the other side, and they will also always be of the same quadruplicity. Thus, the social mask of the ascendant will always be seeking the exact opposite sign in a partner. For instance, Taurus ascendant will want to be seen as diligent and hard-working, but is looking for the dark and intense Scorpio type, while Aries ascendant will want to be seen as ambitious and energetic yet will always be looking for the frivolous Libra.

In the same way, the outward ideals of the midheaven will always be in the opposite sign to the hidden IC. Rather wonderful, isn't it?

How to Weight a Chart

So now you have a full chart in your hand, whether from the Internet, from an astrologer, or someone has given you their chart. For such a simple little drawing, it's a frightening amount of information. When presented with a chart for the first time, even the most practiced astrologers can feel a little overwhelmed.

There are many traps in chart reading for beginners, and this is why it can seem easier to do your own chart first, so that you are not misleading anyone else. You have no doubt done a rough chart already with the tables in the back of this book and gathered some tantalising insights. But I urge you to wait.

Firstly, you have more in-built prejudices and ideas about the way you are and the way you do things than you do on absolutely anyone else. Most of these are put in place during the teenage years. This is like making a little home for yourself so you can go off and explore the world. If you didn't have any core beliefs, you would be thinking through every decision you made from the very beginning. Should I take the bus? Do I take buses? I have a car, I could take that . . . Then again, am I a car sort of person, or a bus sort of person? And so on.

But in this process, we can set in stone a few things that are more to do with our upbringing than our actual personality. If you have been told repeatedly that you are useless at 'thinking things through logically', you are of course going to think that you are not a logical thinker.

You are more likely to skew your results with your own preconceptions of yourself, but if it is the chart of someone else, you may find it easier to be objective.

Of course, your first subject will have to be a few things – easy-going, open-minded, patient and not likely to take anything the wrong way. Siblings are always good because you know them (but not always as well as you might think), and they are bound by blood to love you, but they won't hesitate in standing up for themselves if they think you have gone too far.

So now you have your chart and subject. There are nine steps that you can follow as a guideline to reading it.

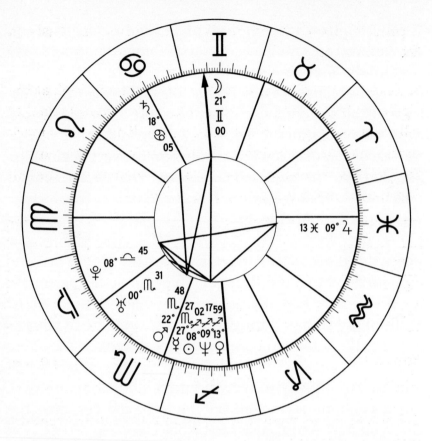

1. The first thing to look at is the shape of the chart. Is it sling shaped, bucket shaped, concentrated in one area or spread evenly? The top half of the chart is considered the conscious social part, the bottom half the subconscious – are the planets all clustered on one side or the other?

2. Check where the ascendant is, and note the position of the ruling planet of the sign on the ascendant. This planet is said to be the 'chart ruler' and flavours the whole chart.

For instance, in the chart above the ascendant is in Virgo. The ruling planet for Virgo is Mercury, so the chart has a 'mental' edge to it. Mercury is in the Third House, of communications, which is the house it rules, in the fixed water sign of Scorpio, so the chart is about someone who is preoccupied with communications with an emphasis on the unknown.

3. Take the ten planets and the ascendant and look at the sign each is in. Using the chart in the Reference section that tells you each sign element and quadruplicity, make a mark in the chart for each sign in the table below – for example, Sagittarius is mutable and fire, so for every planet in Sagittarius make one mark, and so on.

	Fire	Earth	Air	Water
Cardinal	(Aries)	(Capricorn)	(Libra)	(Cancer)
Mutable	(Sagittarius)	(Virgo)	(Gemini)	(Pisces)
Fixed	(Leo)	(Taurus)	(Aquarius)	(Scorpio)

You can see quite easily what is the dominant nature of the chart, and where the cumulative emphasis lies.

4. Look at the signs on the ascendant, the midheaven, the descendant and the IC and list them.

5. Next, look at the houses the planets are in and fill in the table on the following page. Use table 5 in the References section that summarises the houses to help you fill out the last column.

You will end up with eleven statements reading something like: 'Mercury, the planet of Communication expressing itself in an **Aquarian (social networking)** way in the **Sixth House of work**.'

This is a neat little summary. When you become more comfortable at reading a chart, you will still find this a useful construction to fall back on, especially if you come across something you haven't seen before.

Planet = the energy	Sign = how the energy expresses itself	House = where the energy expresses itself
Sun (ego) expressing itself in the	Way in the	House of
Ascendant (social mask) expressing itself in the	Sign	
Moon (emotional) expressing itself in the	Way in the	House of
Mercury (mental communication) expressing itself in the	Way in the	House of
Venus (romance, pleasure) expressing itself in the	Way in the	House of
Mars (energy) expressing itself in the	Way in the	House of
Jupiter (luck) expressing itself in the	Way in the	House of
Saturn (obstacle) expressing itself in the	Way in the	House of
Uranus (eccentricity) expressing itself in the	Way in the	House of
Neptune (fantasy) expressing itself in the	Way in the	House of
Pluto (change) expressing itself in the	Way in the	House of

6. Underline any of the houses that are repeated and take note. A house with many planets will show an area of life where most of the person's energy is concentrated.

7. Next, take a look at the aspects. Some charts will have a little table, like so, in the bottom corner of the page:

Using the reference table in the front of the aspects section to decipher the symbols, circle the major aspects. It is easier to have some coloured pens on hand at this point so you can circle the harmonious major aspects in one colour and the tense major aspects in another.

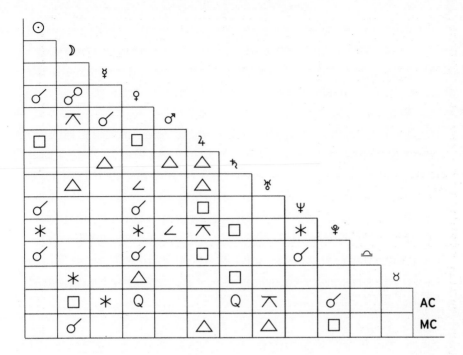

See if there is any one planet with a lot of harmonious aspects. This planet (or planets) should be given special emphasis, because their energy is working well and is free flowing. If a planet has many tense major aspects, this is the energy that the personality has the most trouble expressing, as it has friction with other planets. Mark this planet also for a special mention.

8. Check if any planets make a major aspect to a house cusp, particularly if that cusp happens to be the ascendant, the midheaven, the descendant or the IC. Most computerised charts won't point this out, so you will have to work it out. Planets with a major aspect to an angle cusp (the ASC, MC, IC, or DESC) should be given more weight.

9. Empty houses obviously have less emphasis on the chart than houses that are brimming with life, but this does not mean that this part of the personality lies barren. If you

want to know how these empty houses reveal themselves in the personality, take a look at the sign on the cusp and then the sign following on from that. Then take note of **both** the ruling planets of these signs as the indicators.

For instance, there are no planets in the Seventh House (marriage and relationships) in the chart above. For some reason, people get very anxious about having this house empty, (especially if they are single!), so it is a good one to practice on. Take the cusp of the Seventh House and look at the sign – Pisces, and the sign following on – Aries. The cusp sign is the sign that activates that house (Pisces). Then look at the rulers of these signs – Neptune (for Pisces) and Mars (for Aries).

Neptune is in Sagittarius and Mars is in Scorpio, so it is fantasy expressed in a big-picture way, and energy expressed in emotional intensity. This person doesn't take relationships lightly (Pisces); in fact relationships loom large and are all-encompassing in their fantasies (Neptune in Sagittarius) and once in a relationship, their emotional energy will be highly intense, which could make them possessive (Mars in Scorpio).

Coming to a conclusion from these disparate ideas can be a bit daunting for the novice, but with practice you will be able to relay the general principles in some form.

Another thing to remember in this particular house is the placement of the descendant (the Seventh House cusp). It is said to indicate the sort of person you are likely to marry.

In summary, after following the nine steps outlined above, you should end up with a sheet of paper that looks something like this:

INTERPRETATION

1. Chart Shape – Splayed with concentration of 7 Planets in the first 3 Houses (8 in subconscious).

2. Chart Ruler – **Mercury** (Scorpio, Third House)

3.

	Fire	Earth	Air	Water	
Cardinal			I	I	2
Mutable	III	Asc	I	I	⑥
Fixed				III	3

3	1	2	⑤

Mutable + Water
= **Pisces**

4.   ASC – Virgo
        MC – Gemini
        DESC – Pisces
        IC – Sag

5.   Four planets in the **3rd House.**

Planet = the energy	Sign = how the energy expresses itself		House = where the energy expresses itself	
Sun (ego) expressing itself in the	SAGITTARIUS	Way in the	3rd House of	Communication
Ascendant (social mask) expressing itself in the	VIRGO	Sign		
Moon (emotional) expressing itself in the	GEMINI	Way in the	10th House of	Career
Mercury (mental communication) expressing itself in the	SCORPIO	Way in the	3rd House of	Communication
Venus (romance, pleasure) expressing itself in the	SAGITTARIUS	Way in the	3rd House of	Communication
Mars (energy) expressing itself in the	SCORPIO	Way in the	2nd House of	Material Gains
Jupiter (luck) expressing itself in the	PISCES	Way in the	6th House of	Work
Saturn (obstacle) expressing itself in the	CANCER	Way in the	11th House of	Friends
Uranus (eccentricity) expressing itself in the	SCORPIO	Way in the	2nd House of	Material Gains
Neptune (fantasy) expressing itself in the	SAGITTARIUS	Way in the	3rd House of	Communication
Pluto (change) expressing itself in the	LIBRA	Way in the	1st House of	Self

6. Three major Harmonious Aspects for **Venus, Saturn, Jupiter** and **Neptune.**
Four Major tense Aspects for **Saturn.**

7. **Venus** square the Ascendant, **Moon** coinjunct MC.

8. Empty Houses: Fourth House – Sagittarius, Jupiter/Pisces, Saturn/Cancer
                             Fifth House – Capricorn, Saturn/Cancer, Uranus/Scorpio
                             Seventh House – Pisces, Neptune/Sagittarius, Mars/Scorpio
                             Eighth House – Aries, Mars/Scorpio, Venus/Sagittarius
                             Tenth House – Gemini, Mercury/Scorpio, Moon/Gemini
                             Twelfth House – Leo, Sun/Sagittarius, Mercuy/Scorpio

This will give you the basic material to do a reading, and generally in the right order of emphasis. It is also handy to either keep for later reference, or to give to the person so they will be able to recall some of their reading.

Of course, a reading doesn't stop there. You can then go on to examine what the individual major aspects mean, then onto the minor aspects, the nodes, Chiron and the Pars Fortuna (if the chart shows it), and anything else that might grab your attention.

You will find once you start doing readings that people can get very hung up on minor aspects or empty houses if you don't weight your reading properly. Be assured, if you follow this formula you won't miss anything major and you won't risk overemphasising things that are only light influences.

Things to Think About Before Your First Reading

Astrology is a very powerful tool, and once you have a little knowledge, it can feel a bit like being given the keys to the kingdom. People can be extremely responsive to a reading. More often than not, they will invite you into their confidence and tell you things they would have never have told you otherwise. They feel that you have an insight into their character that other people don't. More importantly, you seem to understand their motives and their behaviour, which makes you more than a sympathetic listener – you are an empathetic ear.

Alternatively, you can really scare people back into their shell. For some, it is very confronting to have someone seeming to peer into their soul and reveal what they see there.

Which of these two responses you get will also depend on your own personality – some people have a knack for tact and some just don't. Ask any Sagittarian!

If you are getting more frightened reactions than tears-and-laughter, take a look at how you are explaining the chart and where you might be subconsciously being negative. It is easy to let your own feelings about certain signs or characteristics show through, but this is not the role of the astrologer. You should be the objective observer, keeping yourself out of it as much as possible and simply telling it like it is.

This is easier said than done, of course. A good way to avoid letting your prejudices show is to acknowledge them in the first place. Take a hard look at your reactions to the different descriptions of the Sun signs. Were there one or two that made you think 'Oh, I can't stand people who are like that . . .'? Listen to yourself when you are talking about other people – what is it that makes you angry? And then write it all down.

Examine why those traits make you cringe. Maybe you had a bad experience with someone, or maybe it is just not the way you do things, or maybe it is something that you don't like in yourself. Sometimes weaknesses that we see in ourselves inspire the most contempt, especially if we have since overcome them. It's a sort of 'if I can do it, why can't you?' reaction.

Once you have all these tendencies down in cold, hard print and have thought through why you dislike them, take a look at each trait and try to see the good side of it. Remember, every failing is just a positive trait overcooked. Moodiness is sensitivity thrice, detachment is the product of a clear and analytical mind, passion can quickly turn into fanaticism and truthfulness can morph into tactlessness.

Having understood the motivations behind these bad traits you will be better equipped to explain them in a more rounded way.

You will become more practised at readings as you go on, but no matter how confident you are, always take a moment to gather your thoughts on how best to express the concept you need to get across.

✧ Concentrate on the positives of any sign or position before easing into the negatives.

✧ Emphasise that problems overcome return far richer rewards than talents frittered away.

✧ Remind the querent that this is not a road map with an inevitable endpoint; rather it is where their strengths and weaknesses naturally lie – what they do with it all is up to them!

✧ Above all, never make a low whistle and say under your breath 'Ooo, . . . that's a doozey . . .' no matter how impressive that Grand Cross might be. People are naturally nervous when laying themselves bare like this, and they are likely to take every little comment very seriously, turning it over and over in their mind in the weeks to come.

Feels great doesn't it? Just remember you are not omnipotent yet . . .

It is certainly a heady rush when you do your first reading and get such an intense response. It can seem like you have put the keys to the kingdom into the lock, turned it, and heard a click. Knowledge is power, said Aquarian Francis Bacon, but just who came up with the saying 'a little bit of knowledge is a dangerous thing' is unfortunately lost in the sands of time.

This is the more appropriate cliche when it comes to astrology. This book has given you a good start, but to call yourself an astrologer takes years of study, so don't get too carried away.

Always keep in mind that astrology is not a science. The most useful thing that astrology can do for you and the people you read for is to act as a circuit breaker. People can easily fall into a rut with how they think about the world and themselves and how they solve problems.

Astrology is a wonderful way of giving someone another perspective, another way of thinking about things, and glimpse at themselves in the mirror through someone else's eyes. Self-awareness is a marvellous thing, and astrology is a very useful tool in that. To think about it as anything more than that is fraught with danger.

Sometimes, knowledge of astrology can actually close rather than open a person's mind. Some people fall into the habit of using their own chart to excuse their bad behaviour. Others become prejudicial against those whose sign doesn't 'gel' with their own and will pick and choose their friends on the basis of their astrological chart. Some astrologers have even been known to adopt different methods of arriving at a chart to make their own chart more favourable!

Don't let any of these examples become you.

Treat astrology with respect but keep it in the context of a myriad of other insightful ways you can think about people and yourself – and always keep in mind that the first principle of astrology is to learn, learn, learn about what makes others tick. You won't get that experience if you close yourself off to people.

Above all, have fun with it and don't let your passion turn you into a zealot.

Dilemmas in Modern Astrology

Myths, Magic and Convenient Lies (Debunking the Debunkers)
Oh! The gravitational pull . . .

'What's your sign?' she breathed over her cocktail, inclining her head ever so slightly.

Captain Capricorn's ears picked up. He may have appeared to her like a relaxed, slightly hippy, Eric-Frampton-wannabe in his brown cable-knit jumper and his caramel cords with just a hint of flare, but really underneath he wore his underpants pulled right up to his belly button.

He was Captain Capricorn, campaigning incognito for truth, justice and the conservative vote.

'So you are into astrology are you?' he said as he pinned her under his keen gaze.

Her eyes widened in fright. She could have kicked herself. It was only now in the dim light she could see that his collar was uncomfortably buttoned down.

'Erm, yes, I suppose so . . .' She shifted from one foot to the other.

'So tell me, why is it that planets thousands of miles away can dictate our daily lives? HUH?!'

Gosh, this guy didn't muck around. She looked around helplessly, fiddling with her straw, garbling about gravity and electromagnetic forces, and the Moon making the tides – 'our bodies are ninety percent water, did you know?' Her voice rang out (too shrill) so she ducked her head, mumbled something about being thirsty, and legged it for the closest exit.

Luckily for her, she got out before he pulled out his Logic Ray Gun and pinned her philosophies to the wall and then pummelled them with his Show-Me-The-Proof punching gloves (last worn by the Catholic Church v. Thomas Huxley, 1860) and snaring any runaway thoughts with his Clap-Trapper 2003.

Don't let this be you. The truth is, there has been no proof found to support the theory of astrology as a science. I can hear your hearts breaking, but this is for your own good. Any theories about the gravity of the planets having an influence over our bodies and minds here on Earth is obviously a bit of a stretch.

Consider Pluto (which can have an extremely powerful effect in your chart). It is no bigger than Europe and sits about forty-one times further from the Sun than the Earth does. To quote Douglas Adams, 'you may think it's a long way down the road to the chemist, but that's just peanuts to space.' It makes the mind boggle doesn't it? But we can't even see Pluto in a telescope, whereas normal everyday things around us also exert a gravitational pull – a pull far greater than that distant little planetoid Pluto.

Sceptics love to quote a book by Roger Culver and Philip Ianna called *Astrology: True or False* when getting excited about the gravitational pull of planets. Their gloating will make you ill when they gleefully point out that the doctor who delivers the baby has about six times the gravitational pull of Mars, and about two thousand billion times its tidal force.

Some well-meaning astrologer postulated that old chestnut about the pull of gravity being the reason for astrology's influence years ago, and it took on a life of its own. Don't get pulled in. Astrology has nothing to do with the gravitational pull of planets. Or their electromagnetic force (whatever that is), or indeed anything we know about, and can take measurements of, with the instruments we have that go 'ping'.

But that *doesn't* mean astrology is a bunk and not worth studying.

It just means science hasn't caught up yet. If you are finding that it works (and you won't be alone in your suspicions) then that's all there is to it. For years science couldn't work out how the bulky body of a bumblebee flew, but the bee kept right on flying anyway, and right on after the scientists caught up. Quantum mechanics flew in the face of everything science had thrown up over the years, but eventually the scientists developed a machine that went 'ping' to prove it.

It's rather ironic that until the beginning of the 20th century the Catholic Church vilified scientists for attacking traditional and fundamental notions about how the world works. Now the scientists are attacking religion for going outside the comfort zone and questioning traditional scientific notions and suggesting all may not be as it seems.

But there is light on the horizon. Science is discovering all the time that no thing exists in isolation and that we are all interconnected. The well-known slogan for the chaos theory (a theory about as misunderstood as the theory of astrology) goes that a butterfly flapping its wings in one part of the world can cause a tornado in another.

Hopefully one day astrology will find its machine that goes 'ping' and there will once again be a place in science books for that wonderfully evocative word 'synchronicity'.

Mythology – myths getting in the way of a good yarn

It is often said that astrologers rely an awful lot on mythology to come up with their conclusions. It's a good point. How can the names of the planets that the Greeks came up with more than two thousand years ago be anything to do with the effect of the planets on the personality?

Well, it is just a way of telling a complex story simply, and astrologers have been guilty of relying solely on them for too long. There are some nice correlations between the actions of the first five planets and their namesakes in mythology, but this may be because the Greeks (who were quite fond of astrology) had observed the influence of stars and planets for some time before naming them. Certainly the last three planets, Uranus, Neptune and Pluto, were named without consideration for their astrological influence.

The myth of Uranus is particularly out of step with its planet. According to mythology, Uranus was leader when Saturn rebelled and overthrew him, but it would be far neater for astrology and the sorts of influences these two planets have if Saturn was the established authority and Uranus the rebellious over-thrower – but you can't have everything.

Mythology is merely a device to make the difficult job of telling the story of astrology a little bit easier. Like using mnemonics to remember a name or sounding out a word when you are first learning to read, relating the myths of ancient Greek and Roman times to the concepts of astrology gives the beginner a handle on these complex, and seemingly disparate ideas and symbols.

But like the archetypes of Jungian psychology, these universal concepts have been a part of our consciousness since year dot, so in fact discovering astrology is often thought of as a relearning rather than a learning process, since we have inherited in our subconscious all the archetypes and symbols.

The Myth of the Cusp

The cusp is the imaginary line between two houses or two signs where they change over from one to the other. People whose Sun lands at the end or the start of a sign are often told they are 'on the cusp', which is usually followed by an airy-fairy explanation of why this person might feel that they straddle two signs, because they are in fact both signs at once.

However, this is not true. There are reasons why someone born close to the cusp will feel as though they embody both signs, but it is not because they are an amalgam of the two.

First, we need to establish what the cusp is. Some people will tell you that you are cusp if you are up to three or four days either side of the changeover. Others will call you cusp only if the Sun is actually touching the imaginary line at the time of your birth (usually no more than twelve hours either side of the cusp).

Some say the influence of one sign gradually fades into the other, others say that a sign is 'unstable' close to the cusp and takes the other's influence. Still others say that a person born at the end of a sign has lived the full breadth of the sign's lessons, whereas someone at the beginning is living the sign for the first time and feels like a foreigner with eyes wide open.

All this conjecture and imagining is not very helpful when you are doing a reading for someone, although the mythology may help you remember the ways in which a personality born on the cusp can manifest itself. But in general, this sort of wishy-washiness does astrology no good. Sceptics quite rightly say you are or you are not a particular sign, and astrology either works or it doesn't work.

And this is the way it works. By now, you will have gathered that a person has more layers to their personality than merely their Sun sign, and people are a combination of many signs, not just one.

We all have every planet in our chart, so when an outrageous Leo born close to the cusp of Virgo tells you earnestly that they sometimes really feel like a Virgo, that they really do have their quiet moments, and that they can be very level-headed should the situation be required, and that sometimes they can be very, very quiet, quiet as a mouse you know, just like a sitting Buddha, no words, nothing to be said, not a sound at all . . .

Before they run out of breath and knock you over with another sweeping hand gesture, you can pat them sympathetically on the arm and say, of course, you are not just a Leo, you are many things, sometimes all at once.

This is not to say it doesn't make a difference being born close to the cusp, only that you are born into one particular Sun sign, not two. Your ego will reflect this sign and this sign alone. But there are reasons why you may closely associate with your neighbouring sign.

One is Mercury. Mercury is always very close to the Sun, either in front or behind, and it is quite possible that if you were born with your Sun at the very end of Leo, your Mercury may have just snuck into the next sign, Virgo, or vice versa. The Sun is your ego and your motivation, a very powerful and obvious part of your personality; but Mercury is your thinking and communication, also a very powerful part of your make-up. If your motivation was all Leo pomp and ceremony, but your mind was Virgo and analytic, it is very easy to see how you could feel that you straddle two worlds.

Another reason for feeling you belong in two Sun signs could be your progressions. Progression is that part of astrology that deals with what is called a 'progressive horoscope'. It is concerned with predicting your path through life from the point of your birth.

Thus your natal chart progresses about 1° per year, showing how your personality will blossom and what lessons you will learn. If your Sun is only 1° away from the next sign, your progressions will put your Sun into the next sign by the time you have turned one, and won't leave that sign until you are in your very late twenties, or possibly early thirties.

By the time you enter the period of self-discovery in your teens, the next sign will be very much a part of your make-up. You will probably feel as though your birth Sun sign is something that you have dealt with, and your daily challenges are more to do with the next sign.

More than likely, it will be one of these things. But if neither of these hold true (perhaps because both your Sun and your Mercury are in the early stages of your Sun sign) and you still swear to having an affinity to both signs, take a closer look at where your other planets lie. They may be clustered in the preceding sign, or in the house that the sign rules (a Virgo with many planets in Leo's house, the Fifth House, for example). You may have a very strongly aspected planet in the sign or the house it rules. Or it may be that the sign's ruling planet (in Leo's case, the Sun) is very strongly aspected. Check which sign the ascendant or the midheaven fall in. There should be a fairly obvious reason why another sign is strongly present; you will just have to do some detective work and find it.

It is easy to see why the myth of the cusp has persisted, when the real explanation is so much harder to decipher, but it is important that we be more accurate when explaining what we know about astrology – it is for the good of the art!

The Age of Aquarius

Are we? Aren't we? When does it start? Since a bunch of actors in cheese-cloth shirts first tread the boards in the musical *Hair* proclaiming that 'this is the dawning of the Age of Aquarius' people have peered into the heavens and wondered what is it, when does it begin, and what on earth does it mean?

The Age of Aquarius has everything to do with the pre-cession of the signs (see the Glosssary for more details). In a nutshell, because of a wobble in the Earth's orbit, when we look up into the sky at the spring equinox (for the northern hemisphere) on 21 March, the Sun is no longer in front of Aries. The signs have shifted backwards and the Sun now sits in front of Pisces. This process will continue, and over 25,920 years the Sun will go through all twelve signs, changing signs about every 2160 years.

So it follows that we are currently in the Age of Pisces, and that our next stop is actually the Age of Aquarius. When that begins, no one knows for sure, because we haven't been keeping accurate records long enough to know exactly. But the date is thought to be between 2060 and 2100, if you assume, as Western astrology does, that the constellations are exactly 30° across.

The problem is, if you take the actual size in the sky of Pisces (which is a comparatively large constellation and takes up 38° of the ecliptic) then the Age of Aquarius does not start until 2600 or thereabouts. We are also not entirely certain that precession is a constant process – the Earth may slow up or go faster.

Another shock is that, while the cast of *Hair* said it was dawning of an age of brotherly love, equality, harmony and understanding, if the early indicators are anything to go by, the Age of Aquarius will probably be more about the indi-vidual, the fall of the Piscean institution of religion, and the rise of technology as an answer to everything! Get a haircut and a job in IT . . .

Hold the front page – horoscopes are a load of bunk

Captain Capricorn is tut-tutting. He almost seems amused by your seeming naivety. 'How,' scoffs he, with a mischievous glint in his eye, 'could you seriously believe that one-twelfth of the population is going to meet a tall, dark and handsome stranger on Tuesday and they will all win lotto if they use the numbers 12, 13, 14, 21, 39 and 6?'

How indeed? Good old Cap'n Cap is, of course, talking about newspaper astrology columns which pretend to predict the course of the lives of everyone with the same Sun sign. He is right to scoff. Nearly all newspaper astrology is absolute twaddle.

I say nearly all, because it is possible (but very difficult) to make some general predictions about how someone with a certain Sun sign will be feeling on a certain day. Most columns do nothing of the sort. In fact very few are written by actual astrologers.

When British astrologer R. H. Naylor invented the daily newspaper astrology column to boost newspaper circulation, it was so popular that there are now very few papers and magazines without their own astrology column.

The worst ones are simply truisms and cliches, construed with the general population in mind. Unless there is a by-line, most newspapers give the astrology column to the copy girl and let her run with it. One example of this has gone down in legend (or is it urban myth?). A hack reporter had been given the job of making up the day's astrological advice. He must have allowed himself a bit of an evil chuckle as he penned this portentous line: 'All the sorrows of yesteryear are as nothing compared to what will befall you today.'

The switchboard went berserk and the journalist was given the boot, but only because he was found out. The situation is changing gradually, with so-called 'star' people – often with a considerable reputation – providing their thoughts. But there are still many editors who don't take astrology seriously enough to employ an astrologer to solely write these columns, when they can get the racing writer to whip them up in his lunch break for an extra tenner. And there is no such thing as a Bureau of Astrology where publications can ring up and get the forecasts for the day ahead, like they can the weather.

Unfortunately, this is pretty much the case for most horoscopes.

Some horoscopes take a step up and give out generally good advice (things that always hold true, such as, 'You should listen to your grandmother, she is wiser than you think' or 'You should always wear clean knickers when playing on the monkey bars'), with the characteristics of the Sun sign in mind. They then couple that with the planetary transits of that day, and in particular, look at the planet that rules that sign and what it is aspecting.

Of course, you really can't give solid predictions on such flimsy information as your Sun sign and the day's planetary transits. But occasionally there is some give good self-help advice that would stand up on its own.

Before you chuck out your subscription to *Horoscope & Predictions Weekly*, there is a way to do general horoscopes, but it is not often employed. You take the chart of that day (using an Equal House System) and place 0° of the Sun sign you are predicting for on the ascendant. You then take note of the relationships of traditional ruling planets (so instead of Pluto you use Mars for Scorpio, Saturn instead of Uranus for Aquarius, and Jupiter instead of Neptune for Pisces). A skilled astrologer should be able to make some fairly specific assertions on the strength of this chart.

If the astrologer really knows their stuff, they will also look at the dispositors of the sign to make a horoscope. A dispositor is the name for a planet that rules the sign that your own ruling planet happens to be in at the time of reading. For instance, if you were doing a reading for Cancer, your subject planet would be the Moon, since the Moon rules Cancer. If the Moon was in Leo, you would look for where the Sun was sitting, as the Sun rules Leo. The Sun would now be called the Moon's dispositor, and an assessment of its position would be made. If the Moon was in Libra, Venus would be the dispositor and so forth. If the Moon happened to be passing through Cancer on that particular day, the Moon would have no dispositor – it would be dispositing itself.

But it must be frankly admitted that very few horoscopes in newspapers and magazines are written using these principles, firstly because many of them are written by people without qualifications and secondly because making an accurate prediction for everyone in the one sign is pretty hit and miss anyway.

It is very rare that an astrologer can make consistent predictions. Predictive astrology is very much in its infancy. Subjectivity clouds the information and the reader will often pre-empt what they want to see, rather than what is in front of them. It is also in the nature of astrology for things not to make sense until they have passed. Unfortunately, our sketchy (but rapidly growing) knowledge of predictive astrology has only cleared our myopia somewhat. The most you can expect from an astrologer in terms of predictions is to tell what you can expect to learn from the events ahead.

A personal horoscope can be illuminating. By using the natal chart and the progressed chart (where the natal chart is progressed by about 1° a year to the present day), plus the chart of the day in question, you can draw up what is known as a daily transit. This type of chart compares where the planets were when you were born to where they are on a given day and what aspects they form. Predictions are made from this information.

The Thirteenth Sign

You may have heard rumours about the 'thirteenth sign'. Like the alien grave in NASA's Area 51, the thirteenth sign gets a fair bit of underground publicity but very few people really know if it exists.

Well, there is a thirteenth sign or, to be more precise, a thirteenth constellation that the planets pass through on their way around the zodiac. Astrology hasn't really been dead straight with people over all these thousands of years. The way astrologers go on about the constellations you would really think they had an innate sense of meaning, and that their placement was as important as the planets. Well, that's not really true.

In fact, the constellations are just arbitrary place-markers. When you think about it, constellations are just stars millions of miles away that have no connection with each other, apart from how they look from here on Earth. When we look up, they appear to be clustered in the same part of the sky.

Of course they are not. No matter our advances in technology, we are never going to be able to travel to Aquarius because Aquarius is not a neighbourhood of galaxies – it just appears that way from here. Just as if you were looking out to sea and saw a dinghy 100 metres away, and sitting directly behind it in your line of sight was a huge oil tanker several kilometres away. The dinghy would appear bigger than the tanker, but that doesn't mean if you swam out to the dinghy you would be very much closer to the oil tanker.

It's the planets that are the real deal in astrology. The constellations are too far away to have a huge impact on us, but they are a useful device to tell us where the planets are. The constellations are also much more poetic to use than the planet's mathematical placements, which don't lend themselves so easily to story-telling. Let us imagine . . . 'OK, Mary, so here we have Venus sitting at the declination 7° 0' from right ascension 9h 15m to 7h 55m 30s in your natal chart. Of course it is well known that having Venus in declination 7° 0' from right ascension 9h 15m to 7h 55m 30s means you will find beauty and love in the home . . .'

Doesn't quite work, does it?

So, here are a few things you should know about how astrology and astronomy differ.

The Subdivison – A Red-tape Nightmare

About 2300 years ago, for the sake of a pleasant day at the office, astrologers divided the Sun's path into twelve sections and ascribed exactly 30° to each sign (12 times 30 equals 360°). But the stars are not so compliant as to rearrange themselves into taking up exactly 30° in the sky. Pisces is huge and hogs a massive 38°, whereas tiny little Cancer takes its place at the table with only 20°. But for the sake of fairness, they were all given 30°.

In those days, astronomers couldn't even agree on where the constellation Cancer began and ended, a problem they only solved last century when the Astronomical Union (which had no interest in issues of astrology) ended the debate. It put out a definitive guide to the constellations' subdivisions that would keep any bureaucrat happy, allotting each constellation its own plot of sky.

Astrologers had always known that the constellations were erratic lengths, but as they were only using them as imaginary pointers in the sky, 30° apart, the Astronomical Union guidelines didn't matter a jot.

Ophiuchus – The Old Kid on the Block

But the new definitions did raise another interesting conundrum for astrologers – they entrenched the thirteenth constellation in the path of the zodiac. This collection of twinkly orbs is called Ophiuchus (pronounced OH-fee-YOO-cuss). It sits right between Scorpio and Sagittarius and it takes up 18°. So the actual backdrop of the ecliptic looks a lot more higgledy-piggledy than the pretty pictures commonly used in astrology texts.

Ophiuchus was well known to ancient astrologers, and there is a tradition of knowledge around Ophiuchus that you can take into account when doing natal charts. A wrap-up of the characteristics of Ophiuchus is given at the end of this chapter.

A Merry Merry Merry-Go-Round

But wait! It gets messier. The path the planets take on their way around the Sun is a lot less regimented than astrologers would like. In fact, it is not really a path that the planets take, it is more like a four-lane highway – and Pluto is asleep at the wheel. The orbit of Pluto is so elliptical that it occasionally comes closer to the Sun than Neptune. It gave up its status as furthest planet form the Sun for twenty years, only recently taking back the title on 11 February 1999. The tilt of Pluto's orbit is also a rakish 17° to the ecliptic.

Mercury could keep its eyes a little more carefully on the road too. Mercury's inclination is about 7° off the ecliptic, although it doesn't go skipping lanes.

So rather than all the planets following the mother duck Sun around the zodiac in strict rotation, they actually take a much more anarchic path, often into uncharted astrological waters.

And if you take in all the constellations that the visible planets venture into (ie, 7° from the ecliptic) you get another eleven constellations – Cetus, Corvus, Scutum, Auriga, Crater, Orion, Serpens (sometimes called a part of Ophiuchus), Pegasus, Sextans, Canis Minor and Hydra.

If you include the constellations that Pluto appears to wobble through, you get another four – Bootes, Coma Berenices, Eridanus and Leo Minor.

So why has Ophiuchus been ignored? Was it superstition about the number 13? Superstition about the sign itself? Was plain-Jane Ophiuchus overlooked for Scorpio's awe-inspiring beauty? The astrologers' obsession with even numbers? Maybe it is just too difficult to pronounce . . . or spell.

Ophiuchus (29 November to 17 December)

Basic characteristics of the sign

Personal creed – *I heal*

Gemstone – Crystal, serpentine

Flower – Peony

Tree – Mistletoe

The constellation of Ophiuchus is often used as a term for two constellations – Ophiuchus and Serpens. It appears that Ophiuchus is holding the snake in Serpens. Ptolemy of Alexandria gave it its Greek name Ophiuchus (ofis 'snake', and echein 'have, hold') and the Romans called it Serpentarius. Both names mean 'snake-holder'. One of the larger constellations, it is flanked by Libra and Scorpio on its southern border, and by Sagittarius to the east with the second part of Serpens. It stretches approximately 18° across the ecliptic.

No one really knows why Ophiuchus went missing, because it rounds out the calendar to a handy twenty-eight days per month (plus one day and one quarter per year). There is some suggestion that it was a 'goddess' month in the Sumerian culture and its symbol was a bare-breasted woman holding two snakes, and that eventually more prudish males took over and tossed it out.

It is also possible that when the Babylonians first named the constellations of the zodiac 3500 years ago, the sky appeared different to the one we gaze upon today. With the precession of the signs and the universe ever-changing, the stars would have been in different positions.

The Ophiuchus Myth

Ophiuchus, in Greek mythology, was Asclepius, healer and the god of wisdom. His name means 'unceasingly gentle'.

Asclepius had rather a rough entry into the world. His mother was a mortal princess called Coronis, his father was the all-powerful Apollo (Mars in Roman mythology). Apollo was so besotted by Coronis that he sent a white crow to look out for her. Alas, she was unfaithful, and the crow came back to Apollo to break the bad news. In a classic case of shoot the messenger, Apollo turned the crow's superb white plumage black for not plucking the suitor's eyes out when he had the chance.

The stories diverge here into two versions – in one, Apollo asked his sister Artemis to kill Coronis. Asclepius was born into the world half-god, half-mortal and running from his vengeful father. They were both captured and the funeral pyre was built and lit, when suddenly Apollo had a sudden change of heart and he saved his son, leaving his mother to burn.

Coronis' father found out and sent an army to Delphi, to Apollo's temple and oracle, and burnt it to the ground. Unfortunately for her well-meaning and justifiably upset papa, you rarely get away with that sort of thing when your enemy is a god. Poor old Dad was sent to Tartarus, which is a kind of dire prison of the Grecian underworld, where he remains in agony for all eternity.

The other version of the story comes from Epidaurus, which is the epicentre of the Ophiuchus/Asclepius cult. Its followers believe that the pregnant Coronis and her father came to Epidaurus, where she delivered her child in the temple of Apollo in the dead of night. Artemis and the Fates helped her. No one knew that she was pregnant and she took the child to the slopes of Mount Titthion, and left him there. A goat and a dog took turns to suckle him and keep him alive.

Both versions then agree that Apollo gave the child to Chiron to raise, from whom Asclepius learnt all manner of godly skills. Chiron passed on to him the art of healing and medicine. Athene, the goddess of reason, gave him phials of blood from a snake-haired monster, one that could turn a human to stone, and one that would bring someone back from the dead.

Ironically, it was the latter phial that caused Asclepius' own death. Hades (Pluto), the god of the underworld, was miffed that the laws of fate were being broken and that the fear of death no longer held sway. When Asclepius tried to bring back Orion the hunter, Zeus (Jupiter) became nervous that Hades would blow his top, so he killed him and put him in the sky and gave him the name Ophiuchus.

After his death, the sick would flock to his temples, which were homes to tame serpents. Priests would perform rituals on them, and after a period of fasting and chewing bay leaves they were allowed to sleep in the inner sanctum of the temple – the 'kline', which is where we get the English word clinic. Asclepius would then appear to them as a dog or a serpent in their dreams, and they would be diagnosed and cured.

The Ophiuchus Character from Ancient Astrology

People born under this sign are naturally empathetic. They tend to see everything in terms of illness and health, and they focus on wellness in others and themselves, both real ills and imagined. They have the potential to be great healers of the mind, body and soul, and once they tap into this wealth of knowledge, they let go of the hypochondria.

They will learn this by learning to listen, which is quite an effort when you are a great talker like the serpent-bearer. People really respond to how the serpent-bearer conveys information. She can speak to anyone on their level, with clarity and pithiness. She can know what to say to cast a light into the darkness, and can make a great therapist or astrologer.

Ophiuchus is endowed with both healing and dramatic powers, and people born under this sign make great actors. They absorb characters as though they are an extension of themselves, and their natural empathy makes it easy for them to throw themselves into the drama with abandon. Sometimes they can empathise a little too well, and will take on the pain of others to their own detriment. They need to work out how much they can carry without burdening their soul to the point of collapse. This is not an easy lesson, as the serpent-bearer's natural impulse is to absorb pain.

Their kindness is often taken advantage of by more ruthless souls, but it is useless to tell them to stop being so naive, they expect to be taken advantage of every now and then.

Often they have some disturbance in their childhood and have an unusual upbringing like the mythological Asclepius. This may not be losing their mother, but some unusual circumstance that they had to grow and learn from. Their preoccupation with illness can lead them from wonder diet to magic potion, and they especially enjoy indulging in naturopathic healing and massage. They are always trying to get others to follow their lead – they live by the creed that you have nothing without your health.

Famous Ophiuchus Sun Signs

29 November 1832 – Louisa May Alcott (writer)

30 November 1835 – Mark Twain (writer)

30 November 1874 – Winston Churchill (political leader)

1 December 1935 – Woody Allen (comedian/film director)

1 December 1945 – Bette Midler (entertainer)

2 December 1981 – Britney Spears (singer)

3 December 1948 – Ozzy Osbourne (entertainer)

4 December 1892 – Francisco Franco (dictator)

5 December 1901 – Walt Disney (animator/film producer)

6 December 1956 – Peter Buck (singer)

7 December 1932 – Ellen Burstyn (actress)

8 December 1925 – Sammy Davis Jr (entertainer)

8 December 1944 – Jim Morrison (musician)

8 December 1967 – Sinead O'Connor (singer)

9 December 1916 – Kirk Douglas (actor)

10 December 1830 – Emily Dickinson (poet)

11 December 1843 – Robert Koch (bacteriologist)

12 December 1915 – Frank Sinatra (singer)

13 December 1925 – Dick Van Dyke (actor)

14 December 1946 – Patty Duke (actor)

16 December 1770 – Ludwig van Beethoven (composer)

16 December 1775 – Jane Austen (writer)

16 December 1899 – Noël Coward (playwright)

16 December 1901 – Margaret Mead (anthropologist)

16 December 1917 – Arthur C Clarke (writer)

17 December 1958 – Mike Mills (musician)

The Precession of the Signs

Let us take another look in the sky, but squint a bit because we are going to look at the Sun. We can't see the constellation that sits behind the Sun at any given time because the Sun's light blocks it out, but about 2300 years ago you could be assured that the Sun was sitting in front of the sign that we were 'in'. For instance, if it was 1 October, you just knew that the Sun was sitting over Libra – you didn't have to think about it.

When the Greeks set their calendar in 300 BC, they decided to pin it on the most obvious dates, the equinoxes, those days so precious to ancient cultures all over the world, when day equals night, in both autumn and spring. When they looked into the heavens that fateful eve, they calculated that the Sun was just moving into Aries on the day of the spring (vernal) equinox, 21 March. Likewise, 0° Libra was placed at the autumn equinox.

This was a difficult enough task without all the instruments we have at our disposal today, but there was one other small issue that the Greeks were unaware of. The Earth is not on a perfect orbit. As we zoom through space at a mind-blowing 18,000 kilometres per second, our Earth makes a small, slow wobble. It is relatively tiny, but has an effect on how we see the sky over time. The constellations appear to move backwards across the sky, very slowly, at about 1° every seventy-two years.

So now during the vernal equinox, the position of the Sun is not 0° Aries but rather less than 10° Pisces.

This is called the 'precession of the equinoxes' and the Greeks appeared to have been unaware of this phenomenon until the second century, although the Egyptians had known about it since 4000 BC and even incorporated it into their religion.

So that's when astrology fixed its charts. The astronomers and astrologers of the day assumed that the universe worked like a clock keeping time. We had an extremely limited concept of the universe until Copernicus and Kepler (a great student of astrology as well as astronomy) came along and set us straight about a few things, and gave Columbus the wacky idea that he might not fall off the edge of the Earth if he took a little look-see around.

But now we know that the universe is expanding and that stars burn out and fade away and a comet isn't necessarily a harbinger of death (unless it is coming straight for you) and all sorts of other wonderful things, and now we also know about the precession of the equinoxes.

So the Sun sits in front of Pisces and is inching its way, bit by bit, into Aquarius. This is why we refer ourselves as being in the Age of Pisces. When the Sun finally does sit in front of Aquarius it will allegedly herald in that age the love, peace and harmony that is the Age of Aquarius (for more detail see the Age of Aquarius earlier in this section).

There is a branch of astrology that takes the precession into account, called sidereal astrology. Starting from where the Sun sits on 21 March, the ecliptic is divided into the twelve 30° slices. Vedic (Indian) astrology uses this method as well.

This table on page 434 shows the differences in dates when comparing where the Sun sits according to tropical, sidereal and actual calculations, including the length of the constellations as we see them in the sky and the constellation Ophiuchus.

So why don't we use the actual placements of the stars?

Very good question. The simple answer is that tropical astrology works.

Over the thousands of years that astrologers have been making observations, the precession of the equinoxes has not seemed to make one jot of difference to the accuracy of the charts. Experiments into sidereal and actual astrology have been just that – experiments. Tropical astrology continues to dominate because it works.

In tropical astrology, the ecliptic is simply measured from

Constellation	Tropical		Sidereal		Actual (2000)		Days
Aries	Mar 21	Apr 20	Apr 14	May 14	Apr 19	May 13	25
Taurus	Apr 21	May 21	May 15	Jun 14	May 12	Jun 22	40
Gemini	May 22	Jun 21	Jun 15	Jul 15	Jun 23	Jul 21	29
Cancer	Jun 22	Jul 22	Jul 16	Aug 16	Jul 20	Aug 10	20
Leo	Jul 23	Aug 22	Aug 17	Sep 16	Aug 9	Sep 16	37
Virgo	Aug 23	Sep 23	Sep 17	Oct 16	Sep 17	Oct 31	45
Libra	Sep 24	Oct 23	Oct 17	Nov 15	Nov 1	Nov 23	23
Scorpius	Oct 24	Nov 22	Nov 16	Dec 15	Nov 22	Nov 29	6
Ophiuchus					Nov 30	Dec 18	19
Sagittarius	Nov 23	Dec 21	Dec 16	Jan 13	Dec 19	Jan 21	34
Capricornus	Dec 22	Jan 20	Jan 14	Feb 12	Jan 22	Feb 16	26
Aquarius	Jan 21	Feb 19	Feb 13	Mar 12	Feb 17	Mar 11	24
Pisces	Feb 20	Mar 20	Mar 13	Apr 13	Mar 12	Apr 18	38

the vernal equinox point and the sky divided into twelve equal slices. So a tropical chart has more to do with the positions of the planets according to the seasons than the position of the constellations. Which to those in the southern hemisphere seems a little odd, as the 'vernal' equinox is actually the beginning of their autumn.

So in the end, astrology comes down to the answer students least like hearing from their science teacher – 'that's just the way it is'. We began this book with the assertion that astrology is a science of observation, in a similar vein to psychology or anthropology. It should be clarified that it is also an issue of faith. Astrology works on premises that we don't fully understand, but its ability to enhance self-awareness is well known. The concept of synchronicity is not foreign to the scientific world, and the chaos theory has moved us on into a better understanding of our interconnectedness; but we are still a long way off understanding why astrology works the way it does. It just does. Use it wisely.

Reference Material

If you are anxious to get started and can't get hold of your full chart, you can use these tables to put together a simple 'Planets in Signs' chart. Following is an outline of the major components you need to put together a chart, and which tables in this reference section to turn to.

✧ Your Sun is in the sign that your birth date falls in.

✧ Your Moon can be found using the Moon Charts (see Tables 1 to 3).

✧ Your Mercury is either the same as your Sun sign, or one sign before or after your Sun sign. For this purpose, it is best to put it in the same sign as your Sun sign.

✧ Your Venus can be found in Table 5 – Venus Tables.

✧ Your Mars can be found in Table 4 – Mars Table.

✧ Jupiter, Saturn, Uranus, Neptune and Pluto can be found in Table 6 – The Outer Planets.

Mark your planets in a simple zodiac wheel. If you know your time of birth, turn the wheel so the Sun is at that spot on the horizon – for instance, if you were born at 6 a.m., the Sun would be almost exactly on the ascendant line; if you were born at midday, turn the wheel so the Sun is at the top of the chart.

Then mark out the houses in the usual way. This chart will be far from exact and is not good enough for marking aspects, but it will get you started.

Moon Chart

1. To use this chart, simply find your year and month of birth in Table 3. Write down the glyph.

2. Then, referring to Table 2, look up your birth date and note down the number.

3. Find your glyph in Table 1 – Zodiacal Glyphs, and then count through the signs the number from Table 2.

4. The one you land on is your Moon sign.

For example, if you were born on 15 April 1945, you would find the glyph ♏ (Scorpio) in Table 3 under April 1945. Under the number 15 (referring to the 15 of your birthday) in Table 2, you find the number 6. Then you find the Scorpio glyph in Table 1 and count down through the chart from Scorpio (Sagittarius is 1, Capricorn is 2, Aquarius is 3, Pisces is 4, Aries is 5, Taurus is 6). The sixth glyph is Taurus so your Moon sign is Taurus.

Table 1   Zodiacal Glyphs

♈	Aries
♉	Taurus
♊	Gemini
♋	Cancer
♌	Leo
♍	Virgo
♎	Libra
♏	Scorpio
♐	Sagittarius
♑	Capricorn
♒	Aquarius
♓	Pisces

Table 2   For Moon Chart

Day	Add	Day	Add	Day	Add	Day	Add
1	0	9	4	17	7	25	11
2	1	10	4	18	8	26	11
3	1	11	5	19	8	27	12
4	1	12	5	20	9	28	12
5	2	13	5	21	9	29	1
6	2	14	6	22	10	30	1
7	3	15	6	23	10	31	2
8	3	16	7	24	10		

Table 3   For Moon Chart

	1930	1931	1932	1933	1934	1935	1936	1937	1938	1939	1940	1941	1942	1943	1944	1945
JAN	♑	♉	♎	♓	♋	♏	♈	♌	♑	♉	♍	♒	♊	♎	♓	♌
FEB	♓	♋	♐	♈	♌	♑	♉	♎	♒	♊	♏	♈	♌	♐	♉	♍
MAR	♓	♋	♐	♉	♍	♑	♊	♎	♒	♋	♐	♈	♌	♐	♉	♎
APR	♉	♍	♒	♋	♎	♓	♌	♐	♈	♌	♑	♉	♎	♒	♋	♏
MAY	♊	♎	♓	♋	♐	♈	♍	♑	♉	♎	♒	♊	♏	♓	♌	♐
JUN	♌	♐	♉	♍	♑	♊	♎	♒	♋	♏	♈	♌	♑	♉	♎	♒
JUL	♍	♑	♊	♎	♓	♋	♏	♈	♌	♑	♉	♍	♒	♊	♏	♓
AUG	♏	♓	♋	♐	♈	♌	♑	♉	♎	♒	♋	♏	♈	♌	♐	♉
SEP	♐	♈	♍	♑	♊	♎	♓	♋	♏	♈	♌	♑	♉	♍	♒	♋
OCT	♑	♉	♎	♓	♋	♏	♈	♌	♑	♉	♎	♒	♊	♎	♓	♌
NOV	♓	♋	♐	♈	♌	♑	♊	♎	♒	♊	♏	♈	♌	♐	♉	♍
DEC	♈	♌	♑	♉	♍	♒	♋	♏	♓	♌	♑	♉	♍	♑	♊	♎

	1946	1947	1948	1949	1950	1951	1952	1953	1954	1955	1956	1957	1958	1959	1960	1961
JAN	♐	♈	♍	♑	♊	♎	♓	♋	♏	♈	♌	♑	♉	♍	♒	♋
FEB	♑	♊	♎	♓	♋	♐	♈	♍	♑	♉	♎	♒	♊	♏	♈	♌
MAR	♒	♊	♏	♓	♋	♐	♉	♍	♑	♊	♏	♓	♋	♏	♈	♌
APR	♓	♋	♑	♉	♍	♒	♊	♎	♓	♋	♐	♈	♎	♑	♊	♎
MAY	♉	♍	♒	♊	♎	♓	♋	♐	♈	♍	♑	♉	♐	♒	♋	♏
JUN	♊	♏	♉	♌	♐	♈	♍	♑	♉	♎	♓	♋	♑	♈	♌	♒
JUL	♌	♐	♉	♍	♑	♊	♎	♓	♋	♏	♈	♌	♒	♉	♍	♒
AUG	♍	♑	♊	♏	♓	♋	♐	♈	♍	♑	♉	♎	♓	♊	♏	♈
SEP	♏	♓	♋	♐	♈	♍	♑	♊	♎	♒	♋	♐	♈	♌	♑	♊
OCT	♐	♈	♍	♑	♊	♎	♓	♋	♏	♓	♌	♑	♉	♍	♒	♋
NOV	♑	♊	♏	♓	♋	♏	♈	♍	♑	♉	♎	♒	♊	♏	♈	♌
DEC	♒	♋	♐	♈	♌	♑	♊	♎	♒	♏	♓	♋	♐	♉	♍	

	1962	1963	1964	1965	1966	1967	1968	1969	1970	1971	1972	1973	1974	1975	1976	1977
JAN	♏	♓	♌	♐	♈	♍	♑	♊	♎	♒	♋	♐	♈	♋	♑	♉
FEB	♐	♉	♍	♒	♊	♏	♓	♋	♏	♈	♍	♑	♉	♎	♒	♋
MAR	♐	♉	♎	♒	♊	♏	♈	♌	♐	♉	♍	♑	♊	♎	♓	♋
APR	♒	♋	♏	♈	♌	♑	♉	♍	♒	♊	♏	♓	♋	♐	♈	♍
MAY	♓	♌	♐	♉	♍	♒	♊	♎	♓	♋	♐	♈	♍	♑	♉	♎
JUN	♉	♎	♒	♊	♏	♓	♌	♐	♉	♍	♑	♊	♎	♓	♋	♐
JUL	♊	♏	♓	♌	♐	♈	♍	♑	♊	♎	♓	♋	♐	♈	♌	♑
AUG	♌	♐	♉	♎	♒	♊	♏	♓	♋	♏	♈	♍	♑	♉	♎	♓
SEP	♍	♒	♋	♏	♓	♋	♐	♉	♌	♑	♊	♎	♒	♋	♏	♉
OCT	♏	♌	♋	♐	♈	♍	♑	♊	♎	♒	♋	♐	♈	♌	♑	♉
NOV	♐	♉	♎	♒	♊	♎	♓	♋	♐	♈	♍	♑	♉	♎	♓	♋
DEC	♑	♊	♏	♓	♋	♐	♈	♌	♑	♉	♎	♒	♊	♏	♈	♌

	1978	1979	1980	1981	1982	1983	1984	1985	1986	1987	1988	1989	1990	1991	1992	1993
JAN	♍	♒	♊	♏	♓	♌	♐	♉	♍	♑	♊	♎	♒	♍	♏	♈
FEB	♏	♈	♋	♐	♉	♍	♒	♊	♎	♓	♋	♐	♈	♍	♑	♉
MAR	♏	♈	♍	♑	♉	♎	♒	♊	♏	♓	♌	♐	♉	♏	♒	♊
APR	♑	♊	♎	♒	♋	♏	♈	♌	♑	♉	♍	♒	♊	♐	♓	♋
MAY	♒	♋	♏	♓	♌	♐	♉	♍	♒	♊	♏	♓	♌	♑	♈	♍
JUN	♈	♌	♑	♉	♎	♒	♊	♏	♓	♋	♐	♉	♍	♒	♊	♎
JUL	♉	♍	♒	♋	♏	♓	♌	♐	♉	♍	♑	♊	♎	♈	♋	♐
AUG	♋	♏	♈	♌	♐	♈	♎	♉	♊	♎	♓	♌	♐	♊	♍	♑
SEP	♌	♐	♊	♎	♒	♊	♏	♓	♌	♐	♉	♍	♑	♋	♏	♓
OCT	♍	♒	♋	♏	♓	♋	♐	♉	♍	♑	♊	♎	♒	♋	♐	♈
NOV	♏	♓	♌	♐	♉	♍	♒	♊	♎	♓	♌	♐	♈	♍	♑	♉
DEC	♐	♉	♍	♑	♊	♎	♓	♋	♐	♈	♍	♑	♉	♎	♒	♋

	1994	1995	1996	1997	1998	1999	2000
JAN	♌	♑	♉	♎	♒	♊	♏
FEB	♎	♒	♋	♏	♈	♌	♐
MAR	♎	♓	♋	♏	♈	♌	♑
APR	♐	♈	♍	♑	♊	♎	♓
MAY	♑	♉	♎	♒	♋	♏	♈
JUN	♓	♋	♐	♈	♌	♑	♉
JUL	♈	♌	♑	♉	♎	♒	♋
AUG	♉	♎	♓	♋	♏	♓	♌
SEP	♋	♏	♈	♌	♑	♉	♎
OCT	♌	♑	♉	♎	♒	♊	♏
NOV	♎	♒	♋	♏	♈	♌	♑
DEC	♏	♈	♌	♐	♉	♍	♒

Table 4 Mars Table

	JAN	MAY	SEPT		JAN	MAY	SEPT
1950	♎	♍	♏	1971	♏	♑	♒
1951	♒	♉	♌	1972	♈	♊	♍
1952	♎	♏	♐	1973	♐	♒	♉
1953	♓	♉	♌	1974	♉	♋	♍
1954	♏	♑	♑	1975	♐	♓	♊
1955	♓	♊	♍	1976	♊	♋	♎
1956	♏	♒	♓	1977	♐	♈	♊
1957	♈	♊	♍	1978	♌	♌	♎
1958	♐	♓	♉	1979	♑	♈	♋
1959	♉	♋	♍	1980	♍	♌	♏
1960	♐	♓	♊	1981	♒	♉	♋
1961	♋	♋	♎	1982	♎	♎	♏
1962	♑	♈	♋	1983	♒	♉	♌
1963	♌	♌	♎	1984	♎	♏	♐
1964	♑	♈	♋	1985	♓	♊	♌
1965	♍	♍	♏	1986	♏	♑	♑
1966	♒	♉	♌	1987	♓	♊	♍
1967	♎	♎	♏	1988	♎	♒	♈
1968	♒	♉	♌	1989	♈	♋	♍
1969	♏	♐	♐	1990	♐	♓	♊

Table 5 Venus Tables

	JAN	FEB	MAR	APR	MAY	JUN	JUL	AUG	SEP	OCT	NOV	DEC
1930	♑	♒	♓	♈	♊	♋	♌	♍	♎	♏	♏	♏
1931	♏	♐	♑	♓	♈	♉	♊	♋	♍	♎	♏	♑
1932	♒	♓	♈	♉	♊	♋	♊	♊	♋	♌	♎	♏
1933	♐	♑	♒	♈	♉	♊	♋	♍	♎	♏	♐	♑
1934	♒	♒	♒	♒	♓	♈	♊	♋	♌	♍	♏	♐
1935	♑	♓	♈	♉	♊	♋	♌	♍	♍	♍	♍	♎
1936	♏	♑	♒	♓	♈	♊	♋	♌	♍	♏	♐	♑
1937	♒	♓	♈	♈	♈	♈	♉	♊	♌	♍	♎	♏
1938	♑	♒	♓	♈	♊	♋	♌	♍	♎	♏	♏	♏
1939	♏	♐	♑	♓	♈	♉	♊	♋	♍	♎	♏	♑
1940	♒	♓	♈	♉	♊	♋	♊	♊	♋	♌	♎	♏
1941	♐	♑	♒	♈	♉	♊	♋	♍	♎	♏	♐	♑
1942	♒	♒	♒	♒	♓	♈	♊	♋	♌	♍	♏	♐
1943	♑	♓	♈	♉	♊	♋	♌	♍	♍	♍	♍	♎
1944	♏	♑	♒	♓	♈	♊	♋	♌	♍	♏	♐	♑
1945	♒	♓	♈	♈	♈	♈	♉	♊	♌	♍	♎	♏
1946	♑	♒	♓	♈	♊	♋	♌	♍	♎	♏	♏	♏
1947	♏	♐	♑	♓	♈	♉	♊	♋	♍	♎	♏	♑
1948	♒	♓	♈	♉	♊	♋	♊	♊	♋	♌	♎	♏
1949	♐	♑	♒	♈	♉	♊	♋	♍	♎	♏	♐	♑
1950	♒	♒	♒	♒	♓	♈	♊	♋	♌	♍	♏	♐
1951	♑	♓	♈	♉	♊	♋	♌	♍	♍	♍	♍	♎
1952	♏	♑	♒	♓	♈	♊	♋	♌	♍	♏	♐	♑
1953	♒	♓	♈	♈	♈	♈	♉	♊	♌	♍	♎	♏
1954	♑	♒	♓	♈	♊	♋	♌	♍	♎	♏	♏	♏
1955	♏	♐	♑	♓	♈	♉	♊	♋	♍	♎	♏	♑

	JAN	FEB	MAR	APR	MAY	JUN	JUL	AUG	SEP	OCT	NOV	DEC
1956	♒	♓	♈	♉	♊	♋	♊	♊	♋	♌	♎	♏
1957	♐	♑	♒	♈	♉	♊	♋	♍	♎	♏	♐	♑
1958	♒	♒	♒	♒	♓	♈	♊	♋	♌	♍	♏	♐
1959	♑	♓	♈	♉	♊	♋	♌	♍	♍	♍	♍	♎
1960	♏	♑	♒	♓	♈	♊	♋	♌	♍	♏	♐	♑
1961	♒	♓	♈	♈	♈	♈	♉	♊	♌	♍	♎	♏
1962	♑	♒	♓	♈	♊	♋	♌	♍	♎	♏	♏	♏
1963	♏	♐	♑	♓	♈	♉	♊	♋	♍	♎	♏	♑
1964	♒	♓	♈	♉	♊	♋	♊	♊	♋	♌	♎	♏
1965	♐	♑	♒	♈	♉	♊	♋	♍	♎	♏	♐	♑
1966	♒	♒	♒	♒	♓	♈	♊	♋	♌	♍	♏	♐
1967	♑	♓	♈	♉	♊	♋	♌	♍	♍	♍	♍	♎
1968	♏	♑	♒	♓	♈	♊	♋	♌	♍	♏	♐	♑
1969	♒	♓	♈	♈	♈	♈	♉	♊	♌	♍	♎	♏
1970	♑	♒	♓	♈	♊	♋	♌	♍	♎	♏	♏	♏
1971	♏	♐	♑	♓	♈	♉	♊	♋	♍	♎	♏	♑
1972	♒	♓	♈	♉	♊	♋	♊	♊	♋	♌	♎	♏
1973	♐	♑	♒	♈	♉	♊	♋	♍	♎	♏	♐	♑
1974	♒	♒	♒	♒	♓	♈	♊	♋	♌	♍	♏	♐
1975	♑	♓	♈	♉	♊	♋	♌	♍	♍	♍	♍	♎
1976	♏	♑	♒	♓	♈	♊	♋	♌	♍	♏	♐	♑
1977	♒	♓	♈	♈	♈	♈	♉	♊	♌	♍	♎	♏
1978	♑	♒	♓	♈	♊	♋	♌	♍	♎	♏	♏	♏
1979	♏	♐	♑	♓	♈	♉	♊	♋	♍	♎	♏	♑
1980	♒	♓	♈	♉	♊	♋	♊	♊	♋	♌	♎	♏
1981	♐	♑	♒	♈	♉	♊	♋	♍	♎	♏	♐	♑
1982	♒	♒	♒	♒	♓	♈	♊	♋	♌	♍	♏	♐
1983	♑	♓	♈	♉	♊	♋	♌	♍	♍	♍	♍	♎
1984	♏	♑	♒	♓	♈	♊	♋	♌	♍	♏	♐	♑
1985	♒	♓	♈	♈	♈	♈	♉	♊	♌	♍	♎	♏
1986	♑	♒	♓	♈	♊	♋	♌	♍	♎	♏	♏	♏
1987	♏	♐	♑	♓	♈	♉	♊	♋	♍	♎	♏	♑
1988	♒	♓	♈	♉	♊	♋	♊	♊	♋	♌	♎	♏
1989	♐	♑	♒	♈	♉	♊	♋	♍	♎	♏	♐	♑
1990	♒	♒	♒	♒	♓	♈	♊	♋	♌	♍	♏	♐
1991	♑	♓	♈	♉	♊	♋	♌	♍	♍	♍	♍	♎
1992	♏	♑	♒	♓	♈	♊	♋	♌	♍	♏	♐	♑
1993	♒	♓	♈	♈	♈	♈	♉	♊	♌	♍	♎	♏
1994	♑	♒	♓	♈	♊	♋	♌	♍	♎	♏	♏	♏
1995	♏	♐	♑	♓	♈	♉	♊	♋	♍	♎	♏	♑
1996	♒	♓	♈	♉	♊	♋	♊	♊	♋	♌	♎	♏
1997	♐	♑	♒	♈	♉	♊	♋	♍	♎	♏	♐	♑
1998	♒	♒	♒	♒	♓	♈	♊	♋	♌	♍	♏	♐
1999	♑	♓	♈	♉	♊	♋	♌	♍	♍	♍	♍	♎
2000	♏	♑	♒	♓	♈	♊	♋	♌	♍	♏	♐	♑

Table 6 **The Outer Planets**

JAN	JUPITER	SATURN	URANUS	NEPTUNE	PLUTO
1950	♒	♍	♋	♎	♌
1951	♓	♎	♋	♎	♌
1952	♈	♎	♋	♎	♌
1953	♉	♎	♋	♎	♌
1954	♊	♏	♋	♎	♌
1955	♋	♏	♋	♎	♌
1956	♍	♏	♌	♏	♌
1957	♎	♐	♌	♏	♍
1958	♎	♐	♌	♏	♍
1959	♏	♐	♌	♏	♍
1960	♐	♑	♌	♏	♍
1961	♑	♑	♌	♏	♍
1962	♒	♑	♍	♏	♍
1963	♓	♒	♍	♏	♍
1964	♈	♒	♍	♏	♍
1965	♉	♓	♍	♏	♍
1966	♊	♓	♍	♏	♍
1967	♌	♓	♍	♏	♍
1968	♍	♈	♍	♏	♍
1969	♎	♈	♎	♏	♍
1970	♏	♉	♎	♏	♍
1971	♏	♉	♎	♐	♍
1972	♐	♊	♎	♐	♎
1973	♑	♊	♎	♐	♎
1974	♒	♋	♎	♐	♎
1975	♓	♋	♏	♐	♎
1976	♈	♌	♏	♐	♎
1977	♉	♌	♏	♐	♎
1978	♊	♍	♏	♐	♎
1979	♌	♍	♏	♐	♎
1980	♍	♍	♏	♐	♎
1981	♎	♎	♏	♐	♎
1982	♏	♎	♐	♐	♎
1983	♐	♏	♐	♐	♏
1984	♐	♏	♐	♐	♏
1985	♑	♏	♐	♑	♏
1986	♒	♐	♐	♑	♏
1987	♓	♐	♐	♑	♏
1988	♈	♐	♐	♑	♏
1989	♉	♑	♑	♑	♏
1990	♋	♑	♑	♑	♏

Reference Tables

Much has been said about the Signs, Planets and Houses throughout this book. For your convenience the most useful information is summarised in the following tables.

Table 1   Keywords of the Signs

Sign	Glyph	Keywords
Aries	♈	Assertive, Impulsive, Aggressive, Innovative
Taurus	♉	Persevering, Materialistic, Stubborn, Sensual
Gemini	♊	Versatile, Communicative, Curious, Superficial
Cancer	♋	Sensitive, Protective, Creative, Manipulative
Leo	♌	Proud, Gregarious, Practical, Self-Absorbed
Virgo	♍	Enterprising, Meticulous, Pedantic, Intellectual
Libra	♎	Affable, Harmony-Loving, Articulate, Aesthete
Scorpio	♏	Intense, Shrewd, Loyal, Partial
Sagittarius	♐	Extroverted, Forward-Thinking, Wasteful, Motivating
Capricorn	♑	Inhibited, Ambitious, Responsible, Staid
Aquarius	♒	Social, Philosophical, Eccentric, High-Strung
Pisces	♓	Romantic, Enigmatic, Reclusive, Wet

Table 2   Details of the Signs

Sign	Date Begin**	Symbol	Ruler	+/-	Mode†	Element†	Psychic Element	Temperament
Aries	21 Mar	Ram	Mars	+	Cardinal	Fire	Intuition	Choleric
Taurus	20 Apr	Bull	Venus	-	Fixed	Earth	Perception	Melancholic
Gemini	21 May	Twins	Mercury	+	Mutable	Air	Thinking	Sanguine
Cancer	21 Jun	Crab	Moon	-	Cardinal	Water	Feeling	Phlegmatic
Leo	22 Jul	Lion	Sun	+	Fixed	Fire	Intuition	Choleric
Virgo	23 Aug	Virgin	Mercury	-	Mutable	Earth	Perception	Melancholic
Libra	23 Sep	Scales	Venus	+	Cardinal	Air	Thinking	Sanguine
Scorpio	23 Oct	Scorpion	Pluto*	-	Fixed	Water	Feeling	Phlegmatic
Sagittarius	22 Nov	Archer	Jupiter	+	Mutable	Fire	Intuition	Choleric
Capricorn	21 Dec	Goat	Saturn	-	Cardinal	Earth	Perception	Melancholic
Aquarius	20 Jan	Water-bearer	Uranus*	+	Fixed	Air	Thinking	Sanguine
Pisces	19 Feb	Fish	Neptune*	-	Mutable	Water	Feeling	Phlegmatic

* Before the discovery of Uranus, Neptune and Pluto: Scorpio ruled by Mars, Aquarius ruled by Saturn and Pisces ruled by Jupiter.
** Dates are approximate and vary from year to year.
† Mode also known as Quadruplicity or Quality; Elements also known as Triplicity.

Diagram 1   Visual Summary of Signs

Use this diagram to quickly identify groups of signs. For example, the whole left side of the diagram represents Positive Signs. We instantly see the six Positive Signs.

If we look in the area of Fire, we see that Aries, Sagittarius and Leo are Fire Signs. Or we can see that the Positive, Fixed Signs are Leo and Aquarius.

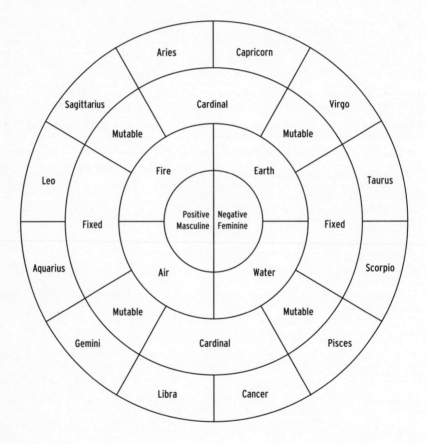

Table 3 Keywords of the Planets/ Calculated Points

Planet	Keywords
Sun	Individuality, Vitality, Potential, Ego, Your outward expression, Your lifeforce
Moon	Personality, Nourishment, Creativity, Intuition, Your emotional expression
Mercury	Communication, Versatility, Expression, Intellect
Venus	Love, Indulgence, Charm, Appearance
Mars	Impulsion, Assertion, Motivation, Aggression, Your energy level
Jupiter	Luck, Generosity, Religion, Wisdom, Your magnanimity and bonhomie
Saturn	Discipline, Lessons, Inadequacy, Challenge, Your obstacles and restrictions
Uranus	Independence, Originality, Humanitarianism, Eccentricities and lateral thinking
Neptune	Spirituality, Illusion, Escapism, Fantasy
Pluto	Birth, Death, Regeneration, Obsession, Change, All or nothing
North Node	Opportunity for growth and development.
South Node	Repression or tendencies that restrict growth.
Ascendant	Outer-self, Superficiality, Social Identity, Your social mask
Pars Fortuna	Prosperity, Physicality, Success, Direction
Chiron	Healing, Restoration of Balance, Independence

Table 4   Details of the Planets/ Calculated Points

Planet	Glyph	Greek God*	Rules	Detriment	Exalted	Fall	Sign Time**
Sun	☉	Apollo	Leo	Aquarius	Aries	Libra	1 Month
Moon	☽	Artemis	Cancer	Capricorn	Taurus	Scorpio	2.5 Days
Mercury	☿	Hermes	Gem'/Virgo	Sag'/Pisces	Virgo/Aqua'	Pisces/Leo	1 Month
Venus	♀	Aphrodite	Taur'/Libra	Scorp'/Aries	Pisces	Virgo	1 Month
Mars	♂	Ares	Aries	Libra	Capricorn	Cancer	2 Months
Jupiter	♃	Zeus	Sagittarius	Gemini	Cancer	Virgo/Cap'	1 Year
Saturn	♄	Cronus	Capricorn	Cancer	Libra	Aries	2.5 Years
Uranus	♅	Ouranos	Aquarius	Leo	Scorpio	Taurus	7.5 Years
Neptune	♆	Poseidon	Pisces	Virgo	Cancer	Capricorn	15 Years
Pluto	♇	Hades	Scorpio	-	-	-	30 Years
North Node	☊	-	-	-	Gemini	Sagittarius	1.5 Years
South Node	☋	-	-	-	Sagittarius	Gemini	1.5 Years
Ascendant	ASC	-	-	-	-	-	2 Hours
Pars Fortuna	⊗	-	-	-	-	-	-
Chiron	⚷	Chiron	-	-	-	-	4 Years

*Planets are named after Roman Gods; here are the Greek equivalents.
*Approximate average time the Planet spends in each sign.

Table 5 Details and Keywords of the Houses

House	Natural Chart	Keywords	Modes*	Elements*	Orientation
First	Aries	Self, Appearance	Angular	Individual	Personal
Second	Taurus	Earnings, Possessions	Succedent	Temporal	Personal
Third	Gemini	Communications, Relatives	Cadent	Relative	Personal
Fourth	Cancer	Home, Parents	Angular	Terminal	Personal
Fifth	Leo	Pleasures, Children	Succedent	Individual	Social
Sixth	Virgo	Health, Service	Cadent	Temporal	Social
Seventh	Libra	Spouse, Partnerships	Angular	Relative	Social
Eighth	Scorpio	Death, Regeneration	Succedent	Terminal	Social
Ninth	Sagittarius	Philosophy, Travel	Cadent	Individual	Universal
Tenth	Capricorn	Career, Status	Angular	Temporal	Universal
Eleventh	Aquarius	Friends, Aspiration	Succedent	Relative	Universal
Twelfth	Pisces	Secrets, Limitations	Cadent	Terminal	Universal

*Division of the Houses is not normally given a unique name, however Angular, Succedent and Cadent Houses correspond to the Cardinal, Fixed and Mutable Signs (Modes); and Individual, Temporal, Relative and Terminal Houses correspond to the Fire, Earth, Air and Water Signs (Elements).

Table 6   Aspects – Major

Aspects	# of Signs	Degrees	Glyph	Diagram	Effect
Conjunction	0	0°	☌		Compound – Union of energies in the Sign and House.
Opposition	6	180°	☍		Great tension and conflict between Planets. A harmonious Aspect between one of the Opposed Planets and a third Planet will help release tension.
Quincunx	5	150°	⚻		Uneasiness and discomfort between the Planets affecting the function of Planetary energy.
Trine	4	120°	△		Great harmony and co-operation between Planets. Expression of energy is unhindered.
Square	3	90°	☐		Similar to the Opposition but to a lesser degree.
Sextile	2	60°	✳		Similar to the Trine but to a lesser degree.

Table 7   Aspects – Minor

Aspects	Degrees	Glyph	Diagram	Comment
Bi-Quintile	144°			2 Quintiles – Rare
Sesquiquadrate	135°	⊞		Common Minor Aspect
Bi-Septile	102.8°			2 Septiles – Rare
Quintile	72°	Q		Common Minor Aspect
Septile	51.4°			Rarely Used
Semi-Square	45°	‹		Common Minor Aspect
Nonagen	40°			Rarely Used
Decile	36°		1/10	Rarely Used
Semi-Sextile	30°	⊻		Common Minor Aspect
Quarto-Square	22.5		1/16	Rarely Used
Semi-Decile	18		1/20	Rarely Used

Glossary

Most astrological terms have greater and lesser usage depending on which branch of astrology you are studying. This glossary contains a wide variety of words to enable you to place the context of many terms you might encounter – in classes, books and especially on the Internet.

You should not randomly look up words in this glossary and begin applying them to your chart or the charts of others, as some terms, while not being officially extinct, are not used in any significant way. Instead, use this glossary as a quick reference when you come across something unfamiliar in your wider reading. See also the reference tables earlier in this section for keywords and other useful information regarding the signs, planets and houses.

accidental dignity
A favourable position (dignity) achieved by a planet with regards to the house it is in, that is, it accidentally finds itself in a house with similar energy.

afflicted
Describes a planet that has a bad aspect, such as square, opposition and quincunx aspects. An ancient but commonly used term.

Age of Aquarius
See *Aquarian Age*.

air signs
Gemini, Libra and Aquarius (all masculine signs). Air represents intellect and thought processes.

In a natural wheel they occupy the Third, Seventh and Eleventh Houses.

Alcabitius House System
Method of house division similar to the more popular Placidus House System, and considered to be accurate for polar regions.

almanac
An annual calendar publication dealing with historical and astrological data, weather predictions and agricultural time-tables.

almuten
Translates as 'The Winner'. A way of scoring points to each planet based on the five essential dignities. Every degree in the chart can be ascribed an almuten and some more than one.

anaretic degree
The final degree (ie, the 29th degree) of any sign. It is also known as the degree of fate.

angle
Any of the four cardinal points are called angles. The cardinal points are the axes of the chart, that is, the horizontal and vertical lines. The eastern angle is also known as the ascendant; the western angle as the descendant; the southern angle is the medium coeli (MC); and the northern angle is the imum coeli (IC).

angular houses
The First, Fourth, Seventh and Tenth Houses and corresponding to cardinal signs. From the term angle (not the common meaning for angle, but referring to lines on the chart – see *angle*).

antipathy
An inharmonious relationship of planets caused by their different natures, by aspect or by detriment or fall.

aphelion
The name given to the point in a planet's orbit when it is furthest from the Sun.

apogee
The point in the Moon's orbit when it is furthest from the Earth.

apparent magnitude
Describes the apparent brightness of a star.

applying aspect
The movement of one planet towards another planet, house cusp or sensitive point in approaching the formation of an aspect between them. Both planets may be in direct motion, or one may be direct and the other retrograde, or both may be in retrograde motion. See also *mutual application*.

Aquarian Age
A period of 2160 years where the vernal equinox is found in the sign Aquarius. We are currently on the cusp of the Age of Pisces and the Age of Aquarius and there is debate about whether the Aquarian Age has already begun. See also *precession*.

Arabic part
A significant calculated point in the sky whose position is derived from a combination of other significant points or planets. Derived from Arabic astrology.

arc
An angular measurement between two celestial planets or points.

ascendant
ASC. The degree of the zodiac on the ecliptic that is rising over the eastern horizon at the time of birth shown in a natal chart. Determines the position of the First House. Its opposite is the descendant.

Defines what the querent believes themselves to be, or shows the superficial face of their personality.

ascension
Signs of short ascension rise quickly over the horizon, while signs of long ascension rise slowly.

Because of the angle of the Earth's axis at 23.45° to the equator, some signs lie north and others south of the equator. Due to the curve that this causes in the zodiac, some signs rise slowly and others quickly.

aspect
The angular relationship between planets and other points in the sky. These are often divided into major and minor aspects.

asteroids
Small bodies located mostly between Mars and Jupiter. There are, at last count, 12,487 asteroids.

astrologer
A professional who studies the positions and aspects of planets and stars, believing these things have an influence over humans and human affairs.

autumnal equinox
The equinox before autumn.

balsamic phase
When a more quickly orbiting planet trails a planet with a slower orbit and appears to 'catch up' with the slower body. Deals with your dedication to your destiny.

barren signs
These are Gemini, Leo, Virgo. Considered to be infertile of body and ideas.

Bary Centre
The point corresponding to the centre of mass of the solar system, which the planets orbit. The Bary Centre is normally close to the centre of the Sun.

benefic planets
The belief among certain astrologers that some planets, especially Jupiter and Venus, are positive and beneficial influences. The Moon's North Node is a benefic point. Opposite of malefic.

besieged planets
A planet is besieged when it lies between two malefics. Traditionally, besieged planets lie between Mars and Saturn, and in the same sign with them.

bestial signs
These are Aries, Taurus, Leo, Sagittarius and Capricorn, because they represent four-footed creatures.

bicorporal signs
Corporale is Latin for 'of the body'. Bicorporal means double-bodied and refers to Gemini, Pisces and Sagittarius.

bi-quintile aspect
An aspect of 144°, arising from a division of the 360° zodiac into two-fifths. This is a minor aspect.

See also *quintile*.

birth chart
See *natal*.

bi-septile aspect
An aspect of 102.8°, the combination of two septiles. This is a minor aspect. See also *septile aspect*.

black Moon
The average lunar apogee (where the Moon is furthest from the Earth). The point opposite the black Moon is called priapus.

black Sun
The average apogee of the Sun (where the Sun is furthest from the Earth).

blocked planet
Where the energy of one planet blocks another.

bound
Also known as 'term'. See *essential dignities and debilities*.

bucket
A configuration of planets in a chart that are grouped closely together. Not reliant on the presence of aspects.

cadent houses
The Third, Sixth, Ninth and Twelfth Houses. These are ruled by mutable signs and are generally associated with the mutable qualities.

Campanus House System
This house system is one of the quadrant systems, so named because they use the ascendant, descendant and MC/IC axes to divide the chart into four quadrants. The Campanus House System is distinguished by using the cusps of the house to mark the centre of the house. This system causes greatly unequal house sizes in charts for polar locations.

cardinal signs and houses
These are Aries, Cancer, Libra and Capricorn; the Third, Sixth, Ninth and Twelfth Houses. Concerning the quadruplicity known as cardinality. Such signs possess initiative and impulsion.

cazimi
A planet within seventeen minutes (ie, in terms of degrees, not time) of the Sun, by conjunction, is said to be cazimi, and at the 'heart of the Sun'. This greatly strengthens the planet. See *combust*.

celestial body
A physical form that exists in space, such as a planet.

celestial equator
The projection of the Earth's equator onto the celestial sphere on the same plane as the Earth's equator (not the plane of the ecliptic). See also *plane*.

celestial harmonics
See *harmonics*.

celestial sphere
The sky as it appears to an observer on Earth.

Ceres
The first asteroid to be discovered. Ceres is associated with the Roman goddess of agriculture and our ability to grow grain, harvest it, grind it into flour and make bread.

Chaldean order
The order of the visible planets from the slowest to the fastest: Saturn, Jupiter, Mars, the Sun, Venus, Mercury, the Moon. An ancient term.

chart
A diagram of the zodiac sky.

Chiron
A small celestial body (planetoid) between Saturn and Uranus. Named for the mythical centaur noted for healing and teaching.

choleric
One of the four temperaments, associated with the element of fire. The choleric personality is believed to indicate an optimistic, youthful, impulsive temperament, prone to spontaneous outbursts of emotion.

See also *temperaments*.

chronocrator
A planet that has governance over an individual's life for a period of time on a given subject.

combust
A planet is combust if it is approaching conjunction with the Sun. Being combust burns up and weakens a planet. Traditionally the Moon is especially weakened (ie, in debility) when combust.

composite chart
Two charts that are merged to form one to show the relationship between the individuals whose charts are combined.

configuration
An aspect involving three or more planets.

conjunct aspect
Originally a planet that is in the same sign as another planet. Later astrologers applied an 'orb of light' standard by which planets outside the orb are not conjunct even if in the same sign. This 'orb of light' is also used with aspects. The conjunction aspect represents the union of planetary energies.

constellation
A group of visible stars named after a figure or animal they are considered to represent.

contraparallel
When two planets are on opposite sides of some line and both the same distance from the line, for example, when one planet is 5° above the equator and the other planet is 5° below it. The 'line' can also be the ecliptic rather than the

equator. Many astrologers regard contraparallels as similar to an opposition aspect.

coordinate system
One of a number of systems used to measure the position of the planets in the sky.

cosmic cross
See *grand cross.*

culmination
A term used to describe a planet reaching its highest elevation (on the midheaven) above the horizon due to the rotation of the Earth.

cusp
The midway point between two signs of the zodiac; also used to refer to the start of a house.

cycle
A planet's zodiacal period, that is, the time it takes a planet or point to make one complete revolution in the heavens.

day houses
Refers to the Seventh to Twelfth Houses (six in all) located above the horizon.

day rulers
The Sun (Sunday), the Moon (Monday), Mars (Tuesday), Mercury (Wednesday), Jupiter (Thursday), Venus (Friday) and Saturn (Saturday).

daylight-saving time
A local time variation that must be considered when calculating a chart.

debility
A weak condition of a planet. See *essential dignities and debilities*.

decan, decanates
A division of the signs into 10° units with different rulers. Also known as 'face'. See *essential dignities and debilities*.

decile aspect
An aspect of 36° of arc, arising from a division of the 360° zodiac into tenths. Sometimes called the semi-quintile.

declination
The arc of measurement in degrees north or south of the equator.

degree
A degree is 1/360th of a circle. In astrology, degrees are the common unit of measurement.

delineation
Meaning 'to draw a line'; in astrology it means to paint a portrait or interpret a horoscope.

derived houses
A method of renumbering the houses in horary astrology.

descendant
The opposite point from the ascendant – the western horizon and the cusp of the Seventh House. It describes interactions with others.

detriment
When a planet is in the sign opposite of the sign it rules, the planet is in detriment. Note that the 'opposite sign' is

in relation to the sign that the planet ruled before the discovery of Uranus, Neptune and Pluto. See *essential dignities and debilities*. See also *ruler*.

diamond
A mathematical point that corresponds to the position of the Sun when it is at perihelion.

dignity
See *essential dignities and debilities*.

direct motion
(Normal) movement of a planet in the order of the signs of the zodiac (Aries, Taurus, Gemini and so on). Retrograde motion is opposite to direct motion.

direct station
The point where a stationary planet begins direct motion.

dispositor
The dispositor of a planet is the ruler of the sign in which the planet is placed.

diurnal
Meaning 'of the day'.

domal dignity
Refers to a planet in its own ruling house and the positive effects of this position.

dome
See *zenith*.

Dragon's Head
The Moon's North Node. See *Moon nodes*.

Dragon's Tail
The Moon's South Node. See *Moon nodes*.

Earth signs
These are Taurus, Virgo and Capricorn (all feminine signs). Earth represents stability, responsibility and practicality. In a natural wheel, they occupy the Second, Sixth and Tenth Houses.

east point
The point where the eastern horizon intersects the path of the Sun. The east point plays a prominent role in how a person projects themselves to others.

easy aspects
A harmonious aspect such as conjunct, trine or sextile.

eclipse seasons
Two times about every six months, when solar and lunar eclipses can happen.

eclipse, annular
See *eclipse, solar*.

eclipse, lunar
An eclipse where the Earth's shadow passes over the Moon. Often instead of seeing a dark shadow, we see a red shadow, due to the Sun's light passing through the Earth's atmosphere.

eclipse, partial
When only part of the Sun or Moon is shadowed over.

eclipse, solar
An eclipse where the Sun is behind the Moon and the Moon's shadow tracks across the Earth's surface.

eclipse, total
When the Sun or Moon are completely overshadowed. A good time for new beginnings.

ecliptic
The apparent path of the Sun around the Earth. This path is at an angle of 23.45° to the equator.

electional astrology
The branch of astrology that deals with selecting the best time to initiate any given activity or project.

elements
The division of the zodiac into fire, earth, air and water signs. Signs of the same element share similar characteristics. Also known as triplicity.

elevated planet
A planet is said to be elevated when it is high in a chart, above the horizon. The most elevated planets are those closest to the midheaven or the Tenth House cusp.

empty house
Referring to a house with no occupying planets.

ending houses
See *terminal houses*.

ephemeris
An almanac listing the zodiacal positions of the planets and other astronomical data.

Equal House System
Method of house division that divides the horoscope into twelve equal 30° sections. In this system, the MC does not coincide with the cusp of the Tenth House.

equator
The circle around the Earth's middle that is equal distance from both poles, marking the angle of the Earth's rotation.

equinoctial
Another name for the tropical or cardinal signs.

equinox
Day of equal day and night. These occur twice a year and mark the beginning of spring (vernal) and autumn (autumnal). 21 March marks the vernal equinox in the northern hemisphere and the autumnal equinox in the southern hemisphere. It also marks the Sun in 0° Aries. 21 September marks the vernal equinox in the southern hemisphere and marks the Sun in 0° Libra.

essential dignities and debilities
Dignities are favourable positions, phases or aspects assumed by a planet. Debilities are the opposite.

The five essential dignities are: rulership (when a planet occupies the house that it rules, ie, is the ruler of); exaltation (when a planet is in a sign that is seen as beneficial to its energy); term, or bound (thought to delimit, or mark the end of things in life); face, or decanate (used to determine physical appearance, using a division of each sign into three faces with rulers based on the Chaldean order); trigon, or triplicity (combining signs and sects).

The debilities are: detriment (being in the physically opposite sign to that which it rules); fall (being in the physically opposite sign in which the planet is exalted); exaltation (the opposite of fall); rulership (the opposite of detriment); essential dignity (dignity by position); accidental dignity (dignity by aspect).

exaltation
Some signs match the energy of certain planets so well that, when the planets enter the sign, they are said to be in exaltation (the opposite is fall). These are: Aries (the Sun); Taurus (the Moon); Gemini (North Node); Cancer (Jupiter, Neptune); Leo (none); Virgo (Mercury); Libra (Saturn); Scorpio (Uranus); Sagittarius (South Node); Capricorn (Mars); Aquarius (Mercury); Pisces (Venus). For example, when the Moon is in Taurus, Taurus is said to be in exaltation. See *essential dignities and debilities*. See also *fall*.

face
Also known as decanate. See *essential dignities and debilities*.

fall
When a planet is in the sign opposite to the sign in which it finds exaltation, the planet's energy is stifled: Aries (Saturn); Taurus (Uranus); Gemini (South Node); Cancer (Mars); Leo (Mercury); Virgo (Venus, Jupiter); Libra (the Sun); Scorpio (the Moon); Sagittarius (North Node); Capricorn (Jupiter, Neptune); Aquarius (none); Pisces (Mercury). For example, when Uranus is in Taurus, Taurus is said to be in fall. See *essential dignities and debilities*. See also *exaltation*.

feminine signs
Feminine refers to receptivity and not gender. These are also referred to as the negative or passive signs, and are the

opposite of masculine signs. They are the earth and water signs: Taurus, Cancer, Virgo, Scorpio, Capricorn and Pisces.

figure
Another name for aspect, or depending upon the context, the birth chart itself.

finger of God
See *yod*.

fire signs
These are Aries, Leo and Sagittarius, all masculine signs. Fire is considered fiery, passionate and spontaneous. In a natural wheel these signs occupy the First, Fifth and Ninth Houses. See also *elements*.

fixed signs and houses
These are Taurus, Leo, Scorpio and Aquarius; and the Second, Fifth, Eighth and Eleventh Houses. Concerning the quadruplicity known as fixity. The influence of these signs lies in maintaining the status quo and resisting change.

fixed stars
These are used by more advanced astrologers. There are many examples, which are usually the brighter stars in the sky. Fixed stars work like the constellations and are said to have a gentle but persistent effect.

flat chart
See *natural chart*.

fruitful signs
These are the water signs: Cancer, Scorpio and Pisces.

galactic centre
The centre of gravity of the Milky Way Galaxy.

geocentric
Concerning a viewpoint from the centre of the Earth. The Geocentric Co-ordinate System is the system most commonly used in astrology. A geocentric model of the solar system places the Earth at the centre.

Geodetic House System
Geodetic means Earth-based. Geodetic houses are linked solely to a place on the Earth's surface instead of the usual date, time and place of birth.

glyph
A symbol denoting a planet, sign or other body or calculated point in the sky.

grand cross
A pattern of aspects consisting of two pairs of opposition aspects forming a cross. Whereby each pair of adjacent planets forms a square aspect. Planets form an opposition and a third planet at their midpoint, in square. It usually will involve all planets in the same quadruplicity (ie, cardinal, fixed or mutable). Seen to create a great deal of tension between the planets involved, with obvious and creative results. Also known as a cosmic cross.

grand trine
When three planets, generally of the same element (ie, all earth, air, fire or water), meet each other to form a triangle of trine aspects. This is a very harmonious relationship between planets.

Great Year
A period of time lasting 25,866 years determined by the precession of the vernal equinox through all twelve signs of the zodiac. See also *precession*.

greater benefic
This is Jupiter, in horary astrology bringing major blessings in signs, houses and aspects.

greater malefic
This is Saturn, in horary astrology causing stress and strain in signs, houses and aspects.

Greenwich Mean Time
The time in Greenwich, England, taken as the reference point for calculating charts based on local time.

Gregorian calendar
Introduced in 1582 by the Roman Catholic Church to replace the previously used Julian calendar. Used worldwide.

hard aspect
Aspects that create tension and friction – squares, oppositions and quincunxes. Inharmonious aspects.

harmonics
Concerning aspects derived from 360 divided by any whole number. Produces many types of aspects not traditionally considered.

harmonious aspects
These are conjunct, sextile and trine. Also referred to as the soft or easy aspects.

harmony of the spheres
Referring to musical tones emitted by heavenly bodies as they travel in space. Devised by the Greek mathematician Pythagoras.

heliacal planets
See *oriental planets*.

heliocentric
Meaning the Sun is at the centre. A heliocentric astrology system would give the planetary positions as seen from the centre of the Sun.

hemisphere
One of two halves of the celestial sphere (Earth) divided by the equator.

horary astrology
The branch of astrology where specific questions are answered by means of a chart drawn up at the time the question is asked. Subject to strict rules. Horary means 'by the hour'.

horizon
The visible or apparent horizon is a circle formed by the sky meeting the Earth from the perspective of the querent.

horoscope
Technically another term for a natal chart. Popularly known as a forecast of (daily) events based on a person's Sun sign. Means 'view the hour'.

house cusp
The dividing line between two houses. Planets on the cusp
will influence both houses. The MC sits on the cusp of the
Ninth and Tenth Houses.

house system
One of a number of ways to divide the sky into houses. The
best-known systems are the Koch, Placidus, Campanus,
Regiomontanus and Equal House Systems.

houses
Division of the sky into twelve parts in the same orienta-
tion as the zodiac. Houses are numbered 1 to 12 where
number 1 is fixed to the eastern horizon from the querent's
point of reference. Houses are numbered in the same order
as the order of the zodiac. Houses add meaning to the sign
in which they fall, and are energised by the planets that
reside in them. See also *house system*.

human signs
These are Gemini, Virgo, Aquarius and the first half of
Sagittarius!

IC
See *imum coeli*.

impeded planet
A badly aspected planet. Mars, Saturn, Uranus and Pluto
are often involved.

imum coeli
IC. On the cusp of the Fourth House, opposite the medium
coeli (MC). See also *medium coeli*.

inconjunct aspect
Now mostly used in reference to a quincunx aspect. Originating as derogatory for certain aspects not considered to be major.

inferior planets
These are Mercury and Venus, located between the Earth and the Sun. They travel very quickly and influence rapid change.

ingress
A planet entering a sign of the zodiac.

inner planets
See *inferior planets*.

intercepted sign
A sign is intercepted when it lies wholly within a single house and does not occupy the cusp at either end of the house. A planet is intercepted when it lies in an intercepted sign. Being intercepted may restrict the freedom of a planet to act.

invariable plane
The central plane of the solar system. It passes through the solar system's centre of mass and makes an angle of about 1°35′ to the Earth's plane of orbit.

joys
The planets are said to rejoice when in certain houses: Mercury (First House); the Moon (Third House); Venus (Fifth House); Mars (Sixth House); the Sun (Ninth House); Jupiter (Eleventh House); Saturn (Twelfth House).

Julian calendar
A calendar introduced in Rome in 46 BC, which overcame calendars based on Moon cycles and politics. It adopted 365 days from the Egyptians and introduced a leap year.

kite
A grand trine (two trine aspects) with another planet in an opposition aspect to one of first three planets. The additional planet acts as an energy channel for the grand trine.

Koch House System
A system that begins by dividing the chart into four quadrants based on the MC and the IC of the chart. These quadrants are then subdivided into the houses by a measure of time (the time it takes for each sign to rise – see *ascension*), as opposed to a measure of space between the signs. The Koch system is also called the Birth Place System and is similar to the older System of Alcabitius.

latitude
See *terrestrial latitude*.

lights
An ancient term used for the Sun and the Moon.

Local Mean Time
LMT. Used before standardised time zones were implemented. Representing the location of birth in relation to the location of Greenwich, England, rather than by a difference in time.

longitude
Measurements from east to west along the surface of the Earth. There is also celestial longitude, which refers to a measurement along the zodiac.

luminaries
The Sun and the Moon. Sometimes referring to some or all of the planets.

lunar eclipse
See *eclipse, lunar*.

lunar mansion
One of twenty-eight divisions of the zodiac circle used to identify the Moon's position on a given day. Often used in horary astrology.

lunar month
There are two types of lunar month. The synodic month is from one new Moon to the next new Moon, that is, the time it takes for the Moon to return to an opposition aspect with the Sun. This month lasts about twenty-nine days. The sidereal month is the time it takes the Moon to do a complete orbit of the Earth, that is, to return to the same star sign. This month lasts about twenty-seven days.

lunar nodes
See *Moon nodes*.

lunation cycle
One lunar cycle of a new Moon to the next new Moon.

major aspects
These are the conjunction, sextile, square, trine and opposition – the group of aspects usually known as the major aspects. All other aspects are known as minor aspects.

major planets
These are Mars, Jupiter, Saturn, Uranus, Neptune and Pluto because they are on the outer side of the Earth from the Sun.

malefic
A negative or unfortunate planet, traditionally Mars and Saturn. Modern astrologers include Uranus, Neptune and Pluto. The Moon's South Node is a malefic point.

mansions
An old term meaning houses.

masculine signs
Masculine suggests aggression and action, not gender. Also referred to as the positive or active signs, these are the fire and air signs: Aries, Gemini, Leo, Libra, Sagittarius and Aquarius. Opposite of feminine signs.

MC
See *medium coeli.*

medium coeli
MC. The midheaven on a birth chart, and the point in the sky where the path of the Sun intersects the meridian line (the South Pole then overhead to the North Pole). Also at the cusp of the Tenth House. Should not be confused with the zenith, which is where the meridian line passes directly overhead.

melancholic
One of the four moods or temperaments, associated with the element earth. The melancholic personality indicates a conservative, practical temperament and one prone to be stubborn. See also *temperaments.*

meridian
A circle that runs north-south. It is found by drawing a line from the South Pole, through the zenith (directly overhead) and to the North Pole. The prime meridian is 0° at Greenwich, England.

midheaven
See *medium coeli*.

midpoint
Or halfsum. The halfway point between two planets, usually measured in longitude.

minor aspects
Aspects considered less important or influential than major aspects, eg, the quincunx. See also *harmonics* regarding other minor aspects.

modality
See *quadruplicity*.

modes
See *quadruplicity*.

Moon nodes
The astronomical calculation of when the Moon's orbit intersects with the Sun's orbit. The two intersecting points located opposite each other in the zodiac are termed the North and South Nodes. If the Sun and the Moon are positioned at one of these nodes, there is a solar eclipse. The North Node (Dragon's Head) is considered a good influence, with the nature of Jupiter. The South Node (Dragon's Tail) is seen as undesirable, with the nature of Saturn.

movable signs
See *cardinal signs and houses*.

mundane astrology
The branch of astrology that deals with places and events in the world, as opposed to dealing with people. From the Latin 'mundus', meaning 'world'.

mutable signs and houses

These are Gemini, Virgo, Sagittarius and Pisces; the Third, Sixth, Ninth and Twelfth Houses. Concerning the quadruplicity known as mutability; these signs are seen as versatile and changeable.

mutual application

An aspect in which two planets are moving towards one another because one is advancing (direct motion) and the other is reversing (retrograde motion). Concerns bringing matters to perfection, and often brings a speedy, unforeseen result.

mutual reception

When two planets are in the sign of each other's rulerships (see *ruler*). A beneficial situation that often negates the negative influences of either planet.

nadir

The point opposite the zenith and directly below you through the centre of the Earth. Not to be confused with the imum coeli. See also *zenith* and *imum coeli*.

natal

Meaning 'birth'. Natal chart and birth chart are interchangeable terms. Also a 'map' detailing the position of the planets in the stars signs and around the Earth at the specific moment of birth.

native

See *querent*.

natural chart

A chart in which the First House is set at 0° Aries. Frequently used when the birth time is not known.

natural houses
The houses when aligned with the corresponding signs:
Aries with the First House and through to Pisces with the
Twelfth House.

negative signs
See *feminine signs*.

night houses
The First to Sixth Houses, because they are located below
the horizon on the opposite side of the globe to the location
of birth.

nodal degree
The same degree between 0 and 30 as the Moon's nodes
(the nodes are always at the same degree as each other).
The sign position does not matter. So 17° Aries correlates
with 17° Taurus.

nodes
The two points in a planet's orbit that intercept the Sun's
apparent path around the Earth. See *Moon nodes*.

North Node
See *Moon nodes*.

north point
The north intersection of these two lines: the meridian (line
around the Earth from south to north and passing through
the zenith); and the geocentric horizon (equivalent to the
line of the horizon circling around you, but passing through
the centre of the Earth instead).

obliquity
The angle made between the plane of the ecliptic (Earth's
orbit) and the plane of the Earth's equator.

occidental planet
A planet that can be seen in the west after sunset, and which will be overtaken by the Sun. A planet so placed has a weak position (ie, it is accidentally weak in dignity). Also called vespertine.

occultation
The eclipse of a star or a planet, by the Moon or another planet.

opposition aspect
An aspect based on an arc (section of a circle) of 180°. Planets exactly opposite each other in the chart; this creates stress. The difference between two planets in opposition is six stars signs. Balance by way of additional aspects to either of the opposed planets is needed in the presence of an opposition. This is a major aspect.

orb
Aspects are distinct relationships between planets (eg, a square is 90° apart). An orb is the number of degrees that the relationship can differ and still be effective (eg, 94° is still a square).

orbit
The path travelled by a planet around the Sun, or by a Moon around a planet, and so on. The orbit is a balance between the planet's desire to go straight (velocity), and the attraction (gravity) of the Sun. Its shape is elliptic (like an oval, but with distinct mathematical properties), which means that the planet is sometimes closer and sometimes further from the Sun.

oriental planet
A planet that has just been overtaken by the Sun and can therefore be seen in the east before sunrise. A planet so

placed is in a strong position (ie, it is accidentally strong in dignity).

orientations
Along with the elements (triplicity), polarities and modalities (quadruplicity), the orientations are a way of grouping the signs and houses. The three orientations are personal, social and universal, and they describe a way of orienting energy in time and space. See *personal signs and houses; social signs and houses; universal signs and houses*.

orthogonal referent
A term used to describe a planet's position north and south of the celestial plane or the plane of the ecliptic. See *plane*.

out of bounds
Planets that are outside the usual north or south boundaries of the zodiac.

out-of-sign
Certain planetary aspects (configurations) coincide with the planets being in specific signs. For example, two planets in conjunction (0°) will generally share the same sign. However, if one planet is 29° Aries and the second planet is 1° Taurus then, although the two planets are in conjunction, they are in different signs and therefore out-of-sign. Also known as a dissociate aspect.

Pars Fortuna
The point in the zodiac that is the same distance from the ascendant as the Sun is from the Moon. For example, if the Sun and Moon are in conjunction, the ascendant and Pars Fortuna will also be in conjunction. Derived from Arabic astrology and used in varying degrees in modern Western astrology.

part of fortune
See *Pars Fortuna*.

partile aspect
An aspect that is not exact, but is within orb. For example, one planet at 1° and a second planet at 4° are not exactly conjunct, but are still considered conjunct, and the aspect is therefore partile.

peregrine planet
A planet that has no essential dignity in its current position. It is considered to be a 'wanderer', with the tendency to be problematic.

perigee
Perig. The point in the Moon's orbit when it is closest to the Earth.

perihelion
The name given to the point in a planet's orbit when it is closest to the Sun.

personal signs and houses
Oriented towards the self. The personal signs are Aries, Taurus, Gemini and Cancer and the personal houses are the First through to the Fourth. See also *social signs and houses; universal signs and houses*.

phlegmatic
One of four moods known as temperaments, associated with the element of water. The phlegmatic personality indicates a withdrawn, sensitive, emotional, somewhat unstable temperament prone to moodiness and self-protective behaviour. See also *temperaments*.

pivot
See *angular houses*.

Placidus House System
A system that begins by dividing the chart into four quadrants based on the MC and the IC of the chart. This house system is one of the most complicated to calculate. It is considered a time-based system, based on trisections of arcs. The Placidus system is one of the most widely used. This is largely due to the widespread availability of Placidus House tables.

plane
If you cut a ball in half, the flat surface is a plane. The celestial plane is derived from the line of the equator (ie, the Earth cut in half along the equator). The plane can then be stretched out into the surrounding universe.

plane of the ecliptic
A plane based on the Earth's orbit around the Sun. If the Earth's orbit is extended out into the surrounding universe, then everything in its path would lie on the plane of the ecliptic. The plane of the ecliptic defines the Sun's orbit around the Earth.

planet
From the Greek word 'planetes' meaning 'the wanderer'. Describes any body that appears, from Earth, to move in relation to the fixed stars. Astronomy recognises nine planets in the solar system and the term indicates a celestial body that orbits the Sun.

planetary strength
The power of a planet in a (horary) chart due to the sum total of the planet's strengths (dignities) and weaknesses (debilities). See *essential dignities and debilities*.

platic aspect
See *partile aspect*.

polarity
Opposing forces or energies. In astrology, polarity describes dichotomies such as life/death, physical/mental, beneficial/malevolent. These opposites are fundamental to astrology, like the paired signs on opposite sides of the zodiac. However, polarity also often refers to feminine (negative, passive, yin) and masculine (positive, active, yang) energy.

Porphyry House System
A system that begins by dividing the chart into four quadrants based on the MC and the IC of the chart. These quadrants are then divided into equal thirds.

positive signs
See *masculine signs*.

post-ascension
See *succedent houses*.

precession
At the vernal equinox (around 21 March), the zodiac sign occupied by the Sun slowly changes in reverse zodiac order (Pisces, Aquarius, Capricorn and so on). The sign changes once every 2160 years. The Sun at 21 March is slowly moving into Aquarius (hence the Age of Aquarius). This phenomenon means that the constellation currently found in the sign of Aries is Pisces. However, Western astrology

maintains that Aries is assigned the first month after the equinox. Also called precession of the equinox.

precessional ages
See *precession*.

primary direction
The movement of the planets across the sky due solely to the rotation of the Earth.

prime meridian
Circles the Earth, running north-south, and intersects the North and South Poles and is in line with Greenwich, England (0°). See also *meridian*.

profection
An old method of predictive astrology that involves turning a chart by distinct steps to see how the nature of a planet changes.

progression
A method of advancing the planets and points of a natal chart to a particular time after birth. Used to illustrate a person's evolution. Also called progressive horoscope.

prolific signs
These are the water signs: Cancer, Scorpio and Pisces.

Ptolemaic aspects
Those aspects first established by the Greek astrologer Ptolemy. See also *major aspects*.

quadrants
The zodiac wheel is divided into four quadrants by the intersection of the horizon (vertical) lines and meridian

(horizontal) lines. The first quadrant contains houses 12, 11, and 10; the second quadrant contains houses 9, 8, and 7; the third quadrant contains houses 6, 5, and 4; the fourth quadrant contains houses 3, 2, and 1.

quadrate aspect
See *square aspect*.

quadruplicity
Qualities of the zodiac signs defined as cardinal, mutable or fixed. Also pertains to the natural house qualities. Also known as modes and qualities. See also *cardinal signs and houses; fixed signs and houses; mutable signs and houses*.

qualities
See *quadruplicity*.

quarto-square aspect
A 22.5° aspect determined by dividing 360° by sixteen. A minor aspect based on the sixteenth harmonic. Also see *harmonics*.

querent
Inquirer. The person who asks a question in horary astrology. The subject of a natal chart.

quesited
What one queries about. The person or matter asked about in horary astrology.

quincunx aspect
An arc of 150°. This aspect is also known as the inconjunct. It creates uneasiness and a feeling of discomfort. The 150 is not derived from the division of 360 by a whole number, so is therefore considered an inharmonious aspect (see

harmonics). However, it represents a difference between planets of exactly five star signs. It is a minor aspect.

quintile aspect
An aspect of 72°. It is an easy minor aspect often signifying human endeavour and accomplishments.

A harmonious minor aspect not normally considered in natal charts although, as opposed to the septile, it is a whole number of degrees.

rational horizon
The rational horizon is the geocentric horizon (a great circle parallel to the apparent horizon but passing through the centre of the Earth) projected onto the celestial sphere (the sky).

reception
A planet, when in one of the dignities (beneficial positions) of another planet. Receives one of the classical Ptolemaic (major) aspects from that other planet. See *essential dignities and debilities*.

rectification
The process of adjusting or determining a birth time. By referencing known events and dates and progressing planets, the birth chart most likely to match the person is identified.

Regiomontanus House System
A system that begins by dividing the chart into four quadrants based on the MC and the IC of the chart. These quadrants are then subdivided into the houses by dividing them into equal spatial arcs (division of distance on Earth) and projecting them back onto the ecliptic. (As opposed

to dividing the quadrants by the measure of time it takes for the signs to rise.) The beginning of each house is then 5° before each chart division, so the chart divisions represent points of maximum intensity, rather than the entrance to the house.

rejoicing
See *joys*.

relationship chart
Often confused with a composite chart, the relationship chart presents in a single drawing the planetary information of two individual horoscopes based on their midpoints (halfway points) between planets in time and space.

relationship houses
These are the Third, Seventh and Eleventh Houses. Associated with the air signs. Also called relative houses.

retrograde motion
When a planet appears to be travelling backwards from the perspective of Earth. The energy of a retrograde planet is less assertive and more internalised.

retrograde station
The point where a planet stops moving forward (direct motion) and begins retrograde motion.

return chart
A chart based on the time and place that a planet returns to the exact position it was at the moment of birth or an important event.

rising degree
See *ascendant*.

rising planets
The first planet of the First House. If none are present, then the rising planet is the planet in the Second House, and so on. Some planets indicate good things (see *planets*) and some bring stress and tension (see *planets*).

rising sign
See *ascendant*.

ruler
Every sign is allocated a planetary ruler: Aries (Mars); Taurus (Venus); Gemini (Mercury); Cancer (the Moon); Leo (the Sun); Virgo (Mercury); Libra (Venus); Scorpio (Pluto); Sagittarius (Jupiter); Capricorn (Saturn); Aquarius (Uranus); Pisces (Neptune). Before the discovery of Uranus, Neptune and Pluto, Scorpio was ruled by Mars, Aquarius by Saturn and Pisces by Jupiter. Venus in Taurus means Taurus in Dignity. See *essential dignities and debilities*.

sanguine
One of the four moods known as temperaments, associated with the element of air. The sanguine personality is individualistic, relates to the world using the intellect and is likely to disconnect from the emotions. It is freedom-loving, friendly, communicative, cool and dry.

satellitium
See *stellium*.

semi-decile aspect
An aspect of 18° of arc, formed by a division of the 360° zodiac by twenty. See also *harmonics*.

semi-sextile aspect
An arc of 30° representing a difference of one star sign. This

aspect is said to create unease, but others claim it is a natural division and a milder form of the harmonious sextile aspect. It is a minor aspect.

semi-square aspect
An aspect of 45° of arc, formed by a division of the 360° zodiac by eight. Interpreted usually as a milder or more subtle form of square aspect. Represents planets 1.5 signs apart.

separating aspect
An aspect that was recently perfect (eg, the planets were at 90° – a square) but is becoming less perfect as the planets continue on their paths.

septile aspect
An aspect of 51.4° of arc, formed by a division of the 360° zodiac by seven. An harmonious minor aspect not normally considered in natal charts.

sesquiquadrate aspect
An aspect of 135° of arc, the combination of a square aspect and a semi-square aspect. The sesquiquadrate is usually interpreted as providing an influence of irritation or agitation on the planets involved. Planets in this aspect are not an equal number of star signs apart (4.5) and it is not derived from dividing 360° by a whole number. However, it is considered more important in charts than the quintile and septile aspects.

sextile aspect
An arc of 60° and a favorable major aspect. Planets in this aspect are exactly two star signs apart and are usually in compatible elements. A sextile allows the influences of the planets to work in harmony; it brings forth opportunity.

sidereal month
The time it takes the Moon to make one revolution around Earth. See *lunar month*.

sidereal time
Linked to the rotation of the Earth on its axis relative to the fixed stars. (Unlike solar time, or normal time, which is linked to the rotation of the Earth relative to the position of the Sun.) The sidereal day is about 23 hours and 56 minutes, hence the reason for leap years.

sidereal zodiac
A zodiac based on the placement of the stars, not the vernal equinox. It is used in Eastern, Hindu or Vedic astrology.

sign
See *zodiac*.

sign ruler
See *ruler*.

significator
A planet symbolising a person or a matter. Used when answering a question in horary astrology.

social signs and houses
Oriented towards others. The social signs are Leo, Virgo, Libra and Scorpio, and the social houses are the Fifth through to the Eighth. See also *personal signs and houses; universal signs and houses*.

soft aspects
See *easy aspects*.

solar chart
A chart devoid of houses due to the subject of the chart not knowing their time of birth.

solar eclipse
See *eclipse, solar*.

solar return
A horoscope cast for the moment when the Sun returns to the exact place in the sky that it occupied at birth. Approximately one day after birth. Considered symbolic of the coming year.

solid signs
The signs of the fixed quadruplicity. See *quadruplicity*.

solstice
When the Sun reaches its maximum declination (distance from the equator). This occurs twice a year, marking the longest and shortest days in each hemisphere.

South Node
See *Moon nodes*.

south point
The south intersection of these two lines: the meridian (line around the Earth from south to north and passing through the zenith); and the geocentric horizon (equivalent to the line of the horizon circling around you, but passing through the centre of the Earth instead).

square aspect
An arc of 90° traditionally regarded as unfavourable. A square brings stress and denotes obstacles as it represents the struggle of two forces with dissimilar purpose. Growth

can be obtained through concentrated effort. Planets in this major aspect are exactly three star signs apart.

star sign
See *Sun sign*.

station
A planet makes a station when it appears motionless in relation to the fixed stars behind it. See also *retrograde station* and *direct station*.

stellium
Three or more planets linked together by conjunct aspects. The outer planets of the chain are not necessarily conjunct, but are joined by the planets between them. A stronger configuration when the planets are grouped in one sign or house.

substance houses
See *temporal houses*.

succedent houses
The houses that follow the angles, namely the Second, Fifth, Eighth and Eleventh Houses. See also *angular houses* and *cadent houses*.

Sun sign
Popularly known as a star sign. Refers to the sign which the Sun was in at a person's birth, presenting a generalised description of their personality.

sunrise chart
A natal chart calculated for sunrise on the day of birth at the birthplace. Can be used when the time of birth is unknown.

superior planets
See *major planets*.

synastry
A branch of astrology that studies relationship potential. Uses calculations made from the birth dates, birth locations and information about when and where the two people met.

synetic vernal point
The precession of the equinox, this represents the current longitude of the equinox. Also known as the sidereal longitude of the equinox.

synod, synodic
Means 'ruling'.

synodic month
Equals the time from one new Moon to the next new Moon. See also *lunar month*.

syzygy
Term used to describe the situation when three or more planets or fixed stars align.

T-cross
See *cosmic cross*.

temperaments
The early Greek theory of four 'humours', linking bodily fluids with moods or dispositions. A person's temperament was said to be affected by a lack, or excess, of a particular fluid. The fluids were phlegm, black bile, yellow bile and blood, which correspond to phlegmatic, melancholic, choleric and sanguine temperaments, respectively.

temporal houses
These are the Second, Sixth and Tenth Houses. Usually associated with the earth signs.

term
Also known as 'bound'. See *essential dignities and debilities*.

terminal houses
These are the Fourth, Eighth and Twelfth Houses. Associated with the water signs.

terrestrial latitude
Latitude on Earth is the measured distances north and south of the equator. There is also celestial latitude, which refers to a measurement along the zodiac.

Topocentric Co-ordinate System
Topocentric means 'as viewed from the observer's place'. This coordinate system should not be confused with the Topocentric House System. This is a modern technique where planet positions are calculated as seen from the actual surface location of the Earth. This normally has little effect on the calculated positions of the planets. For the Moon, the difference can be up to 1°.

Topocentric House System
Method of house division which is capable of identifying house cusps for any place on Earth. The system determines cusps by projecting known events onto a chart, as opposed to other house systems that are calculated mathematically.

transit
The position and movement of a planet or point on any given day.

trigon
See *essential dignities and debilities.*

trine aspect
With an arc of 120° of the 360° zodiac, this is the most harmonious aspect. It separates planets with a total of four star signs and therefore, in most cases, it joins planets in congenial signs of the same element. These energies combine well. However, there can be a lack of challenge and complacency as benefits are gained without effort.

triplicity
See *essential dignities and debilities.* Also referring to the four elements. See also *elements.* Also known as trigon.

Tropic of Cancer
During the summer solstice in the northern hemisphere, this is as far north of the equator as the Sun will travel. The Tropic of Cancer is a calculated line on the Earth's surface that corresponds with the position of the Sun during the solstice.

Tropic of Capricorn
During the summer solstice in the southern hemisphere, this is as far south of the equator as the Sun will travel. The Tropic of Capricorn is a calculated line on the Earth's surface that corresponds with the position of the Sun during the solstice.

tropical zodiac
See *zodiac, tropical.*

T-square
A configuration of an opposition aspect, both squared by a third planet. Someone determined that it looked like a 'T',

and not a triangle. The hard opposition aspect generates stress which can be sporadically passed through the third planet. Generally seen as a difficult configuration.

universal signs and houses
Where energy is oriented towards the universal or the social collective. The Universal signs are Sagittarius, Capricorn, Aquarius and Pisces and the universal houses are the Ninth through to the Twelfth. See also *personal signs and houses; social signs and houses.*

vernal equinox
The equinox before spring.

vernal point
The beginning of the northern hemisphere summer, when on 21 March, the Sun is over the horizon and moving north into the northern hemisphere. The Sun during the vernal point is always 0° Aries. However, the actual constellation occupied by the Sun is Pisces cusp Aquarius. See also *precession.*

vespertine planet
See *occidental planet.*

void of course
Describes a planet that does not make a major aspect before changing signs. It is used primarily with respect to the Moon.

wandering stars
Another term for the planets (including the Moon but not the Sun). Some astrologers and horoscopes still refer to these simply as 'the stars'.

waning Moon
The Moon is waning (decreasing in light) in the fourteen days after the full Moon (Moon opposite the Sun) until its face is in shadow (Moon conjunct the Sun). Considered a time for reaping the rewards of plans implemented during the waxing Moon.

water signs
These are Cancer, Scorpio and Pisces, all feminine signs. Water is considered emotional, sensitive and intuitive in nature. In a natural wheel they occupy the Fourth, Eighth and Twelfth Houses.

waxing Moon
The Moon is waxing (increasing in light) in the fourteen days after a new Moon (Moon conjunct the Sun) until it becomes a full Moon (Moon opposite the Sun). Considered a good time for making and putting plans into action.

west point
The point (also called the equatorial descendant) where the western horizon intersects the path of the Sun.

yod
Triangular pattern of planets that is formed by three planets. Planets A and B are quincunx aspects and planets A and C are also quincunx; planets B and C are sextile to each other. Also known as the Finger of God.

zenith
The highest point directly above your head, opposite the nadir. This is opposed to the midheaven (Medium Coeli, which is the high point of the Sun's path).

zodiac
Greek for 'circle of animals'. The belt of constellations in the sky roughly above the equator.

zodiac, sidereal
This system is most commonly used in Eastern astrology. Each spring the constellations have moved. In the sidereal zodiac, the boundaries of each star sign move with the constellations. So the start date of each star sign slowly changes. See also *precession*.

zodiac, tropical
This system is most commonly used in Western astrology. The star sign boundaries are dictated by the same date and fixed to the start of spring. See also *precession*.

Useful Websites

www.astrology-numerology.com – explains the essential elements of astrology and the zodiac

www.astrology.com – profiles on star signs, planets, houses and other astrology-related information

www.bobmarksastrologer.com – an online tutorial in creating star charts

www.nasa.gov – NASA's site with scientific info on the planets, constellations etc

www.astrologycom.com – lists symbols associated with the star signs, such as flowers, gemstones, colours

www.alabe.com/freechart/ – an easy to use free chart service that will even e-mail your chart to you

Index